Soviet Military
Strategy in
Europe

Pergamon Policy Studies on the Soviet Union and Eastern Europe

Related Titles

PERGAMON POLICY STUDIES ON THE SOVIET UNION AND EASTERN EUROPE

Soviet Military Strategy in Europe

Joseph D. Douglass, Jr.

An Institute for Foreign Policy Analysis Book

Pergamon Press
NEW YORK • OXFORD • TORONTO • SYDNEY • FRANKFURT • PARIS

Pergamon Press Offices:

U.S.A Pergamon Press Inc., Maxwell House, Fairview Park, Elmsford, New York 10523, U.S.A.

U.K. Pergamon Press Ltd., Headington Hill Hall, Oxford OX3 0BW, England

CANADA Pergamon of Canada Ltd., 150 Consumers Road, Willowdale, Ontario M2J 1P9, Canada

AUSTRALIA Pergamon Press (Aust) Pty. Ltd., P.O. Box 544, Potts Point, NSW 2011, Australia

FRANCE Pergamon Press SARL, 24 rue des Ecoles, 75240 Paris, Cedex 05, France

FEDERAL REPUBLIC OF GERMANY Pergamon Press GmbH, 6242 Kronberg/Taunus, Pferdstrasse 1, Federal Republic of Germany

UA
770
D66
1980

Library of Congress Cataloging in Publication Data

Douglass, Joseph D
  Soviet military strategy in Europe.

  (Pergamon policy studies)
  "An Institute for Foreign Policy Analysis book."
  Bibliography: p.
  Includes index.
  1. Russia—Military policy. 2. Strategy. I. Title.
UA770.D66 1980   355.03'347   79-19320
ISBN 0-08-023702-9

Printed in the United States of America

Contents

Acknowledgments

In 1975 I conducted a study of the Soviet threat to NATO for the Office of Net Technical Assessment in the Department of Defense. This study, The Soviet Theater Nuclear Offensive, was published under the auspices of the United States Air Force as volume 1 in a new U.S. Government Printing Office series, Studies in Communist Affairs.

Shortly after that monograph was published, I learned that a large volume of classified Soviet General Staff material was about to be released. This presented an unusual opportunity to expand the scope of this earlier study, place greater emphasis on the combined arms character of the Soviet offensive, rewrite portions of the study about which I had developed second thoughts, and make extensive use of this new and important material of that Soviet agency responsible for overall planning for war in Europe.

This book is the product of this "second effort." It was made possible by a grant from the Earhart Foundation of Ann Arbor, Michigan, to the Institute for Foreign Policy Analysis of Cambridge, Massachusetts. In the process, I have benefited greatly from many discussions and arguments with numerous colleagues on both sides of the Atlantic, and have been most fortunate in receiving invaluable critiques and assistance on the manuscript. In this regard, I am especially grateful to Dr. James Dougherty, Dr. Leon Goure, Dr. Wynfred Joshua, Dr. Richard Pipes, Mrs. Harriet Fast Scott, Dr. William F. Scott, and Dr. Milton Weiner. Special thanks also goes to Dr. Robert L. Pfaltzgraff, Jr., and Mr. Walter F. Hahn of the Institute for Foreign Policy Analysis, and to Mr. Richard Ware of the Earhart Foundation, for sponsoring this current effort. Without their interests, encouragement, support, and patience, this book would never have been completed.

Introduction

Soviet military strategy toward Europe: What is its form and content? What guidance underlies its development? Where is it headed? These questions form the subject of this study.

The motivation for asking these questions is simple. Since 1960, nearly all United States and NATO actions in Europe have been designed to pull away from the brink of war and as President Kennedy put it, "To put the nuclear genie back in the bottle." The types of actions in mind include the removal of long-range "provocative" missile systems, such as THOR, JUPITER, and the high accidental-war-risk DAVY CROCKETT missile; the pullback of forward-based nuclear weapons; the relative absence of extensive deployments of major new systems; the cancellation of several planned systems, such as the SKYBOLT air-to-surface missile designed to increase the effectiveness of the British bomber force and a mobile medium-range ballistic missile (MMRBM) designed to provide Europe with a long-range survivable strike force; the shift away from the NATO massive nuclear retaliation strategy of the 1950s to a flexible response strategy accompanied by efforts to modernize NATO's conventional defense capability; and the acceptance of Soviet hegemony over Eastern Europe and of the boundaries of the Federal Republic of Germany. While some force improvements have taken place, the main trend in Western capabilities appears to have been downward.

Soviet actions stand in marked contrast to those of the United States, not only because they are headed in a different direction, but because the major growth - quantitatively and qualitatively - in their theater capabilities does not appear to have started until the mid-to late-1960s, by which time most of the above United States actions were clearly evident. The types of Soviet force improvements in mind included a significant expansion in deployed forces, particularly in Czechoslovakia; major expansion in nuclear-capable tactical aircraft; completely modernized tank and motorized rifle divisions (all equipped and trained for nuclear and chemical war); new highly redundant and hardened command/control capabilities; significant upgrading of chemical warfare capabilities; impressive growth in land-based, air-defense surface-to-air missiles (SAMs); expansion of airborne assault forces; the deployment of the new sophisticated SS-20 IRBM, improved or new tactical (FROG) and operational-tactical (SCUD) nuclear missiles, and so forth. All this occurred while the Soviets made major improvements in their strategic and other theater forces (e.g., Far East and naval) - the sum total of which reflects a defense budget that had expanded to at least 12 percent of the Soviet GNP in 1976 and will perhaps exceed 15 percent by 1980. (1)

How does one explain this continuing growth in Soviet capabilities? This question has been raised in all of the recent annual United States Secretary of Defense Posture Statements. This study will seek an explanation of this Soviet expansion by examining Soviet military strategy, for it is that which underlies the growth of their capabilities and guides their planning.

Soviet military strategy toward Europe also deserves increased attention and analysis as part of NATO's continuing self-assessment process. While none of the major NATO nations appears interested in developing a new NATO strategy at this time, certain reassessments are necessary. The existing strategy, formally adopted in the late 1960s, is now ten years old - and older if one considers the duration of the effort that went into changing it from the previous massive retaliation strategy of the late 1950s. Since the existing strategy was adopted, the world has changed. Besides the types of changes in the theater capabilities enumerated above, there has been a basic change in the strategic nuclear balance - a change from dominant Western superiority, upon which the current NATO strategy is based, to what most people now view as "rough" or essential equivalence, at best. If the current trends continue, and most indications are that they will, some changes appear unavoidable. NATO may well be entering a new and quite different phase in its life. The direction it takes, or should take, must depend on the best possible perception of Soviet capabilities and strategy toward Europe - a strategy which NATO should be prepared to defeat, or at least to counter. NATO's future success in achieving its goals, particularly when the pendulum is swinging in favor of the Soviets, may hinge on its understanding of Soviet strategy, on identifying Soviet vulnerabilities, and on exploiting both NATO strengths and Soviet weaknesses.

This study of Soviet military strategy toward Europe is based almost wholly on Soviet literature dealing with military doctrine and military science, which includes military geography, organization, training, strategy, operational art, and the art of war itself - i.e., military tactics. It is, therefore, broader than pure military strategy and includes considerations of several related subject areas that make up the Soviet study of military affairs.

As a study of Soviet military literature, the focus of this book is on Soviet thinking - not capabilities. The objective is to understand better the thinking (doctrine) that underlies Soviet capabilities. As such, the study embraces Soviet objectives, which in many regards may exceed current Soviet capabilities. In so doing, there is a tendency to credit the Soviets with more than they are capable of at this time. Certainly in the military field, Soviet objectives often have exceeded their capabilities, and it is important not to overestimate their actual capabilities simply because of their written statements. On the other hand, these objectives should not be cast aside as unimportant merely because they appear to be currently unattainable. They are objectives or goals toward which the Soviets are striving. One of the strengths of the Soviet system may well be the long-term nature of their planning and commitment and the associated continuity of leadership. In numerous areas we see steady Soviet progression toward desired capabilities that reflect long-term plans of ten to fifteen years and more.

In this regard, it is important not to discount the value of older Soviet military literature. This literature is of special importance today because many Soviet goals established in the early sixties are as valid now as they were then; moreover, it shows how the Soviets were thinking when the capabilities we see today were being planned and when the critical concepts of nuclear war fighting, limited nuclear war, initial conventional phase, and escalation were first being structured and formulated.

Further, as part of the long-term commitment and continuity reflected in Soviet military literature, the possibility also exists that the rationale for developing and procuring a system may also underlie its planned utilization. This is quite different from the process in Western countries, particularly in the United States, where it has been recognized explicitly that the weapon system acquisition policy or rationale may differ sharply from the associated employment policy or rationale. There is a tendency to discount Soviet literature on the grounds that it is also designed with acquisition rather than utilization in mind and hence is of little value in explaining how the Soviets really plan to employ their capabilities. It is important neither to reject outright nor accept as gospel what they say; rather, it is necessary to consider it, weigh the possibilities, and ultimately compare it with the capabilities that emerge. (2) Above all, it should be recognized that the Soviet system is quite different from the American, and this difference is particularly evident in their literature.

A distinction of special importance in Soviet literature is the institutional origins of the research material - particularly the role of the Main Political Administration of the Soviet Army and Navy, which reports to the Central Committee of the Communist Party of the Soviet Union (CPSU) and, as such, acts as the party control over and conscience of the Ministry of Defense. There are two basic types of military officers (hence, writers) in the Soviet Union: line and political. Line officers are in charge of military operations, units, tactics and so forth. They report up through the military chain of command to the Ministry of Defense, and are the counterpart of the military officers in the West.

Political officers have no counterpart in the West; they are, in effect, in charge of political indoctrination, loyalty and morale in the Soviet Armed Forces. They insure complete understanding and adherence to Marxist-Leninist ideology at all levels in the Soviet military system. They report up through their own chain of command to the Main Political Administration of the Soviet Army and Navy. Nikita S. Khrushchev, the principal party leader from 1956 to 1964, Leonid I. Brezhnev, the party leader since 1965, and Dmitriy F. Ustinov, current minister of defense, were all political officers. While they may not be military officers in the traditional Western sense, neither do they represent civilians in the Western sense.

Similarly, Soviet military literature is quite different from Western military literature in the extent to which it bears the imprint of the Main Political Administration. If an article by a military officer does not properly reflect the political will of the party, it generally does not get printed. Furthermore, if the officer is a political officer, he is speaking for the Party rather than the military. Insuring that all articles properly reflect Marxist-Leninist teachings, in addition to providing explicit guidance on these teachings, is among the responsibilities of the political officers.

Perhaps the single most important Soviet book on strategy used in this study is Soviet Military Strategy, which was prepared by an authors' collective headed by Marshal V.D. Sokolovskiy, who had been the head of the Soviet General Staff. First published in 1962 with subsequent revised editions in 1964 and 1968, (3) this book was the first Soviet work on strategy published for a wide group of readers since before World War II. It represented the Soviet strategy that was arrived at in the early 1960s following an intensive study of the impact of nuclear weapons on the nature of modern war. Soviet Military Strategy set forth the questions of modern military strategy, discussed the problems of special urgency, and "assisted in working out common views on an entire array of problems." (4) It is one of the few Soviet books for which two excellent translations are available in English.

Other Soviet books of particular importance to this study, and for which excellent translations are now available as part of the United States Air Force translation series, "Soviet Military Thought," are selected texts from the Soviet series entitled, "The Officer's Library." This series, announced in 1964 by the Ministry of Defense publishing house, Voyenizdat, is designed to "arm the reader with a knowledge of the fundamental changes which have taken place in recent years in military affairs." These books are written largely by senior officers and generals of both political and line types. The more valuable ones used in this study are The Officer's Handbook, Marxism-Leninism on War and Army, Scientific-Technical Progress and the Revolution in Military Affairs, Decision Making and Automation: Concept, Algorithm, Decision, and Dictionary of Basic Military Terms. (5) Other Soviet military textbooks of particular value in the Air Force series that were used in this study are The Armed Forces of the Soviet State by Marshal A.A. Grechko, The Offensive by A.A. Sidorenko, and Basic Principles of Operational Art and Tactics by V. Ye Savkin. (6) The latter two are principally concerned with war in Europe; thus, they are of special

significance to this study, ranking with <u>Military Strategy</u> and <u>Voyennaya</u>
<u>mysl'</u> as the more important sources.

<u>Voyennaya mysl'</u> – known in English as <u>Military Thought</u> – is
published monthly as the official military-theoretical organ of the
Ministry of Defense.(7) Regarded as the official organ of the Soviet
General Staff,(8) it is a "restricted or classified journal" written for
senior officers of the Soviet Armed Forces and is usually not available
to Western researchers.(9) This journal is particularly significant to this
study because extensive use was made of the issues from 1963 to 1969
that were recently declassified by the director of the Foreign Press
Digest and made available to the public through the Library of
Congress.

<u>Voyennaya mysl'</u> is the principal journal in which military affairs are
discussed and debated. It contains articles on doctrine, strategy,
tactics, organization, management, and other topics, written by members of the Academy of the General Staff, the Frunze Political
Academy, and the Lenin Military-Political Academy, as well as members of the General Staff, Ministry of Defense, and the Main Political
Administration of the Soviet Army and Navy. As set forth in the
journal, it is designed to aid senior officers, generals and admirals
"studying the basis of Marxist-Leninist philosophy and working on
broadening the military-theoretical outlook and raising their methodological culture."(10)

Finally, use has been made of the numerous newspapers such as
<u>Pravda</u>, <u>Izvestia</u>, <u>Kommunist</u>, and <u>Krasnaya Zvezda</u> (<u>Red Star</u>), and
journals such as <u>Kommunist Vooruzhennykh Sil</u> (<u>Communist of the</u>
<u>Armed Forces</u>), <u>Voyennyy Vestnik</u> (<u>Military Herald</u>), which is concerned
with low-level tactics, <u>Aviatsiya i Kosmonavtika</u> (<u>Aviation and Cosmo-</u>
<u>nautics</u>), and <u>Voyenno-Istoricheskiy Zhurval</u> (<u>Military Historical Journal</u>)
– although these are of less importance to this study.

The methodology employed in preparing this study was to examine
Soviet literature meticulously for the purpose of understanding as much
as possible the Soviet mind-set and isolating the basic principles of the
military literature in the West, the Soviet material was found to be
directed forthrightly to problems of fighting and winning a nuclear war.
Further, there was no evidence of fundamentally opposed schools of
thought as exist in much of Western literature. The Soviet literature
was found to be highly consistent, both between different sources (e.g.,
journals versus textbooks), and over different time frames, subject only
to a few gradual trends, developments or refinements in basic themes.
The second phase in the study was to lay out the common structure of
Soviet thought on war in Europe, allowing for the significant differences between the Soviet and Western approaches so as to com-
municate the Soviet point of view as accurately as possible. Finally, all
the material was reexamined systematically to reassess and challenge
my initial ideas and analyses, and to search for contrary evidence.

In considering Soviet military literature and its use in the subsequent analysis, the natural questions that arise are: Is it credible? Is
it usable? These are not trivial questions. Many people regard this

material as "soft" in contrast to "hard" intelligence on technical systems. However, this author believes that this literature contains some of the "hardest" information on Soviet actions and motives. It is written for Soviet officers and is their basic reference material. It is carefully reviewed by the Soviets to insure that it correctly projects the approved concepts or, in the case of discussion material, the issues approved for discussion. The material is not static, but is subject to change and refinement. Both continuity and change are basic to the Soviet approach: continuity in ideology, and change in implementation in conformance with changes in the political, economic and technical environment. Changes are evident in military doctrine, strategy, tactics, and other areas, but these are prudently considered and orchestrated, and with only a few major exceptions, they are implemented gradually. Also, unlike Western literature, Soviet military literature is very consistent. While most journals contain articles for discussion purposes and even reveal considerable debate and disagreement, eventually the debate is brought to a conclusion and a "correct" line of reasoning is established. These types of discussion are, however, carefully controlled and appear to emerge only when sanctioned or encouraged.

Soviet literature, however, is not without its problems. Words, while used precisely, often have different meanings from their Western counterparts. Sometimes it is difficult to determine what is meant due to the inherent ambiguities in the language and the extremely conservative approach the Soviets often take in discussing what may be potentially crucial issues. Secrecy guidelines are tightly applied and the three levels of censorship (Ministry of Defense, Main Political Administration, and KGB) certainly inhibit creative thought. Yet what eventually emerges represents the accepted position.

The result is a body of literature which is highly redundant, often couched in historical settings (e.g., lessons of the Great Patriotic War) that apply to today, or presented as analyses of the threat. It is often difficult to know when the Soviets are discussing Western concepts or when they are using such discussions as a cover for disseminating ideas. It has been necessary to comb many pages to find those nuggets that provide the additional detail and structure required to add credibility to what would otherwise be rejected as mere repetitive platitudes. Examination of this material is a laborious and time-consuming task, especially when one is researching a specific question: the Soviets do not believe in indexes and each time a new question comes up, one must virtually reread all the material. If however, an analyst is willing to spend the time and effort, and do so with an open mind, there is no shortage of information in this material, waiting to be analyzed.

1 The Basis of Soviet Military Thought

Soviet military thought differs from military thought in the West in several important ways. First, there is the Soviet political philosophy or ideology, Marxism-Leninism. This structures the thought processes of Soviet officials and sets up the framework of their military thought. Understanding their military thought is facilitated if one starts with an understanding of some of the basic precepts of this ideology.

The second difference is the highly structured nature of the Soviet study of military affairs. The Soviets have a well-defined hierarchy of topics - ideology, doctrine, military art, strategy and so forth - which structures military affairs literature. Terms such as military doctrine, military science and military strategy have carefully defined meanings and relationships that should be appreciated. At the same time, there is considerable overlap or redundancy. Ideas tend to flow downward; discussions at one level (e.g., strategy) involve considerable refinement and restatement of higher level discussions (e.g., ideology and doctrine). Ideas are restated and reinterpreted to suit the subject under discussion and, in effect, to justify it by tying it to a higher authority, which ultimately is Marxism-Leninism.

Throughout this examination, it is important not to impute Western ideas and practices to the Soviets in interpreting their literature. Their approach is very different, their use of words and the underlying meanings of these words are often quite different, and their thought processes may be difficult to grasp. In a book attributed to Soviet Army Colonel Oleg Penkovskiy, who had turned over to the British a large volume of Soviet military papers in the early 1960s, there is a graphic description of these differences:

One thing must be clearly understood. If someone were to hand to an American general, an English general, and a Soviet general the same set of objective facts and scientific data, with instructions that these facts and data must be accepted as unimpeachable, and an analysis made and conclusions drawn on the basis of them, it is possible that the American and the Englishman would reach similiar conclusions - I don't know. But the Soviet general would arrive at conclusions which would be radically different from the other two. This is because, first of all, he begins from a completely different set of basic premises and preconceived ideas, namely, the Marxian concepts of the structure of society and the course of history. Second, the logical process in his mind is totally unlike that of his Western counterparts, because he uses Marxist dialectics, whereas they will use some form of deductive reasoning. Third, a different set of moral laws governs and restricts the behavior of the Soviet. Fourth, the Soviet general's aims will be radically different from those of the American and the Englishman. (1)

At the same time, their analyses of military problems and principles are eminently logical, given their ideology, its clear goals, and their highly organized and objective approach to the study of military affairs.

BASIC CONCEPTS OF THE MARXIST-LENINIST IDEOLOGY

The Soviets describe Marxist-Leninist teaching on war and the army as sociopolitical instruction on the origin and the essence of war, on the character and types of war, on its origin in contemporary times, on the facts that determine the course and outcome of the war, on the attitude toward it of various strata of society, and on the social nature and purpose of the Army. (2)   The teachings of Marxism-Leninism are supreme and unchallengable. As stated very simply in Voyennaya mysl': "The Marx-Engels-Lenin teaching is omniscient because it is true." (3) Marxist-Leninist ideology is the basis and justification of Soviet military power. It stands behind the development of their strategy, operational art and tactics, weapon systems, force deployments, and even behind their technological research and development.
    In the Soviet study of war, one of Lenin's most salient teachings is that war is a continuation of politics. War is political, is to serve political aims and is undertaken to achieve definite purposes.

The class character of politics determines also the class nature of war. Lenin wrote: "War is a continuation of policy by other means. All wars are inseparable from the political systems that engender them. The policy which a given state, a given class within that state, pursued for a long time before the war is inevitably continued by that same class during the war, the form of action alone being changed.(4)

Thus, war cannot be understood without first understanding its connections with the policies preceding it, without a study of the policies pursued by two warring sides long before the war. War is other of combatants. Therefore, being developed and introduced simultaneously with the development and introduction of methods of achieving surprise are opposing methods for preventing (disrupting) surprise of attack and surprise of strikes in the course of a war.

...to prevent and disrupt a surprise enemy attack, it is necessary to have, besides combat-ready forces and means, data on his preparation for a war and the thorough analysis of it. The chief thing is to delve deeply by means of individual and even insignificant intelligence indicators into the content of the intentions and plans of the enemy, foresee the possible nature of operations, not permit oneself to be deceived by a false maneuver and be ready to counter his most unexpected methods. (13)

this use "prevent" has strong, aggressive, action-oriented overtones. "prevent" a surprise attack, it is necessary to stop the enemy, and surest way to do that is by preempting and destroying the enemy's pons before they can be launched. In Soviet strategy, prevention, aration, and preemption are closely related and not dissimilar cepts.

The third meaning ascribed to the word prevent is in the sense of erting," which implies a turning aside. It does not mean, however, a king down or unwillingness to face up to the prospects of nuclear , as suggested by the word "avoid" - a word rarely encountered in Soviet literature.

As implied in the way in which they use the word prevent, the ets are not against war. On the contrary, they view military force war as a vehicle to use to the fullest in pursuit of their political ctives. The Soviets oppose only those wars that do not serve their ctives, i.e., "unjust" wars; "just" wars, those that advance the Soviet e, are to be promoted and supported. As explained in _Izvestia_ in ,

War can and must be banned as a means for resolving international isputes. But we must not "ban" civil and national liberation wars, e must not "ban" uprisings and we by no means "ban" revolutionary novements aimed at changing the political and social status uo. (14)

epeat a quote used earlier, "Capitalism...should be eliminated by revolutionary struggle...under conditions of peaceful co-ence." (15) Further, the Soviet Union must be prepared for wars do not serve its interests, i.e., the wars it would like to prevent, cularly nuclear wars. As explained in _Voyennaya mysl'_, nuclear war two aspects: "...the necessity of its prevention and the possibility being waged." (16) Moreover,

position which, in our view, is erroneous on the theoretical level nd harmful on the practical level is that which counts only on the ossibility of preventing war and ignores its being unleashed.... In a

the continuation of politics by violent means. It is an implementation of politics by armed struggle, and its main feature. At the same time not all armed struggle should be considered war. Without a political aim even the fiercest struggle will not be a war, but simply a fight. The political interests of the classes at war and of their states determine the war aims, while armed struggle is the means of achieving these aims. Together they comprise the essential aspects of war as a social phenomenon. The essence of war, that is, the decisive feature that expresses its nature, i.e., the qualitative difference from the peaceful state of society, is that war is the continuation of the politics of definite classes and states (coalitions) by violent means. (5)

This principle applies equally to both nonnuclear and nuclear war. While many people in the West view nuclear war as the end rather than the continuation of the political process, the Soviets explicitly take issue with this line of "bourgeois" reasoning.

. . . this does not mean that nuclear war . . . has ceased to be an instrument of politics, as is claimed by the overwhelming majority of representatives of pacifist, anti-war movements in the bourgeois world. This is a subjective judgment. It expresses merely protest against nuclear war.(6)

The politics they refer to and believe in is the struggle for the preservation and consolidation of the state system or for its overthrow. Their enemy is capitalism — not just the United States or NATO, but all capitalism. The Soviets view the world as a struggle between two differing social systems, socialism and capitalism. The "socialism" they refer to is, of course, that represented by the Soviet Union and its allies.

The types of war in our time are determined by the main lines taken by the social struggle. These lines are: the struggle between the two world social systems - socialism and capitalism; the revolutionary struggle of the proletariat against the bourgeoisie; the general democratic struggle of the popular masses against monopoly associations; the national liberation struggle of the peoples against the colonialists; the struggle between capitalist countries for strengthening the positions of monopoly capital. The main, decisive line of the social struggle is the struggle between socialism and imperialism.(7)

This struggle is a total military, political and ideological conflict:
...the Leninist legacy remains fully applicable: "Our task is to beat down the resistance of capitalists, not only military and political but the deepest and most powerful ideological resistance as well."(8)
It is a relentless struggle in which the Soviets intend to give no quarter:

The struggle with the bourgeois ideology is the most important sector of the class struggle. It is emphasized in the decree of the CPSU Central Committee that in the struggle with this ideology, there is not and cannot be any neutralism or any compromises". (9)

A war in Europe would likely be pursued with this guidance in mind, and would encompass those territories considered to be of strategic importance to the outcome, with little regard for the neutrality of the country.

The ultimate Soviet goal is the destruction of capitalism on a worldwide scale. Marxism-Leninism is a revolutionary ideology. In it, the historical train of social events is seen to be clear, predetermined and inevitable. Briefly, feudalism gave way to capitalism, the highest form of which, imperialism, has now passed. Capitalism will give way to socialism, the highest form of which is communism. The final transition from capitalism to socialism is, in fact, the Soviet definition of the modern epoch.

> Of basic importance for the Marxist-Leninist doctrine of war and the army under modern conditions was the scientific definition of the modern epoch as a transition from capitalism to socialism, an epoch of the downfall of imperialism and the triumph of socialism and communism on a worldwide scale which was given by the CPSU and other Marxist parties in 1960. (10)

The major contemporary task is to bring about this transition. While this transition is inevitable, one cannot simply wait for it to occur. Marxism-Leninism is not a passive but an active ideology; it is not theoretical, but practical. Further, in the early 1970s, Soviet literature began to call for increased effort toward an active role in the process, perhaps recognizing the impact of the shift in the strategic balance on the Soviets' freedom of action.

As can be deduced from the above, military power plays a most important role in Soviet ideology. This role of the military is called its "external function."

> It must be seen that socialism's military might objectively assists the successful development of the revolutionary, liberation movements and that it hinders the exportation of imperialist counterrevolution. In this lies one of the most important manifestations of the external function of the armed forces of a socialist state. (11)

In examining the nature of the Soviet Armed Forces, particularly those facing Western Europe, it is important to recognize the various dimensions of this external function, for this will help us to understand the nature of the recent buildup in their capabilities. The Soviet (and Warsaw Pact) forces are designed for several different types of war. Wars for which conventional capabilities are essential include the "counterrevolutionary" movements, such as those in Hungary in 1956, Czechoslovakia in 1968, and perhaps in the future in Yugoslavia. Another type of war for which nonnuclear forces are preferred is the "national revolution or liberation movement." The crucial areas where Soviet forces might be needed for this type of activity include various

Middle East countries and selected European NATO c which nuclear capabilities are essential include glo NATO/Warsaw Pact war in Europe, and certain lc nuclear powers. Soviet conventional capabilities a capture and occupy territory in any war, local or wor or nuclear. Thus, Soviet forces serve a variety of p not be regarded as either nuclear or conventional, as do in the West. Rather, Soviet military forces are forces, where the importance of using all forces and best advantage, in combination to achieve victory is (

The Soviets would prefer to achieve their worl peacefully, without major or dangerous armed conf. world nuclear war is one of their major objective appreciate the risks that attend any modern armed cc a nuclear conflict. The destruction that would detrimental to the "progressive development" of soci tion of communism.

> It is especially important to have this in mind in where imperialism is threatening humanity with with the employment of nuclear weapons can t foundation for the existence of human so tremendous damage to its progressive developme most important requirement for progress in prevention of a new world war. Capitalism, as tl the way to the progressive development of humai should be eliminated by the revolutionary strug masses under conditions of peaceful coexister different social systems - world war is not necess

Because Western Europe would constitute a majc objective in a world war and because the threat of war has been a cornerstone of NATO doctrine, preventing world nuclear war are highly relevant to strategy.

The concept of "prevention" in Soviet literatu problem because of the inherent Western tendency with "avoid." The Soviets, insofar as war is conce war from the threat of war, such as the Berlin Cr "prevent" in three principal ways. First, the Soviets to have such a preponderance of strength that no r would challenge them. This is not quite the deterrence, which is most often used in the West, be survival and recovery underlie the Soviet meaning of

Second, "prevent" is used in the sense of "seizing "preempting" in order to "disrupt" the enemy's surpri

> An armed conflict is a bilateral process. A pu possible counteraction of one side is organized fo

growing situation when the aggressiveness of imperialism is growing it would be intolerably complacent not to take into account the possibility of new wars being unleashed by the imperialists. (17)

While peaceful coexistence may be the preferred path for the Soviets, and while nuclear war may be regarded by the Soviets as a catastrophe to be prevented, this does not reduce the importance of military forces or preparation for war, particularly world nuclear war. Quite the contrary, military force, particularly nuclear forces and nuclear war-fighting capabilities - again in contrast with Western logic - become more important. Military force and armed conflict in all their dimensions are most important to the world revolutionary process and to Marxism-Leninism.

In sum, the basic message imparted by Soviet ideology is that Soviet socialism is a world revolutionary force. World socialism directed from Moscow is the objective and the defeat of capitalism is the main means to that end. This objective is to be pursued actively, using all means available; there can be no peace and no diminishing of goals until capitalism is destroyed. There can be no accommodation; the two social systems are opposed and irreconcilable. All actions and means in any form that further that objective are justified by Soviet ideology. Military force is a most essential tool to use in winning the struggle. Military superiority at all levels is a top priority. The most important military capability in this regard is what the revolution in military affairs is all about - the nuclear capability. As explained in the book Marxism-Leninism on War and Army.

The most specific feature of the present-day revolution in military matters is the enormous influence it exerts on social life, on all the aspects or elements of the state's military power.

It was already evident in the past that the transformations in military affairs exert a strong influence on social relations by changing their form. Frederick Engels said: "...the introduction of firearms had a revolutionizing effect not only on the conduct of war itself, but also on the political relationship of domination and subjection." It helped to smash feudalism and promoted the victory of capitalism.

The present revolution in military affairs has an even bigger effect on social relations. In the past, changes in military affairs affected only separate countries, those in which they were taking place; now, however, they affect the fate of many people, of all of mankind. Moreover, the modern revolution in military affairs forms part of the content of our epoch and comprises a definite aspect of it. It has important economic and socio-political consequences which are indissolubly linked with the main content of our epoch - the revolutionary transition from capitalism to socialism. Therefore, its influence on the military potential, on the military power of states (coalitions) is enormous and many-sided. (18)

This quote comes from the basic Soviet reference text for military doctrine. The clear message is that military power is central to the socialist revolution, and if capitalism gets in the way of the revolution, military force may be used. Military superiority and combat readiness, i.e., war-fighting ability, have been and remain primary Soviet goals both to prevent wars that could interfere with the building of world socialism and to use in achieving their political aims in wars that they choose to fight or are forced to fight. The need to build superior military forces and to be prepared to use them is a major theme throughout Marxist-Leninist ideology.

THE SOVIET STUDY OF MILITARY AFFAIRS

The Soviets take military power and war most seriously, and over the years they have developed a comprehensive structure for its study. The two fields of that study most relevant to this one are military doctrine and military science, the latter including such topics as strategy, operational art and tactics.

Military Doctrine

In the United States, military doctrine is a flexible word that means different things to different people. There is national doctrine, Allied doctrine, Army doctrine, Air Force doctrine, and tactical nuclear doctrine, to mention but a few. In contrast, in the Soviet Union, there is only one military doctrine - the official Soviet military doctrine. Its closest equivalent in the United States is national security policy.

As set forth in Military Strategy, military doctrine is

the expression of the accepted views of a state regarding the problems of political evaluation of future war, the state attitude toward war, a determination of the nature of future war, preparation of the country for war in the economic and moral sense, and regarding the problems of organization and preparation of the armed forces, as well as of the methods of waging war. Consequently, by military doctrine one should understand the system of officially approved, scientifically based views on the basic fundamental problems of war. (19)

As stated in The Officer's Handbook in 1971:

The Central Committee of the Party...works out Soviet military doctrine.

Military doctrine is worked out and determined by the political leadership of the state.

Military doctrine is a system of guiding views and principles of a
state on the character of war under given specific historical
conditions, the determination of the military tasks of a state, the
armed forces, and the principles of their construction, and also the
methods and forms for the solution of all these tasks, including
armed conflict, which issue from the goals of the war and the socio-
economic and military-technical capabilities of a country. (20)

In the Soviet Union, military doctrine is drawn up with the participation
of key political, party and military leaders. (21) This doctrine is then
officially approved by the Central Committee of the Communist party.
When approved and disseminated, this doctrine is official and is used in
preparing the country for war. It identifies the "character of the
modern war and military tasks facing the state, and also the methods of
resolving them." (22)
    The basic characteristic of contemporary Soviet military doctrine is
its "offensive" nature.

Soviet military doctrine has an offensive character.... The Soviet
Union...will conduct the war which the enemies impose on them in
the most offensive manner in order to attain the smashing of the
enemy in short times.... Soviet military doctrine allocates the
decisive role in contemporary war to nuclear missile weapons. At
the same time it considers that along with the nuclear missile
strikes of a strategic and operational-tactical character, the armed
forces will employ conventional armament.(23)

And, as presented in a theater war context,

The Leninist ideas of the decisive role of the offensive in armed
conflict find reflection in Soviet military doctrine which considers
the offensive as the basic type of combat actions of troops. Only a
decisive offensive conducted at high rates and to a great depth
achieves the complete smashing of the enemy in short times and the
seizure of important areas, objectives, and political and economic
centers. (24)

Soviet military doctrine begins with a detailed appreciation of the
military and economic capabilities of the enemy to wage war. (25) The
economic capability is important both in preparing the nation for war in
peacetime and in meeting the needs of the armed forces during war.
The attainment of military superiority, by building up the armed forces
in times of peace as well as during war, is a most important national
task. (26)

Our military doctrine and strategy require constant consideration of
the economic capabilities of a probable enemy for waging war, and
of the strong and weak sides of his economic basis. A fundamental

problem in the interrelationship of military doctrine and the economy is the creation and maintenance of military technical superiority over the probable enemy. (27)

Determining the character of a possible war is pivotal in Soviet military doctrine, and in the event of a war between the two opposing social systems,

> it will be a world war, a supreme armed conflict in which both sides will pursue extremely decisive objectives.   In its socio-political essence it will be a war of two powerful coalitions of states. (28)

Because the principal antagonists have acquired large stocks of nuclear weapons and because of the character and range of these weapons, it is believed that a new world war "will more than likely be a nuclear war." (29)

> One of the important tenets in Soviet military doctrine is that a world war, if the imperialists initiate it, will inevitably assume the character of a nuclear war with missiles, i.e., a war in which the nuclear weapon will be the chief instrument of destruction, and missiles the basic vehicle for their delivery to target. (30)

Considering the tremendous combat capabilities of these weapons, under certain conditions the war can be of short duration. However, it is also recognized that if a country is large, such as the Soviet Union or the United States, and prepares itself and its economy for war, the war cannot be won "in one blow" and will become protracted. This accounts for the emphasis placed on the ability of the economy to meet the needs of the armed forces during the war. While it is clear that the Soviets understand the possible consequences of nuclear war, this does not mean that they do not believe it can be won and should be prepared for. Quite the contrary, as indicated earlier, because the consequences are so severe, preparing for such a war is the most important task for military strategy.

> Of all wars which are possible in the modern era, a world nuclear rocket war, which the imperialist aggressors, primarily the USA are preparing against the socialist community, chiefly against the Soviet Union, as the most powerful of the socialist states, presents the main danger. Therefore, in the content of Soviet military doctrine, the chief place is occupied by positions pertaining to problems of preparing and waging world nuclear rocket war. (31)

Moreover, as stated in the 1962 edition of Military Strategy,

> we conclude that the Soviet Union's Armed Forces and those of the other socialist countries must be prepared above all to wage a war where both antagonists make use of nuclear weapons. Therefore,

the key task of strategic leadership and theory is to determine the correct, completely scientific solution to all the theoretical and practical questions related to the preparation and conduct of just such a war. (32)

The unmistakable tenet of Soviet military doctrine is that the Soviet Union will strive both to "prevent" and prepare for such a war, so that, if war comes despite all Soviet efforts to prevent it, the Soviet Union will be victorious and will recover from it.

The most important subsequent elaboration to this basic military doctrine formulated in the late 1950s and early 1960s was the admission soon thereafter that war might begin conventionally and might even continue in this manner for some time. The conventional war possibility is present in several Voyennaya mysl' articles in 1964 as well as in the open literature, and by 1967 the message was clear: Soviet military science was to consider war in four dimensions - nuclear and nonnuclear, worldwide and local. In reviewing the progress of Soviet military science, Marshal of the Soviet Union M. Zakharov stated in February 1968:

> In entering into our second half-century we take account of lessons of the past and look steadily into the future, stressing the modern problems of Soviet military science. They consist in further, more thorough research into the nature and features of possible armed warfare - both nuclear and nonnuclear - in worldwide and local clashes, in wars of various types inherent to the epoch in which we are now living. (33)

The degree and nature of Soviet interests in keeping a war involving NATO and the Warsaw Pact conventional is an important contemporary issue.   For a variety of reasons, considerable caution should be exercised in the analysis of this issue.   First, the notion of a long conventional war is usually cast as an imperialist, rather than a Soviet, notion: "It is possible that war can begin by gradual escalation of a limited conflict into a world conflict.   Imperialists can begin it and wage it for any time without using nuclear weapons with only conventional means." (34) Second, conventional war is really discussed, for the most part, as just a "phase," not a war; that is, it is only the beginning of a war that is most likely to escalate to a nuclear war. Of particular danger to the United States, a conventional phase could be used to cover preparations for a surprise intercontinental nuclear strike. (35) Finally, conventional operations are usually addressed in the context of unit and subunit (a military division and below) operations within a larger war that itself is most often nuclear.   That is, the distinctions made by Marshal Zakharov, if taken too literally, can be misleading because they tend to obscure important nuclear aspects of conventional war, conventional aspects of nuclear war, global aspects of local engagements, and regional aspects of global war.

In the late 1950s, the Soviets adopted a doctrine based on the importance of nuclear weapons. They were then, and indeed remain, the decisive weapons. The basic statement that remains valid today is: "Soviet military doctrine allocates the decisive role in contemporary war to nuclear missile weapons. At the same time it considers that along with the nuclear missile strikes of strategic and operational-tactical character, the armed forces will employ conventional armament." (36)

Military Science

As discussed above, military doctrine provides political guidance to the military on the type of war for which it is to prepare. The remainder of Soviet military thought is military science, and it is indeed treated as a science. The field is well organized and well researched; advanced degrees are granted in it at and beyond the doctorate level. Professors of military science are highly respected and are mostly military officers, many of whom are general or flag rank officers. These officers make up the bulk of the professionals who write the military textbooks referred to in the foreword.

Soviet military science is defined in The Officer's Handbook as a unified system of knowledge on the preparation and conduct of armed conflict in the interests of the defense of the Soviet Union and other socialist countries against imperialist aggression. Its functions include:

- the discovery and investigation of the objective laws of armed conflict;

- the development, on the basis of the knowledge of these laws, of the means and forms of armed conflict for the achievement of victory over the enemy;

- the investigation of the problems and determination of the methods for the preparation of the territory of the country and the Armed Forces for war, and the comprehensive support of the armed struggle economically, politically, morally, materially, technically, scientifically, and in other ways;

- the development of the bases for the organization, training and education of the troops in accordance with the requirements of contemporary war; and

- the development of the method of military science as a whole, its general theory, theory of military art, the military-technological sciences, and its other parts and branches. (37)

Although military doctrine and military science have much in common, it should be clear that there are important differences. As described in Methodological Problems of Military Theory and Practice:

Military science studies a much wider circle of problems than necessary for realization of the practical problems of construction of the armed forces of the state during the given period. It considers all the probable means and conditions of waging armed struggle, including those which are not typical for the given country and do not entirely coincide with its means. But the conclusions of military science use doctrine, proceeding from the real conditions and means of the country. No contemporary military science can disregard the appearance of nuclear missiles and their determining effect on the means and forms of armed struggle. However, for states without nuclear missiles, military doctrine had to show ways of military construction different from those which countries having very modern means of armed struggle can go. And these ways are developed by military science.

Military science studies the development of military affairs in many countries and evaluates the state of the armed forces and military means of states and coalitions and condition of waging armed struggle in various theaters of military actions. The doctrine considers only those factors which affect the construction of the armed forces in its country. In other words, of the entire variety of phenomena and trends studied by military science, of all its generalizations and recommendations, military doctrine takes only those which correspond to the political course of the state and to its strategic means. (38)

In addition to those differences, military science focuses on the past, present and future, while doctrine is pointed to the present and immediate future - that is, to foresee the nature of war and the probable enemy in order to provide guidance to military science regarding the immediate course to follow. Furthermore, it is especially important to recognize that while military doctrine guides military science, military doctrine also is developed from the conclusions of military science. Doctrine is not developed independently of the sound laws, principles and conclusions of military science.

Military doctrine exploits the conclusions of various sciences. The doctrine rests upon the conclusions of military science particularly as regards determining the nature of a future war and the methods for conducting it, and for determining the structure and preparation of the armed forces. (39)

The final distinction of importance is that

doctrine, being developed and accepted by the state, is a single system of views and a guide to action free from any particular subjective views and evaluations. Inherent to science, in its development, is the struggle of opinions. In the system of military theories which comprise military science there may be several different points of view, different scientific ideas, and original hypotheses which are not selected by doctrine for practical application and they thereby do not acquire the character of official state views on military questions. (40)

The identification of issues, questions, problems and "contradictions" is integral to the process of Soviet military science. The Soviet approach is to identify problems and expose them to study and debate, as they did in the 1950s in the process of reevaluating their basic doctrine and strategy in light of nuclear weapons. In the 1960s, considerable attention was devoted to the goals, the initial period and the character and duration of nuclear war; the merits of centralized versus decentralized control in nuclear war; concentration versus dispersal requirements for attack in nuclear war; the role of the tank, and so forth.

The object is not to bury problems, but rather to uncover them. In the Soviet military press, individuals - by name - and their points of view are sharply criticized or supported, as the case may be. However, this debate is not completely free flowing, but is carefully structured and kept within precisely defined bounds insofar as it is reported in the military press, which is carefully censored by at least three agencies, the General Staff, the Main Political Administration, and the KGB.

Soviet military science is divided into the following principal branches: general theory, theory of war or military art, theory of training and education, military-historical science, military administration, military geography, and military-technical sciences. It is organized independently of the military services. There is one, integrated, unified school of military theory and knowledge in the Soviet Union - not one for each service. This combined approach is central to the Soviet military system, which includes the concepts of the combined armed forces - the combined application of all means and forces for victory - and the unified system of knowledge known as military science.

The most important branch of military science is military art, which comprises general theory, strategy, operational art and tactics. Of these, the most significant is strategy. (41) Strategy is concerned with "the preparation of the armed forces and the country as a whole for war, the methods and forms of waging war, and the leadership of the armed forces in it." (42) As explained in Voyennaya mysl' by the dean of Soviet strategy, Marshal Sokolovskiy, "In its broadest form the subject of strategy is war as armed struggle, its theory, or more concretely - the theory of the comprehensive preparation for war, methods for conducting it and the assurance of victory over an aggressor." (43)

The scope of the theory of military strategy includes:

- the laws governing armed conflict which are inherent in strategy;

- the conditions and nature of a future war;

- the theoretical foundation for preparation of the country and of the armed forces and the principles of military planning;

- the services of the armed forces and the basis of their strategic utilization;

- the fundamentals of civil defense;
- the methods of conducting armed conflict;
- the basis of the material and technical support for armed conflict;
- the basis of leadership of military forces and of the war in general; and
- the strategic attitudes of probable opponents. (44)

As with military doctrine, there is only one military strategy in the Soviet Union to which all the services adhere.

> Strategy is general and single for all the types of the armed forces of the country because war is conducted, not by some one type of armed forces or combat arm, but by their combined efforts.   The coordination of the actions of all the types of armed forces in war is possible only within the framework of a single military strategy. (45)

Moreover, like military doctrine, military strategy is developed by the top political and military leaders in the Soviet Union: "Strategy is the mission of the highest military and political leadership, of the supreme command and highest headquarters, and pertains to preparation of the country for war and the conducting of armed struggle under specific historical conditions." (46)   The General Staff and the General Staff Academy, both of which are joint service organizations, play the major role in the analysis and development of strategy. Their most important concern is the character of modern war and its waging: "The most important problem of strategy is the determination of the character of modern war, the possible means of its emergence and conduct, its stages (periods) and targets (problems), which are landmarks for its planning."(47)
   While strategy and doctrine appear similar in several respects, the principal difference is one of direction:

> Military strategy occupies a subordinate position with regard to military doctrine.   Military doctrine determines overall policy in principle, while military strategy, starting from this overall policy develops and investigates concrete problems touching upon the nature of future war, the preparation of a country for war, the organization of the armed forces, and the methods of warfare. (48)

Further, "in practice it [strategy] is policy's direct weapon. With respect to strategy, policy plays the leading and directing role." (49) The second significant difference is in detail: doctrine provides the more general propositions while strategy manages the detailed implementation.
   The principal similarity between military strategy and military doctrine is their common task: to determine the character of modern

war, and the means and methods of its conduct. A second common ground is that they both proceed from a detailed understanding of the nature and capabilities of the probable enemy - a practice which, while quite logical, has not been easy to achieve in the West.

Soviet military doctrine and strategy are often confused in Western literature. A common fault is to suggest that the Soviets will not adhere to their doctrine in case of war. This type of error stems from several possible causes: 1) the United States' assumption that its use of "doctrine" is the same as that of the Soviets; 2) skepticism of the Soviets' belief in their own doctrine; and 3) a belief that some word other than doctrine is intended. In any case, the basic suggestion that the Soviets will change their doctrine - their national security policy - at precisely the moment for which it is designed is not credible. Their doctrine is their guide for the preparation of war; it is not a set of rules to follow after the outbreak of war. When war breaks out, strategy takes over.

> During the war, military doctrine withdraws somewhat into the background because in armed conflict they are guided primarily by military-political and military-strategic considerations and by the conclusions and generalizations which follow from the conditions of a specific situation. Consequently, war and armed conflict are guided not by doctrine, but by strategy. (50)

Hence, Soviet military strategy is the most important field to study in evaluating the Soviet threat to NATO and the prospects for controlling and terminating a NATO/Warsaw Pact war in Europe. At the same time, because of its response to doctrinal dictates, it is essential to understand the doctrinal basis of the strategy.

The two other important elements of military art are operational art and tactics. It is within these areas that the individual services and branches develop their own theories - subject, of course, to the general laws of armed conflict and strategy.

Operational art is described as the binding link between strategy and tactics. It relates to the development of the theory and practice of the preparation and conduct of contemporary operations carried out by large units of various services, both independently and jointly. (51) Operational-size units are front, army, and division-size units, and operational art is concerned with operations at these levels and with joint operations, including their character, organization capabilities, principles of application, questions of operational support, principles of control of troops in operations and their rear support. (52)

In the past, operational art and operational-level command seem not to have played as major a role in the Soviet military system as in that of the United States, apparently largely because of the extensive and detailed role played by the General Headquarters and Soviet General Staff. As described in the Soviet General Staff at War, the General Staff was concerned with routine operations and plans down to division level, and representatives of General Headquarters with decision authority were constantly in the field at front and army level. At the same time, these commands (e.g., front and army) were prohibited from inserting themselves similarly in the affairs of their subordinates -e.g., the corps and divisions. In effect, operational art is practiced by both senior commanders in the theater, such as front and army, the command and General Staff organizations in Moscow, and their representatives in the field. Thus, while operational art is described as the link between strategy and tactics, it appears to be closer to strategy. It is regularly discussed in Voyennaya mysl' and very seldom treated in Voyennyy Vestnik (Military Herald), which is primarily concerned with the subunit-level tactics.

Tactics, the third component of Soviet military art, consists of the direct study of the preparation and conduct of the combat actions of small units (squad, company, battalion) and larger units (regiment and division), of all combat arms and types of armed forces, land, air and sea. (53)

Tactics deals with all aspects of battle as one of the most important phenomena of war. (54) Tactics is subdivided into general tactics and the tactics of the various types of armed forces. The combat arms - the motorized rifle troops, artillery, armored and engineering troops, as well as the services - each have their own tactics. (55)

This hierarchy of strategy, operational art and tactics, the category of conflict, and the command level involved are shown diagramatically in Figure 1.1. This diagram also uses several words that are important in Soviet literature, but have no counterpart in Western literature. These words, podrazdeleniye, chast, soyedineniye and obeyedineniye, refer to various sizes and compositions of force elements. Briefly, they may be defined as follows:

- Obeyedineniye is a Soviet term which refers to a major field force, such as a front or an army.

- Soyedineniye is used by the Soviets to refer to a corps, a division, or brigade. The components may be from a single arm or from various arms and services. The term also is used loosely for an army.

- Chast is a Soviet term which designates any unit of regimental or smaller size that is administratively self-contained and separately numbered. Examples of this are a rifle regiment, an engineer battalion of a rifle division, and a signal corps battalion.

- Podrazdeleniye is a Russian term for subdivision. It is used to refer to a subordinate unit of a chast, and it is any unit which cannot be fully identified numerically except by reference to the larger unit of which it is an integral part: battalions, companies and platoons of a rifle regiment; the battalions and batteries of an artillery regiment; the companies of an engineer or signal battalion.

Throughout this book, these Soviet words will be retained, as they usually are in English translations. Additionally, the type of Western "equivalents," e.g., company, battalion, regiment and so forth, that are most appropriate in the context of the quote, will be included in brackets after the Soviet word.

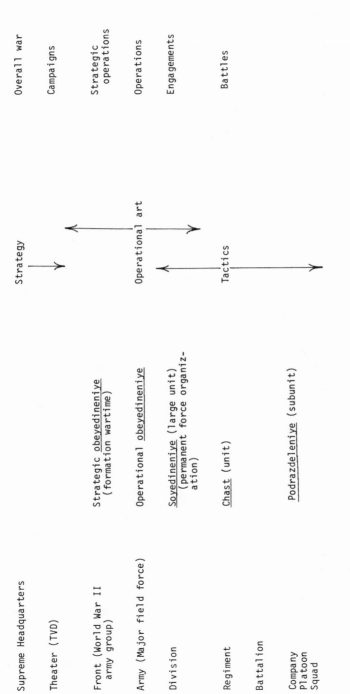

Fig. 1.1. Military art hierarchy and relations.

2 The Revolution in Soviet Military Affairs

The evolution of Soviet military science since the October Revolution of 1917 has been marked by a series of phases. Although this evolution has seen several major transformations, none was as massive nor as rapidly introduced into practice as the changes brought about by the mass introduction of nuclear weapons into the armed forces - changes which are referred to as the modern revolution in Soviet military affairs. While this revolution was, and is, largely a nuclear revolution, it has expanded to include the application of all science and technology in the Soviet drive for across-the-board military-technical superiority.

The nuclear push in Soviet military research and development had begun under Stalin at least by late 1942 when a civilian and military scientific team was established to work on "the uranium problem." (1) The mid-1940s are noted in the Soviet literature as the time their work on long-range rockets and missiles was initiated in earnest (coincident with the capture of German scientists and V-2 rocket technology).

However, during and following World War II, the study of Soviet military science apparently ignored this effort and instead focused strictly on conventional conflict. That study - which was merely a "lessons learned" type of study - is regarded as the first postwar phase in Soviet military science. As described in a Voyennaya mysl' article on the development of military science:

> In the first post-war period the development of Soviet military theory predominantly proceeded along the traditional path of generalization and analysis of the experience of the past war, of working out on this basis conclusions and recommendations for the conduct of armed conflict by ordinary (conventional) means. This period may be considered as 1946-1953. (2)

Three events in 1953 are credited as having brought about the second postwar period in Soviet military science: the death of Stalin, the development of the H-bomb, and the Soviet decision to mass produce long-range missiles as the main means of delivering nuclear warheads.

The next stage in the development of the Armed Forces began in 1953. At that time a hydrogen bomb test took place in our country, and the mass production of various types of rockets was organized, which were to serve as the principal carriers of nuclear weapons. There was a high-speed development of various types of rocket and nuclear weapons, atomic energy, electronics, automation, and many different technical means of armed combat. This made it possible, in a relatively short period, to supply the Soviet Armed Forces with the most modern combat equipment, including such formidable weapons as intercontinental ballistic rockets with powerful thermonuclear charges. (3)

After the death of Stalin, changes did not take place immediately. A year was required to begin to break loose from the traditional thought processes that characterized the first postwar period; and it has been stated that this process was not completed until the Twenty-second Party Congress in 1961. Nonetheless, the second main postwar period in the development of Soviet military science is defined as 1954 to 1960.(4) Generally, this period appears to have had two rather distinct phases. The first phase was 1954 to 1957. At the end of 1953, the work schedule for the General Staff academy was altered radically; the nuclear weapon was to be studied, and plans for its employment were to be developed. By 1957, nearly 1,000 pages of material on modern wars and military science had been written and presented to the Chief of the Soviet General Staff, Marshal V.D. Sokolovskiy.(5)

The second phase of this period, 1957 to 1960, was characterized by the production and deployment of long-range rockets, and by an increasingly focused and creative study of the implications of nuclear weapons.

In 1958 a seminar-discussion began in the General Staff on problems of military art and a future war. All high-ranking officers, from army commanders up, representatives of all arms of troops, participated in these seminars. The seminars were of a secret nature, and the conversations and discussions that took place there must not be revealed to any outsiders. The basic questions discussed were those of a future war and the state of Soviet military art.

By 1959 all the top military brains of the General Staff agreed that Soviet military doctrine needed to be revised. Future strategy must be developed on the basis, first of all, of the availability of nuclear weapons and missiles. (6)

In December 1959, the Strategic Missile Force was formed as a separate force component; the next month, the Kremlin announced its creation as well as the new nuclear doctrine. This event is viewed in the Soviet literature as a milestone in Soviet military development and the beginning of the modern era in Soviet military science, with "its main content the recognition of nuclear weapons as the chief means of combat." (7)

Military strategy, along with doctrine, was the chief subject under examination in the rethinking that took place in the late 1950s and early 1960s.   Although there were many differences of opinion, the basic tenets were formulated and adopted as part of the "revolution in military affairs."

THE NUCLEAR REVOLUTION

The nuclear revolution is the most significant phase in the modern development of Soviet military doctrine and military science. Understanding this revolution is the sine qua non for comprehending contemporary Soviet military affairs (and those in the West for that matter). This revolution was exactly that - a revolutionary change, not an evolutionary adoption. As stated in Red Star in 1963,

> The revolution in military affairs is an accomplished fact. It led to basic quantitative and qualitative changes in the military-technological base of the Armed Forces and in its structure. It marked a revolution in the methods of waging war, a revolution in the theory of military art and actual combat training of the troops. (8)

In the book Problems of the Revolution in Military Affairs, (9) which was published in 1965:

> Soviet military doctrine takes into account that the appearance of the nuclear rocket weapon signifies not a conventional change in the technical equipment of the troops but a basic revolution, a genuine revolution, in military affairs. (10)

This was not simply a revolution in the material basis for waging war, but also a revolution in ideas.

> The revolution in the military field has taken place not only in the field of material means of waging war, but also in the realm of ideas.   It has required a radical review of existing military-theoretical views, a working out of new principles of military science, and a thorough development of all its constituent parts and branches on a new basis. (11)

In sum, it was a total revolution in the mechanism of waging war - a revolution in strategy, operational art and tactics. These characteristics set the Soviet revolution apart from the corresponding effects of the introduction of nuclear weapons in the United States. The Soviets embraced the nuclear weapon, while the United States shied away from it and held back its development. To the United States, the nuclear weapon was clearly a different element of the force structure, and in general, it was not regarded as anything but a more powerful weapon. Hence its introduction was not accompanied by associated revolutionary changes in tactics, force structure and equipment. (12)   Further, in comparing the impact of the nuclear weapon on the Soviet and American approaches to war, in the Soviet Union it changed the mechanism of waging war.   In the United States, however, it appears more to have changed views on the possibility or utility of war - that is, nuclear war became "unthinkable," the end of the political process, and the basic force objective became deterrence in contrast to the Soviet objective of war fighting and winning.

The most important strategic aspect of the Soviet nuclear revolution - an aspect that characterizes their overall approach and is particularly important in the European war context - is the change in the correlation of strategy, operational art and tactics. Prior to the nuclear revolution, victory in war was achieved through the gradual accumulation of tactical successes. Armed conflict occurred primarily in the theater of military operations between the armed forces and involved the combat actions of the front-line troops who held the weapons of war. Successful battles added up to operational success, which in turn would accumulate into strategic victory.

The nuclear weapon transformed radically the traditional nature of war. With the mass employment of nuclear weapons, strategic results could be realized immediately. These, in turn, would be used to assist in the achievement of operational goals, which, in turn, paved the way for tactical success. Thus the correlation is reversed, with strategic results now leading the way. Operational art and tactics are called on to complete the strategic assaults. (13)

> The frontline ground troops in conjunction with frontal aviation and with the fleet in coastal regions, using the results of strikes by Strategic Rocket Troops, long-range aviation and rocket-carrying submarines against objectives and enemy groups in the theaters of military operations will destroy the remaining groups of enemy troops, occupy enemy territory, and protect their own territory. (14)

As a result of the nuclear revolution, nuclear weapons are regarded first as weapons for direct use by the strategic leadership.

> With the appearance of the nuclear-armed rocket weapon the position was radically changed. The strategic leadership for the first time in military history obtained its own means of destruction, by massive application of which it is possible directly to accomplish major strategic missions, creating favorable conditions for carrying out operations and battles on the land and naval theaters and changing their character. (15)

The Soviet nuclear revolution put the principal means of waging war in the hands of the strategic leadership; nuclear weapons are first the weapons of the strategic leadership and the nuclear doctrine is a combined political-military doctrine. This is not to suggest that the Soviets view nuclear weapons as strictly political and therefore unusable military weapons; on the contrary, they were incorporated into the force as valuable, usable, effective military weapons.

Of particular importance in the nuclear revolution at the operational and tactical level is the manner in which nuclear firepower is regarded and introduced into the force - more specifically, its impact on the approach to force concentration and maneuver, its difference from conventional fire support, and, as a consequence, its integration into the forces via new dedicated units with specialized command and control capabilities and practices.

The first consideration is the impact of nuclear weapons on the traditional notions of force concentration and maneuver.

A new and most important element of battle has appeared - the nuclear strike in which the fire, maneuver, and shock action of the troops seem to merge into one and, consequently, the capability to accomplish a mission independently in the destruction of one enemy force or another. (16)

Under these conditions, the excessive massing of men and combat equipment or over-crowding of combat formations ceases to be necessary and, moreover, becomes dangerous. It is obviously more correct to speak primarily not of the massing and concentration of forces, but of concentration of main efforts on the main axis by means of maneuvering the trajectories of missiles. (17)   [Emphasis added.]

Now maneuver is accomplished not only by troops and fire, but also by nuclear strikes. (18)

[The] ... principle of mass in the contemporary offensive is expressed in the concentration of the main fire efforts on the main direction and, primarily, a large portion of the nuclear power, and in the rapid exploitation of the results of the nuclear strikes by the troops. (19)

Troops no longer concentrate to achieve the required mass for attack in the traditional sense. To do so would invite a nuclear strike for which they would be a most lucrative target. Instead, mass is achieved principally by the nuclear strike and the terms mass and maneuver no longer refer merely to the troops, but also to the nuclear strike itself.

The "exploitation" of the nuclear strike introduces the second aspect that is central to the Soviet concept: the relationship between nuclear firepower and the troops. The approach taken in the Soviet Union is different from that taken in the United States. In particular, the Soviet nuclear weapons do not provide "fire support" for the infantry or armor.

The destructive effect of nuclear weapons and their capability to inflict complete destruction on the enemy within a specific radius go beyond the framework of former impressions about the fire of conventional means of destruction. Nuclear weapons do not "assure" and do not "support" the motorized rifle and tank podrazdeleniye (subunits) chast (units) but accomplish missions for the destruction of the enemy independently. (20)

Nuclear weapons are not just larger and more powerful artillery shells; they differ from them in many respects. For example, the traditional role of artillery fire support is suppression; it causes troops to cover up and "softens" them for the subsequent attack. Artillery is rarely used to hit or kill a specific target as it simply is not sufficiently accurate. A nuclear weapon, on the other hand, does not merely suppress; rather, it kills and should be used to kill. Moreover, due to the ineffectiveness of single artillery shots, conventional artillery is organized to produce mass fire, with many tubes coordinated to send many tens, hundreds, or even thousands of shells to a target area in a short time. With nuclear fire, only a few shells are required. Further, misdirected conventional shots are not uncommon and, while not desirable, are certainly tolerable. Misdirected nuclear shots, however, can be disastrous. Finally, conventional artillery shells cost a few hundred dollars each, while a nuclear shell costs in the range of tens to hundreds of thousands of dollars. Those differences demonstrate that nuclear "fire support" cannot be regarded as "fire support" in the traditional sense.

To provide the nuclear fire, a new combat arm has been added - the operational-tactical nuclear missile troops, the impact of which is unmistakable.

Technical progress has also produced serious changes in the Ground Forces. Although earlier their basic firepower was artillery, now the chief means of firepower has become the rocket units, able to carry to the enemy decisive defeat with nuclear attacks,on enormous areas and at great depths. Such possibilities of nuclear rocket weapons determine their role in the Ground Forces. This is not a support means, such as was and remains cannon-type field artillery. The team of the launch position of tactical or operational-tactical rockets is able to independently decide combat problems. (21)

These are specialized units which should not be confused with artillery units. "The operational and tactical missile units comprise the basis for the firepower of the Ground Troops. This is a qualitatively new branch of arms which is the basic means for employing nuclear weapons in combat and operations." (22)

One of the most definitive statements that captures the essence of these new capabilities and their relation to the "conventional" forces is the following quotation from Tactics, published in the mid-1960s as part of the important Soviet "Officer's Library":

Nuclear strikes are not included in the usual concept of fire. They are decisive means of destruction of the enemy, a new element for construction of the defense, and should be applied primarily for the destruction of enemy means of nuclear attack, destruction of major groupings of his troops, and the solution of other most important problems. Therefore, nuclear strikes fall outside the framework of a fire system. (23)

Succinctly stated, "The motorized infantry will be just as important, although it will not be the 'queen of the battlefield' as in past wars. On the battlefields the decisive role will be played by fire of nuclear weapons." (24)

The overall impact of the revolution on military art as a whole was summarized in 1970 in a Red Star article by Lt. General I. Zavyalov titled "New Weapons and the Art of War" - an article that might well be regarded as a summary of The Offensive, also published in 1970 in the Soviet Union:

> The creation of the nuclear warhead and its combination with a missile carrier of varying class and with varying launching methods facilitated the swift introduction of new weapons in all categories of the armed forces. These weapons produced a complete revolution in military affairs, introduced radical changes in the methods of conducting warfare, and made necessary a review of the established principles of the art of war.
>
> ... But what are these changes? First, the limits of the tactical, operational and strategic zones of combat actions have become considerably wider, the depth of modern integrated combined-arms battle and operation is greater, the scales of war are broader, the process of destroying any of the enemy's objectives is ten times quicker, and the dynamism of combat actions is greater, thus predetermining swift and distinct changes in the situation. (25)

Tasks requiring large numbers of munitions, troops and hours can now be accomplished almost instantaneously by a single, medium-yield missile. Whole units and formations can lose their combat capacity in a few minutes and command/control can be disrupted. "Second, the employment of nuclear weapons introduces the most substantial changes not only into the nature of the battle and operation, but in definite way changes the correlation of strategy, operation skill, and tactics." (26) In particular, the simultaneous resolution of tactical, operational and strategic tasks is now possible. "Third, nuclear weapons have increasingly confirmed the role of attack as the decisive form of military actions and have given rise to the necessity of resolving even defense tasks by active offensive actions."(27) This attack is especially decisive, dynamic and relentless.

> ... nothing must stop the troops in the course of fulfilling the assigned missions. Not even a break in coordinated actions and the loss of control from a superior officer can be justification for the slightest inactivity. Success on the battlefield is possible when all the decisions of the commanders and the actions of the troops are imbued with the aspiration to achieve the assigned aims whatever the cost.
>
> Fourth, the principle of concentrating the efforts of troops in a decisive direction undergoes a change in content. The massing of nuclear strikes, and not of conventional forces and equipment,

assumes prime importance. Furthermore, under these conditions not the concentration, but the maximum permissible dispersal of troops is needed because of the danger of nuclear strikes being delivered at them. Naturally, this dispersal is not boundless; its limit is the maintenance of the combat stability of the units and formations and also the maintenance of the possibility of reliable and uninterrupted control of the troops.

Fifth, the role of surprise is increased and the length of the effect of its consequences on the conduct of further military actions is greater. While in the past armies needed considerable time to repel the enemy's unexpected strikes and shift to the counter-offensive, in nuclear warfare surprise can have still more serious consequences. The growing importance of surprise has particularly acutely posed the problem of maintaining the constant high combat readiness of troops and their ability to commence combat actions to repel enemy strikes swiftly and in an organized manner.

Finally, the emergence of nuclear missiles has assigned a material basis to the principle of the simultaneous strike at the enemy's entire combat and operational formation and also the destruction of the most important military economic objectives deep in the rear of the belligerent states. (28)

An important theme that General Zavyalov used to begin and conclude his discussion of important changes brought about by the nuclear weapon is the notion of striking in depth. This, closely coupled with the notion of mass employment, is the strikingly new capability provided by the combination of nuclear warheads and missiles, enabling one to attack and destroy the enemy throughout the depth of his deployment. As explained in Military Strategy:

One of the characteristic features of a future war will be its enormous spatial scope. The decisiveness of the political and military goals of the adversaries will cause armed combat to be waged not only in the zone of contact between the adversaries, but, in essence, over the entire territory of the countries in the belligerent coalitions, since both sides will strive to completely disorganize the enemy rear. The mass nature, the high degree of strategic maneuverability, and the long-range nature of the means of destruction will assure the placing of the enemy under fire over his entire territory, including its most remote regions. (29)

At the theater level:

The employment of nuclear weapons in itself is also accomplished according to particular principles - suddenly and en masse, to the entire depth of the enemy's combat deployment, with the aim of destroying important objectives, tank, artillery, and motorized infantry groupings, major command posts, junctions of lines of communication, and rear area objectives. (30)

This change is so crucial that it is recommended for consideration as a basic principle of military art:

> The enumerated principles have become the most important ones, although of course, they cannot encompass the entire diversity of combat activity. Even, now, and moreover, as there is further development of means of warfare and military art, other principles can be formulated.
>
> For example, the principle of simultaneous action upon the enemy to the entire depth of his deployment and upon objectives of the deep rear has acquired an increasingly realistic basis with the adoption of nuclear weapons. The range of nuclear missiles and their enormous destructive force permit delivery of irreplaceable losses and defeat not only on troops, but also on objectives of the deep rear. The importance of this principle steadily grew with the introduction of nuclear weapons and longer range means of warfare. (31)

The significance of these quotations lies in their relationship to the possibility of limiting nuclear operations to a localized engagement area such as the immediate battlefield. Although the "in-depth" notion began as a clear message that the United States would not escape nuclear devastation in the event of a nuclear war, it applies with equal force and consistency to Europe. Nuclear strikes into the depth of Europe would, at a minimum, include strikes against all enemy nuclear storage sites, nuclear air strike bases, nuclear missile bases, NATO reserves and SACEUR command posts - most of which are "deep" in Germany close to the French border, in France, in England and elsewhere:

> It is believed that nuclear weapons, as the main means of destruction, should be employed in all cases for the destruction of the most important targets and objectives. These include, first of all, enemy means of nuclear attack, large concentrations of his troops and especially armored troops, reserves, in particular tank reserves, artillery in firing positions, bridges, crossings, control posts and communications centers, objects in the troop rear area, defensive structures, and others. (32)

The final point of importance concerning this nuclear revolution is that of numbers or mass. The revolutionary change involves not the limited, but the mass introduction of nuclear weapons.

> It should be noted, however, that the degree of influence of new means of warfare on methods of conduct of combat operations is directly related to the number and quality of these means. New forms of weapons and military technology employed in small numbers cannot have a substantial influence on the character of combat operations. (33)

The importance of mass - as contrasted with limited - employment of nuclear weapons appears consistently as an inseparable part of the Soviet revolution in military affairs.

THE CYBERNETIC STAGE IN THE NUCLEAR REVOLUTION

Three stages can be identified in the Soviet revolution in military affairs: 1) the development of atomic and nuclear warheads; 2) the development of long-range missiles to carry the new warheads; and 3) the cybernetic or control stage, with control used in the broadest sense of the word. The cybernetic stage is simultaneously one of the most important and one of the most neglected aspects in our understanding of Soviet military science. As discussed in the principle Soviet doctrinal reference Marxism-Leninism on War and Army, the cybernetic stage in the revolution was characterized, "by the comprehensive automation of military equipment, the automatic control of equipment and the combat actions of troops, the intensive introduction of scientific knowledge into the military field, notably for the control of the troops." (34) The major distinction between the Soviet approach to military affairs and that of the West lies in the emphasis of the Soviets on combat actions and troop control under conditions of nuclear war and in their application of cybernetics to the associated problems.

In the Soviet view, the cybernetic stage of the revolution began in the mid-1950s both in the Soviet Union and in the United States. While basically true, this view appears quite simplistic. In the late 1940s and early 1950s, cybernetics was a new and vigorous field in the United States and other Western countries. In effect, it exploded into the computer field, which continues to expand rapidly.

In the Soviet Union of Stalin's time, however, cybernetics was regarded as anti-Marxist-Leninist and officially was frowned upon as a frivolous capitalist pursuit. This situation changed only after Khrushchev's rise to power when an eminent scientist explained to the premier that cybernetics practitioners were not charlatans and that rather than being anti-Marxist-Leninist, cybernetics might be essential to the growth of worldwide communism, particularly in terms of centralized planning and control. In response, Khrushchev called a meeting of several hundred top Soviet scientists to reassess the Soviet position on cybernetics. The meeting lasted over a week, and concluded that cybernetics should constitute a third and indispensable component of the nuclear revolution.

In the field of military science, the need for cybernetics was directly tied to the problem of how to fight a nuclear war. As stated by Marshal V.D. Sokolovskiy in Military Strategy in 1962:

Now, in addition to nuclear weapons and missiles, still another new and very important military and technical factor has emerged which undoubtedly will exert a marked influence on the nature of war. We refer to the use of electronic gear, in particular, electronic computers and various other types of equipment, by the armed forces, and other devices for automizing and mechanizing control and command over weapons and troops as a whole. (35)

In the third edition in 1968, it was noted that

Military radioelectronics assures not only the use of missiles, antimissiles, and other technical means of combat, but also reconnaissance, the control of troops, forces, and weapons as a whole. It is the basis of the solution of the problem of complex automation of the processes of staff activity. Without complex automation, effective command of the armed forces and consequently their successful use in a modern war will be impossible. (36)

More specifically, the nuclear revolution brought about the information explosion and the concomitant need to process quickly and accurately large volumes of data. The following is from a 1967 <u>Voyennaya mysl'</u> article on the use of science in troop leadership:

The conditions and the nature of combat activities in modern war will be sharply different from those experienced in the Great Patriotic War. The fast-moving nature of battle, the need for fast concentration and dispersion of troops, and the constantly changing situation - these are the main things to be expected. In this connection, obviously, the volume of work to be done by a commander will greatly increase. It will be necessary to make complex calculations demanding great knowledge and skill in order to make the necessary decision in a short period of time for conducting a battle, for a march movement, or for dispersal with subsequent re-assembly of troops. It is quite obvious that any mistake, even the most minor one, may result in serious consequences. All this makes it necessary to use both mathematical and other scientific methods for a quick solution of problems. (37)

This point was summarized in 1972 by General Shtemenko:

However, it is not a simple thing for the military commander to analyze an abundance of facts. The volume of information that staffs must process has increased manyfold since World War II, and the time allowed for decision making has decreased manyfold. As a result, the requirements on the "brain capacity" of commanders and staffs have increased vastly. To meet these requirements by simply expanding the administrative apparatus is fundamentally impossible, since this would require an inordinate increase in the number of headquarters. Organization of efficient operation within such vast management offices would become a very difficult task.

The only escape from this incompatible situation lies in the extensive application of automation, primarily computers. (38)

In 1973 an article in <u>Kommunist Vooruzhennykh Sil</u> stated that

> the development of military affairs today is characterized by a
> sharp increase in the data necessary for decision-making. It has
> been calculated that, during combat action where nuclear missiles
> are being used, the headquarters of a division will receive more than
> three times as much information as the headquarters of an analogous
> large unit (<u>soyedineniye</u>) received during World War II. And this is
> not just a matter of increase in the volume of information, but also
> a question of the fact that it becomes obsolete extremely fast.
> However, in order to make a decision the commander needs only
> fresh data which reflects the actual situation exactly. All this leads
> to an increase in the time necessary for processing information and
> evaluating enemy and friendly forces. But in modern warfare
> decisions must be made in very short times, often simultaneously.
> The matter is further complicated by the incompleteness of data on
> the enemy and the probablistic nature of the information which the
> commander possesses. But still, the decision should be error-
> free. (39)

To provide for centralized management of this new and important field,
the Scientific Council on Cybernetics was established under the
chairmanship of engineer Rear-Admiral Berg in 1959. At the Twenty-
second Party Congress in 1961, Khrushchev announced that the introduction of highly perfected systems of automatic control would be
accelerated and that cybernetics, electronic computers and control
devices would be widely applied. Later that year Minister of Defense,
Marshal Malinovskiy, announced that new means of troop control,
including computers, were being widely used in Warsaw Pact exercises.

The decade of the 1960s witnessed the large-scale development of
Soviet military operations research, combat modeling, control process
analysis and design and the production of a family of third-generation
computers, the RYAD family, patterned after the IBM 360 series.
These new techniques were first introduced in those areas - missile
guidance, auto pilots and air defense - that could most readily utilize
the capacity.

> The second important circumstance is the "predisposition" of the
> particular area of military affairs to automation of control. There
> are branches of the armed forces which by their very nature, present
> greater opportunities for the introduction of automation than do
> others with the current level of development of technology. Among
> them are the missile forces and the air defense forces.

The second application of this new technology was in the use of
computers to target and direct the nuclear strike. This involves the
development of a target intelligence data base, force-effectiveness
calculations, warhead selection and weapon allocation, effects prediction - both prompt and delayed - and decision transmission. For
example:

Under modern conditions the factor of time acquires very great importance. In connection with this great demands are made on the complete range of actions taken by commanders, staffs, reconnaissance units, and attacking troops. Learning information about the targets, transmitting this information to missile units, and assigning concrete missions to destroy important enemy targets constitute a single process which in each case must be carried out in compressed periods of time. An important factor in the effective use of operational-tactical missiles is the precise coordination among forces and means involved in destroying the enemy's nuclear potential. (40)

Later in 1972 and 1973, it was noted that:

Ordinarily this will involve a calculation of the time for making nuclear strikes or preparing combat operations calculating the balance of forces and means, calculations related to the results of using one's own nuclear weapons and forecasting of the radiation situation, calculations for moving up forces, and so forth. (41)

Using whatever information is available on the enemy and his forces, electronic computing equipment is employed to select within a matter of minutes the best methods for conducting combat operations and to immediately make the operational or battle plan available to subordinates. Any time saved during this stage could ensure a sudden strike being carried out against the enemy and thus the enemy would find himself at a disadvantage. (42)

The third and most difficult application was for troop control - decision making, maneuver, logistic support and so forth. The extent to which the Soviets are applying cybernetics to that area is illustrated by their focus on the command decision process itself. The basis for control of troops is the decision for operations and combat. Analyses of the troop control process indicate that over 40 percent of the time is required for the decision process itself. "It is not by chance that great attention is devoted to the method for making a decision in operational and combat training." (43)

The Soviets have modeled the decision process in detail and applied operations research techniques to improve it. They recognize that there will be gaps in input information and place considerable attention on decision making based on incomplete and even erroneous information. Finally, they apply correlation and "predictive" mathematics to help "foresee the course of events with a high degree of reliability," and "uncover the essence of enemy intentions." (44) These are not just theoretical studies; the procedures designed to handle such problems are tested in Soviet field exercises.

One of the most impressive aspects of the cybernetic revolution is the depth and breadth of the activities subsumed within it. In addition to technology, it includes mathematical modeling, analysis of control processes, establishment of criteria, testing and evaluation, information reporting and organization, noise immunity and secrecy of communications, and optimization techniques.

Of particular interest is the Soviet use of network analysis and PERT management techniques. A major portion of the modeling and analysis activity and scheduling of oriented staff work has relied heavily on network techniques. The processes involved are modeled in flow diagram form. Critical paths are identified and then the process adjusted or restructured to reduce the critical time and thus insure the optimum utilization of personnel and minimum time delays. This process is applied to the scheduling and organizing of staff work itself, river-crossing operations, a tank battalion's march, and even maintenance and supply of petroleum, oil, and lubricants (POL) and ammunition for entire front operations across Europe.

In 1972, the Ministry of Defense published 30,000 copies of the sixteenth and final volume of the "Officer's Library," Concept, Algorithm, Decision. The foreword was written by General of the Army, S.M. Shtemenko, a first deputy chief of the General Staff as well as the first deputy commander-in-chief of the joint Armed Forces of the Warsaw Pact Nations. In it, he states quite explicitly that, "The time for extensive adoption of automation in the entire chain of command has arrived." (45)

By 1976 articles in Soviet military journals were recommending that computerized command/control facilities be built for student use and training purposes at the service academies.

The revolution in military affairs has so increased the significance of troop control and the demands placed upon it that it is on the way to becoming a major sector of military affairs. (46) Cybernetics -including modeling, special analytical techniques such as network analysis, and computers - has become the primary means of meeting demands caused by the greatly increased scope and pace of combat. The focus on combat - on the use of these new techniques to improve the war-fighting ability - is evident throughout the Soviet literature. The Soviets are applying mathematics to the field of actual combat. There is no known counterpart to this approach to the use of cybernetics in the NATO ground forces or, for that matter, very much appreciation in the West of its significance in terms of capabilities or vulnerabilities. The importance of cybernetics to the Soviets, however, is quite clear - accuracy, speed, and flexibility.

THE CONTINUING SCIENTIFIC AND
TECHNICAL REVOLUTION

The primary Soviet objective in both peace and war is to achieve and maintain military-technical superiority over the imperialist enemy. This superiority begins with nuclear weapons. However, it is definitely not limited to them.

The nuclear weapon is already the basis of the combat might of all services of the armed forces. Creating the advantage over the enemy in this weapon and methods of its use is the most important task in the building up of the armed forces in peacetime as well as during the course of a war. (47)

The Soviets view the nuclear revolution as the beginning of a literal explosion in science and technology that embraces all facets of military capability from armor to small arms, reconnaissance, communications, air defense, space or cosmic weapons, and ships.   Science and technology have become major determinants of military power and the military-technical superiority of the Soviet Union, an essential goal.

The need for military-technical superiority has been a constant theme of lead editorials and articles throughout the Soviet military and party press.   For example, as stated in 1968 and 1969 in Voyennaya mysl':

> The party constantly is concerned that the Soviet Army and Navy have military-technical superiority over the armed forces of our probable enemies, the imperialist aggressive states. (48)

> No lags will be allowed in the military field; maintaining reliable military-technical superiority is a task conditioned by the international duties of the Soviet Union. (49)

As implied by the title of the last text in the Soviet "Officer's Library" series, Scientific-Technical Progress and the Revolution in Military Affairs, the revolution extends well beyond a nuclear revolution to include a complete scientific-technical revolution as well.

One of the leading Soviet spokesmen on this subject is Colonel V.M. Bondarenko, Candidate of Philosophical Sciences, who is associated with the Lenin Political Military Academy.   Colonel Bondarenko has written numerous articles on science and its application throughout all aspects of military development and has contributed to several Military Affairs, Methodological Problems of Military Theory and Practice, and The Philosophical Heritage of V.I. Lenin and Problems of Contemporary War.   Writing in 1974 for Communist of the Armed Forces, he stated:

> The increasing role of science in military development has led to its transformation into one of the decisive factors in the achievement of victory in modern war.   Science has become an independent element in the system of the defensive might of the country. Military-scientific potential together with the economic, social-political, moral-political and the war potential itself determine the military (defensive) might of the country.(50)

The Soviets recognize the fundamental importance of the national technology base to economic, political and military strength.   The quantity and quality of equipment is a major component in assessing the correlation of forces at any level - tactical, operational and strategic. The Soviets have made a major commitment to shift decisively the correlation of forces at all levels in their favor.   One of the major aspects of this process has been the buildup of the technology base and equipment reserve.

Technology transfer is extremely important to the Soviets in this regard because it is simpler to buy the "start-up capability" than to develop it from scratch.   As stated by Kosygin at the Twenty-third Party Congress in April 1966:

> We can, and must...assume our due place in the world's license market...we, too, could profit by purchasing licenses, rather than developing the problem concerned ourselves...(which) will enable us to save hundreds of millions of rubles on scientific research during the coming five years.

In terms of scientific and technical progress in Soviet military development, the early 1970s appear to represent the important transition from building a technology base to applying that base. As stated in numerous articles in the 1970s, Soviet science and technology has now matured to the point where it can be directed to solve important problems. (51) This "newly matured" Soviet capability is not isolated in the laboratories or separated from the real world; rather it appears to have a very pragmatic, focused and integrated approach with the military sector. Science and technology are most important to military capability, and as such, impact greatly on military strategy.

> Scientific-technical progress forces military strategy to devote ever greater attention to problems of military formation, in the process of which the latest scientific-technical achievements materialize in the form of latest models and systems weapons. Strategy is called upon to provide a purposeful, planned character to this process and to ensure continual military-technical superiority over imperialist blocs. Scientific-technical progress arms Soviet military strategy with new methods of research which, if not mastered, leave it in no position to fulfill the difficult tasks before it.(52)

The Soviet approach to scientific progress in military affairs may be difficult for the West to match in the years ahead. Among the vital aspects of that approach are the careful identification of goals and selection of priorities - goals and priorities that are not subject to the rapid shifts resulting from the vagaries of the political process that often seem to characterize the United States approach. Long-range planning is not only a possibility, but a reality. It is also practicable because it is carefully directed by high-level managers who do not change jobs every two or three years. Further, Soviet goals and objectives appear to be well thought out and their design philosophy, very pragmatic. Items are generally not developed merely for technological or public relations; military operations and combat and military superiority over the enemy are the primary criteria. Finally, technical talent is encouraged inside as well as outside the military; technological expertise furthers rather than curtails a military officer's career in the Soviet Union.

The 1950s and 1960s can be viewed as the era in which the Soviets built their technology base. The 1970s are now seeing the application of this base to achieve their primary objective - decisive control over the correlation of forces at all levels. This may be what the West is just beginning to experience and question.

3 The Soviet Study of Laws and Principles of Military Art

> The goal of any science is understanding of the laws of the field of phenomena it is studying and use of this knowledge in practical activity. (1)

Soviet military science is treated as a science in much the same sense as physics, chemistry and biology. It has equal if not superior status, is an honored academic discipline, is the subject of intensive study, and has its own set of laws the investigation and understanding of whose essence, nature, and dialectical correlation with principles of military art is viewed as a central military-theoretical task.

The importance of the study of these subjects to the Soviets cannot be overstated. The major task of military science is to understand the nature and essence of future war and to prepare to win it. The laws of warfare and principles of military art comprise the basis of this understanding and planning and are an essential practical input to the formulation of military doctrine. Although military doctrine represents the state's guidance to the military, at the same time it is to be based on a firm foundation of carefully researched military principles. This is one more example of the strong link between military science and national security policy - that is, military doctrine. Military science is also the basis for military strategy. The Soviets believe that victory emerges from an understanding of the laws of warfare and the skillful application of the correct principles of military art in both the preparation for and conduct of war. The Soviet military strategy is a war-winning strategy in every sense of the word. As stated by Marshal Sokolovskiy in 1968, "The subject of strategy itself has not infrequently been defined as the art of achieving victory in war with armed forces." (2)

The laws and principles are studied from all conceivable angles as they contribute to every subject - tactics, strategy, training, staff operations, education, research and development, and so forth. The investigation of these laws and application of the principles constitute a major portion of Soviet textbooks and articles. These laws and principles are studied and taught at the major academies including the Lenin Political-Military Academy, the Frunze Military Academy, and the Academy of the General Staff, among others. To the Soviets these laws and the correct application of the principles are an essential qualitative component of military strength, and as such, receive the attention of senior and general officers as well as younger officers. "The best armament and technical equipment of the army will not bring victory if they are not used in complete conformance with the laws of armed conflict...." (3)

The importance of the Soviet study of these laws and principles to the West cannot be overemphasized as it reflects the manner in which the Soviets are trained to think and plan. This presents a problem, because the study of laws and principles of military art does not appear to have comparable status in Western military organizations. This even appears to confuse the Soviets, for in an uncharacteristic full-page quote of a United States Army text dealing with military principles, they indicate that in the United States Army these principles have not changed since 1924, despite the subsequent introduction of nuclear weapons, advanced electronics, modern air power and armor.

At the same time, there is a tendency in the West to view the seemingly endless debates over military principles in the Soviet literature as part of the dialectical fog or chaff that must be discarded to reveal significant kernels of thought; it is seldom recognized or accepted that this "chaff" is the basis of Soviet thought and that its reiteration signifies its constant refinement and reinterpretation for practical application. Soviet military force development, organization, training and plans are based first and foremost on the application of these principles.

> Objective laws of war and armed conflict lie at the basis of principles of Soviet military art. The principles of military art stem directly from these laws. The principles are correct only when they answer objective laws. Therefore, knowledge of the laws of war and armed conflict and an understanding of the character of their action is an important condition for skilled use of the principles of military art in accordance with the concrete situation, and it comprises the basis of military-theoretical training of generals and officers, just as it comprises the basis of all military practice involving both the resolution of tasks of military development and the organization and conduct of armed warfare. (4)

LAWS OF THE FIRST ORDER

The study of these laws and principles is highly complex; they are not static but subject to constant evolution. In a sense the laws of military science have their own "statistical" probability character. Rather than being independent, they are highly interactive; frequently, the effects of some laws contradict those of others. Thus, in order to understand them, it is necessary to investigate the widely diverse and complex phenomena of war and military affairs. (5)

The first and politically most important law of war derives from Clausewitz and reflects the dependence of war and its conduct on politics. This law is based on the essence of war as a special social phenomenon. A typical statement of this law is: "The nature of a political goal has a decisive influence on the conduct of war." (6)

The second and militarily most important law of war is the impact of the correlation of forces on the course and outcome of war. The correlation of forces is highly emphasized in Soviet texts and journals. Simply stated, the stronger of the two sides generally wins the war provided it acts with the intelligent strategy called for by the situation. Thus, achieving the superior correlation of forces is a primary Soviet goal, both in peace and in war.

The correlation of forces, in general, is not limited to simple quantitative force comparisons, but is determined equally - if not more so - by qualitative factors. The advantage may accrue to the belligerent possessing a smaller number of troops and different types of equipment if he is able to make better use of them as a result of more skilled command, better application of military principles, more stable troops, and other factors. (7) The outcome of war between countries and coalitions of countries depends on the correlation of their military might and "on the ability of the military and political leadership of each to create a superiority in this correlation and to use it to their advantage." (8) This emphasis on using as well as creating superiority is fundamental to the Soviet way of thinking, and applies to all elements of a conflict: "...each military action - battle, engagement, or operation - is also determined by its specific correlation of forces and by the skill of the leaders to create and fully use the conditions for victory."(9) From this law have emerged several crucial principles of military art, including those of surprise and force concentration at decisive times and places.

This law has gone through considerable development. The first and second world wars were a contest not only of forces, but of economies as well, and superiority in the correlation of forces was largely achieved during the course of the war. Currently, the Soviets stress the importance of distinguishing between military potential and in-place military forces. Of primary significance at present is the correlation of forces that exists in place and is usable at the outset of the war. With the mass introduction of nuclear weapons into the armed forces, Soviet military science arrived at the conclusion that the war may not be long in duration, that the outcome may be determined by the very first massive nuclear strikes, and that war can begin with available groupings of troops, rather than await extensive mobilization of armed forces. Hence, the more recent formulation of this law:

...the course and outcome of war waged with unlimited employment of all means of conflict depends primarily on the correlation of available, strictly military forces of the combatants at the beginning of the war, especially in nuclear weapons and means of delivery.

Victory in war will be formed not so much from the sum of particular successes, but as a result of the effective application of a state's maximum power at the very beginning of armed conflict. The simultaneous defeat of the armed forces, including strategic nuclear means, and enemy installations of economic potential to attain war goals in a short time - this is what was advanced to the fore in 1959. (10)

The third law is that the course and outcome of war depends upon the correlation of military potentials of the combatants. Military potential means the maximum capability of a state to maintain and improve armed forces, increase their combat power, man them with trained personnel, and supply them with military equipment. The critical potentials are scientific, economic and moral-political.

This law applies both in peacetime and during the course of the war. In its peacetime use, the law expresses the dependence of achieving the desired correlation of forces on the scientific, economic and moral-political capabilities of nations, and in so doing, ties them into the process. Its wartime application refers more particularly to the importance of military potential if the war is not a short war. While nuclear missiles permit the attaining of war goals in a relatively short time, the Soviets recognize that if nations are large, such as the Soviet Union and the United States, and if they prepare properly for war, then the war will undoubtedly become protracted. Hence, while the short war is the desired goal, the protracted war must be anticipated. In this case its outcome will depend not only on the strictly military forces available at the outset, but also on the military potentials of the countries to continue the war effort.

This post-initial strike period - consisting of reconstitution and recovery generally - is perhaps one of the most neglected aspects of war in the West, and simultaneously, one of the most vital aspects of war in Soviet thought. It serves to reemphasize the difference between Western deterrence and Soviet war fighting, between Western and Soviet views on the impossibility and possibility of war and the consequent need to prepare for it. The Soviets regard "the stability and mobility of the economy, and the ability of a country quickly to restore destroyed economic connections in the event individual elements have been attacked and to make efficient use of all available resources" to be of critical importance. The Soviet approach to war, while recognizing that the crucial economic efforts in preparation for nuclear war occur largely in the period preceding the outbreak of war, (11) also emphasizes the link between victory and recovery. The Soviets do not regard nuclear war as apocalyptic, but rather as involving great destruction that can and will be survived and result in the triumph of communism and defeat of capitalism. Accordingly, the correlation of forces also gives considerable weight to the ability of the country to recover after the war.

This law is sometimes broken into two components that emphasize the careful attention to be given to the correlation of the scientific-technical and moral-political potentials. The former emphasizes the increased role of science in modern times, which makes "the struggle for scientific-technological superiority over the probable enemy a matter of primary importance," (12) while the latter relates to the dictum that superiority is on the side of the progressive social system (communism), which is conducting a just war, and which is psychologically prepared for the rigors of nuclear war.

A fourth law - also cast as a principle - is that forestalling the enemy in the deployment of his forces and in the initiation of combat operations can provide a decisive advantage. This is closely related to, if not a corollary of, the second law on the importance of superiority. It is believed useful, however, to regard it as a separate law because of the emphasis the Soviets place on it. The Soviet literature is replete with discussions of the need to forestall the enemy; it is as indispensable as building up one's own forces and, in both conventional and nuclear attack variants in modern times, is of critical importance. This law is regarded as a rule of "practical activity" of the military commander at all levels. (13) It includes misleading or confusing the enemy and attacking critical points that will actively forestall him, such as command/control facilities and key transportation choke points related to the forward development of reserves. This law also "constitutes the objective basis of the principle of surprise," (14) which receives so much attention in the Soviet literature.

Within these "laws of the first order," war is viewed as much broader than armed conflict, and includes various forms of economic, ideological and diplomatic struggle.

The Soviets also refer to more specific "second-order" laws of which two in particular are worth noting. The first of these is that "...methods and forms of armed conflict depend on the material basis of the battle and operations." (15) The material basis is understood to mean the actual forces and means - armaments, combat equipment and the people that use them. This law is change oriented; it states that as the weapons change, so must the methods and forms of armed conflict.

Weapons are one of the most important and decisive fundamentals of development of military art. They have a substantial influence on methods of conducting military operations and war as a whole. The appearance of new types of weapons increases the combat effectiveness of armed forces, opens up opportunities for accomplishing new and more complex tactical, operational, and strategic missions, and thus involves a change in methods of conducting the battle, operation and war as a whole. Significant changes in means of warfare invariably give rise also to major changes in methods of conducting operations and battles. (16)

The major such innovations in weapons usually discussed in the Soviet literature are firearms, machine guns, tanks, airplanes, and, most important in recent times, nuclear weapons. The Soviets point out, however, that capabilities and change depend not merely on the introduction of new weapons, but also their introduction in sufficient quantity. If new weapons are employed in insufficient numbers, they do not reveal their true capabilities. In general, the Soviet acquisition strategy has been one of quantity first, then quality. There is a particularly interesting quote in The Basic Principles of Operational Art and Tactics concerning the required numbers:

> The number of new means needed for a change of methods of combat operations is inversely proportional to their combat power. For machine guns this figure reached hundreds of thousands of units, and for tanks and aviation - several thousand. The production of several hundred nuclear weapons and means of delivery at one time caused a need for fundamental revision of methods and forms of combat operations. The number of nuclear weapons is constantly building up. (17)   [Emphasis added] .

One might infer from this quote that the Soviet stockpile of nuclear weapons in the mid-1950s amounted to several hundred and that if modern war is to be conducted differently from World War II, at least several hundred nuclear weapons must be used. The use of relatively few weapons would result in a war of a transitional nature - part conventional, part nuclear. Most of the discussion of laws and principles focuses on either nuclear or conventional war and particularly the differences between the two. Seldom is the in-between area discussed except as a transition or in relation to United States or NATO concepts of limited nuclear war.

The second specific law of armed conflict is: "...any battle or operation at any given moment of its development takes shape in favor of that opposing side whose troops possess the greater combat power in comparison with the enemy." (18)   This relates once again to the correlation of forces concept, but in more specific terms. It reiterates the essential motivation for superiority that is present throughout the Soviet military literature.

Combat power measures the ability of the troops to deliver an attack against the enemy, repulse enemy attacks, and the extent of their combat readiness. The elements that enter into Soviet calculations of combat power include the quantity and quality of available nuclear weapons and means of delivery; the technical outfitting and especially the degree of mechanism, motorization and mobility; firepower; numbers of people and their condition (radiation exposure history); the moral-psychological preparation of soldiers and officers; their state of training and coordination; the condition of their military art and the correspondence of its principles to the character of war; training of command personnel, system of control; and so forth. (19)

Superiority can be achieved in two ways: by building up the elements that comprise the combat power of the friendly forces; and by undermining the enemy's combat power. Traditionally, efforts to achieve superiority over the enemy in a particular sector were accomplished by increasing the number of friendly forces and means.

The attacking forces would strive to create a superiority on the axis of main attack of at least three or four on the breakthrough sector. This provided the local superiority required to break through the defenses or win the battle. Superiority was generally gained by the cumulative effect of piecemeal defeat of the enemy in numerous such battles - as many as were required to achieve total success. Thus, the change in the correlation of forces proceeded gradually "from bottom to top."

An examination of the impact of nuclear weapons on the laws of combat reveals significant alteration of that traditional approach. Nuclear weapons can be used to change the correlation of forces almost instantaneously on a particular axis or sector and throughout the entire depth of the enemy's disposition. Moreover, as a result of high troop mobility, it is possible to exploit these strikes over great distances throughout the enemy's ranks. Thus, nuclear weapons became the chief means of changing the correlation of forces.

The Soviets recognize that to some extent, the laws apply to both sides, although their application and interpretation can vary because of the differences in the underlying social-political system. (20) Regardless of these differences, the Soviets emphasize the need to evaluate correctly their own strength as well as that of the enemy. They clearly recognize that unrealistic goals for a battle or an operation can result in minor failures, loss of troops and even complete defeat. The need to understand fully the enemy might well be considered a special law.

> The practice of antagonists in obtaining knowledge about the combat situation indicates that scientific foresight is possible only on the basis of such logical thinking as will correctly reflect objective reality. Rules determining the course and outcome of armed combat are manifested through the conscious and purposeful activity of people who place a distinctive mark on all processes of armed combat. Therefore it is so important to study while it is still peacetime not only the capabilities of enemy weapons and combat equipment, his strategy and tactics, but also the mentality and national character traits of personnel in the army of a probable enemy as well as the individual peculiarities of his individual commanders and leaders. Considerably greater attention must be devoted to studying the morale and combat qualities of personnel in the armies of NATO countries and to familiarize personnel of our armed forces with this information. (21)

> But it would be a dangerous mistake to miscalculate the potential of imperialist military ideology and science. Soviet military science should most painstakingly study and assess new features and trends in development of bourgeois military thought in order to achieve even greater superiority over it. (22)

A thorough, detailed understanding of the enemy in all its dimensions, qualitative as well as quantitative, lies at the basis of Soviet military science and is integral to each of the laws of warfare.

PRINCIPLES OF MILITARY ART

As indicated earlier, the principles of military art stem directly from the preceding laws of war and armed conflict and are correct only when they answer those laws. These principles lie at the heart of Soviet military education, training and plans; they are understood by the Soviets to be the basic ideas and most important recommendations for the organization and conduct of battles, operations and war as a whole, suitable for practical use in all basic forms of troop combat activity. The basic principles are valid for all three parts of military art - tactics, operational art and strategy. (23)

One of the best discussions of Soviet principles of military art available in English is the book The Basic Principles of Operational Art and Tactics. Published in Moscow in 1972, it was the most important Soviet military publication of that year. (24) It was listed in the Soldiers Calendar in 1973 and 1974 as recommended reading for the Soviet armed forces. The author had served on the faculty of the Frunze Military Academy and had written several articles and books, two of which are concerned with achieving high rates of advance in offensive operations.

The basic principles examined in this book are:

1. mobility and high tempos of combat operations;

2. concentration of main efforts and creation of superiority of forces and means over the enemy at the decisive place and at the decisive time;

3. surprise;

4. combat activeness;

5. preservation of the combat effectiveness of friendly troops;

6. conformity of the goal and plan of the operation (battle) to the conditions of the actual situation;

7. coordination; and

8. simultaneous action.

These principles are examined in this text as they have evolved through history. The primary emphasis is placed on the changes that occurred as a result of mass introduction of nuclear weapons into all of the forces. Briefly reviewed below, those principles comprise the basic theory that underlies the development of Soviet strategic planning for a war in Europe.

1. Mobility and High Tempos of Combat Operations

Mobility and high tempos of combat operations bring success in a battle or operation. (25)

The development of this concept into the most important principle of operational art and tactics accompanied the total motorization of the Soviet armed forces, the high degree of mechanization, and broad outfitting of the forces with nuclear weapons that occurred in the 1960s.

Mobility does not refer simply to combat and transport vehicles, but involves as well the capacity to accomplish tasks quickly and effectively, including the capability of rapid and effective accomplishment of the combat mission, maneuver and reaction to situation changes, swift identification of targets for strike, flexibility and ease of troop control, flexibility in using firepower and in the commanders' thinking, precision in organizing control, material and technical support, and, generally, the ability to operate at the necessary moment and place faster and more unexpectedly than the enemy. Thus, mobility is closely connected with principles of surprise, concentration of efforts, and preservation of combat effectiveness of the troops. (26)

Time is of the utmost importance in modern conflict. The major effect of nuclear weapons has been one of time compression. Rapid changes in the situation as a result of nuclear weapons use require rapid adaptation both to survive and to win.

Another Soviet "indicator" of mobility is the ability of the commanders and staff to make a rapid and in-depth analysis of a complex situation, reach the most viable decision without delay, bring it quickly to the attention of subordinates, and direct continuously and firmly the actions of troops in the interests of successful accomplishment of the combat mission. (27) In the case of unit commanders, the latter includes the capability to plan operations while moving up to the engagement. (28) As indicated earlier, the application of cybernetic techniques to all phases of military activity plays a crucial role in achieving this capability.

High rates of advance are a major objective of Soviet strategy and an indicator of success. Costs in terms of casualties, consumption of POL, ammunition and so forth, are directly related to the rate of advance. High rates of attack enable one to cross radioactive terrain quickly, thus minimizing the amount of radiation exposure received by the troops.

Most importantly, high rates of advance and flexibility in maneuver permit rapid penetration into the enemy's deep rear where his nuclear means are based and force him to change positions, thus depriving him of the capability to conduct massive retaliatory strikes.

A major concern of Soviet operations research is the calculation of rates of advance - both in terms of increasing and estimating the speed. Nomographs detailing the speed for different units crossing varied types of terrain have been developed, and optimized march orders and estimates of associated times have been calculated.

2. Concentration of Main Efforts

To attain victory over the enemy one must not dissipate his forces and means equally across the entire front, but the main efforts must be concentrated on the most important axis or sector and at the right time in order to form there the necessary superiority over the enemy in men and weapons. (29)

This principle is denoted variously, including, superiority of forces, massing, concentration of superior forces at the right place and at the right moment, shock effect, and the "law of numbers." It is a direct derivative of the law of the correlation of forces.

The principle of concentration has undergone considerable modification as a result of the development of nuclear (and other) weapons of mass destruction. While in the past, the necessary superiority of forces and means was achieved by concentrating forces on the main axis of attack prior to the assault, this approach is no longer permissible. Due to nuclear weapons, long-range delivery and modern reconnaissance means, large force concentrations must be avoided because they present excellent targets and are, thus, very vulnerable to nuclear attack and destruction. Under present conditions, the necessary force superiority is achieved by destroying the opposition with massed nuclear strikes. Concentration and maneuver are terms that are now applied as much to the nuclear means as they were to forces in the past.

> Under these conditions the excessive massing of men and combat equipment or over-crowding of combat formations ceases to be necessary and, moreover, becomes dangerous. It is obviously more correct to speak primarily not of the massing and concentration of forces, but of concentration of main efforts on the main axis by means of maneuvering the trajectories of missiles. (30)

> Now maneuver is accomplished not only by troops and fire, but also by nuclear strikes.

> [The] ...principle of mass in the contemporary offensive is expressed in the concentration of the main fire efforts on the main direction and, primarily, a large portion of the nuclear power, and in the rapid exploitation of the results of the nuclear strikes by the troops. (31)

While this applies to achieving the overall correlation of forces on the main avenue of attack, some localized concentration will still be required. The nuclear strikes referred to above are believed not to represent an indiscriminate "barrage," but rather a fairly discrete targeting of major defensive force concentrations. One does not just blanket an area with nuclear fire, particularly close to one's own troops. Therefore, some localized concentration remains necessary and can spell vulnerability if not approached correctly.

> Under conditions of nuclear missile warfare, the dispersal of troops does not eliminate the need for their concentration at the necessary place at the right time for delivering powerful attacks.

In addition to this, the concentration of forces and means has taken on immeasurably greater importance in time than in space. Moreover, concentration in space now represents a great danger and can be done only for a short time, quickly, and resolutely. A concentration extended over a longer interval of time may be quickly disrupted by nuclear strikes of the enemy and will not give the proper effect. (32)

Thus, massing has become a question of timing and placement; concentration is no longer a mere quantitative measure, but has acquired qualitative characteristics. Further, its interrelation with other principles, in turn reinforcing their importance, is readily apparent. With the introduction of nuclear weapons, success or defeat in a battle or operation is determined by superiority in forces and means, by high speed in the actions of troops and in the employment of nuclear weapons, and by the intelligent use of time. The effect of the principle of concentration is closely interwoven with the principles of mobility, activeness and surprise. The strength of the attack and swiftness and surprise of actions are of decisive importance and characteristic of the principle of concentration under contemporary conditions. (33) This desire for surprise permeates all decisions involved in the preparation for and conduct of operations; the operational goals, direction and time of the attack, forces and weapons to be employed, and methods of operations must be unexpected for the enemy. (34)

3. Surprise

One of the principles of military art, ensuring success in battle and in operations. Surprise makes it possible to inflict heavy losses upon the enemy in short periods of time, to paralyze his will, and to deprive him of the possibility of offering organized resistance. Surprise is achieved in the following ways: by using various types and methods of combat; by misleading the enemy as to one's own intentions; by safeguarding the security of operational plans; by decisive action and skilful maneuver; by unexpected use of nuclear weapons; and by using means and methods with which the enemy is unfamiliar. Surprise may be tactical, operational, or strategic. (35)

Surprise has been a most important principle of military art since olden times. The employment of nuclear weapons has considerably increased the role and importance of surprise. (36)

With the employment of nuclear weapons, the decisiveness and scope of the offensive are increased, the times for the attainment of its goals are reduced, and the significance of surprise and the time factor increases even more. (37)

Surprise in combat makes it possible to catch the enemy unaware, to spread panic in his ranks, to paralyze the will to resist and to sharply reduce the combat capability of troops, to disorganize command, and to create favorable conditions for achieving victory even over superior forces. The presence of nuclear weapons, the increased mobility and maneuverability of tanks and other means of motorization make it possible to achieve surprise strikes and attacks. (38)

The emphasis on secrecy and surprise is reiterated throughout Soviet military literature. Its greatly increased importance in recent times is the direct result of the potentially decisive effect of a surprise nuclear attack. Because such an attack can determine victory or defeat very early in the opening phase of a war, the significance of both achieving surprise and not being surprised is clear.

The efforts contemplated to achieve surprise are comprehensive and, generally speaking, amount to secrecy and deception.

A deciding condition for ensuring the achievement of surprise has begun to be considered the ability to hide from an enemy conducting constant and active reconnaissance, the presence of new weapons and equipment, the concept and plan of an operation or battle, groupings of forces and means which have been created, their missions, axes, time of beginning and methods of actions prescribed. All commanders, staffs, and troops are obliged always to take all steps to deprive the enemy of an opportunity to collect data relative to the actual location and condition of our troops, especially nuclear missiles, aviation, tank groupings, and control points.

The assurance of secrecy of operations has begun to be achieved as a result of an entire complex of interwoven measures having the purpose not only of depriving enemy of information about friendly troops, but also of leading him astray with regard to their incapabilities and planned actions. Secrecy has begun to be achieved by keeping in strict secrecy all data of interest to the enemy, as well as by using all possible camouflage, and definitely the use of military cunning. Demonstrations and misinformation find wide employment. (39)

Accurate interpretation of actions and indicators becomes very difficult as a result of Soviet secrecy about their true intentions and deliberate deception.

Covertness is applied not only to general attack preparations but also to the main axis of attack: "It is extremely important to concentrate the necessary forces and means on the direction of the main strike in a rapid and covert manner, from different directions and only for the time necessary for making the strike." (40)

Although covert mobilization of air missile and naval units is not considered a major problem, the same cannot be said in regard to the ground forces. The implicit conclusion is that the success of a surprise attack would be largely determined by the use of nuclear weapons: first, because the opportunities to defeat the enemy quickly and take advantage of surprise are far greater with a nuclear strike than a

conventional one; second, because the place of the attack is best kept
secret when it is "defined" by the maneuvering of nuclear strikes rather
than the concentration of forces; and third, because the requirements
for ground forces are minimized through the use of nuclear strikes to
destroy large segments of enemy forces and the instantaneous creation
of a favorable correlation of forces. A major factor in the Soviet
decision to attack with nuclear or conventional weapons may be their
assessment of whether or not they could covertly achieve, on the main
avenues of attack, the correlation of ground forces essential to insure a
very rapid advance and short war.

A dominant approach to achieving secrecy in the attack may be the
use of operations undercover at night or during heavy overcast
conditions.

> In order to conceal preparations for the attack and avoid unjustified
> losses even before the initiation of active operations, the
> podrazdeleniye [subunits such as companies, battalions] should
> move out and occupy the attack position at night or under other
> conditions of limited visibility observing camouflage measures. (41)

This nocturnal movement receives major emphasis in the Soviet
literature. It applies not only to movement of ground forces, but also to
that of weapons, particularly nuclear, in from the rear, the dispersal of
aircraft on the eve of the war, and the insertion of air assault and long-
range reconnaissance/sabotage units and subunits throughout the NATO
rear area during the night before the attack. It also applies to the
reinforcement and replacement of units for sustained or continuous
combat operations. As explained in The Offensive,

> ...the role and importance of combat operations at night will
> increase sharply in a future nuclear missile war. Night operations
> will be more frequent. They will develop on a broader scale than
> during World War II, and they will become an ordinary phenomenon.
> This is explained, first of all, by the decisive character of the
> attack, which demands uninterrupted conduct of combat operations
> day and night; secondly, by the wide development and adoption by
> the troops of night observation instruments, which has permitted
> solution of the problem of driving combat vehicles at night and has
> eased the location of objects on the battlefield and the conduct of
> aimed fire; and thirdly, by the specific advantages and benefits
> which stem from a night attack.
>
> Nighttime facilitates secrecy in moving troops up to the forward
> edge and shifting into the attack, and it thus makes it easier to
> achieve surprise of attack, which in turn deprives the enemy of the
> possibility of orienting himself correctly and in a timely manner in
> the situation of night combat. The defender here is forced to
> operate at random, without knowing what the attacker's goals are.
> The feeling of the unknown, actions in the blind, and heavy
> dependence on the initiative of the attacker paralyze and demoral-

ize the defender, often throwing him into confusion. All this favors the rapid seizure of objectives and positions which are tactically important and the swift defeat of the enemy grouping even by inferior forces.

Surprise is a basic characteristic of night operations. In any situation it is necessary to attempt to take advantage of this factor to the maximum. The experience of the past war shows that at night even relatively small podrazdeleniya [subunits] can use sudden and decisive offensive actions to achieve a level of success which in the daytime would require considerably more forces and weapons.(42)

The Soviet recognition that bad weather hinders the offense as well as the defense can lead to the conclusion that they would prefer not to attack in unfavorable weather conditions.   However, the Soviet assessment would be relative and if they felt better prepared than NATO to operate in bad weather or at night, then that is precisely when they would attack.

4. Combat Activeness

Success in a battle or operation is achieved by that side which, with all else equal, acts more actively and resolutely, takes the initiative, and holds it firmly. (43)

This principle of combat activeness increased in significance with the nuclear revolution and the Soviet view of nuclear war as extremely dynamic, fast-paced and possibly decisive in the initial phase. It is directly related to the possibilities for negotiation should a Warsaw Pact/NATO war develop. As stated in the discussion of this principle in the Soviet book, The Basic Principles of Operational Art and Tactics:

The sharp class character of war, which precludes any possibility of any sort of compromise, predetermines the extreme decisiveness of its political goals, which in combination with the specific features of contemporary means of warfare will determine the exceptionally active and decisive character of military operations. (44)

The notion of decisiveness is a basic tenet of Soviet military thought; partial victory as an objective in war is seldom, if ever, encountered. If one is to wage war, then one must win it.

The basic mission of the Soviet armed forces is to defend the socialist system against the encroachment of reactionary forces, to serve humanism, and they will strive in the future to limit the number of thoughtless sacrifices in war. At the same time they will carry out a decisive struggle against those who are attempting to disrupt the peaceful labor of the builders of Communism. And if the war is begun then it must be conducted decisively, actively, to full victory over the imperialist. V.I. Lenin said of this: "Conduct war properly or not at all." (45)

In specific terms, the key to decisiveness is the destruction of enemy forces.

Lenin considered the chief goal of attack to be not the pushing back of the enemy, not the occupation of territory, but the total defeat of enemy troops. Lenin believed that all possible development of a planned success and bringing it to total victory was a most important condition for a successful attack. (46)

Total victory includes the capture of the enemy's territory.

Only a decisive attack conducted at high tempos and to a great depth ensures total victory over the enemy. The goal of the attack lies in the total defeat of the defending enemy and capture of vital areas of his territory.(47)

Because Soviet military doctrine is offensive in nature, the primary method of attack is the high-speed offense. Important advantages accrue to the attacker because he is able to shift combat actions to enemy territory.

In moving into the enemy disposition, the attacking troops capture or destroy his means of nuclear attack, stores of nuclear weapons, and bases, and thus reduce his opportunities for employing weapons of mass destruction. They also seize conventional weapons and combat equipment of the enemy as well as supplies, take personnel prisoners, and use the resources of the territory they have occupied. (48)

A side which only defends is inevitably doomed to defeat. (49)

The offense has incomparable advantages, particularly in the initial period of the war, which can be decisive under modern warfare conditions.

The offense has indisputable advantages over other forms of combat actions. The chief one is that the initiative belongs to the attacker in choosing the axis, time, and methods of delivering attacks against the enemy, which makes it possible to impose one's will on him and thus achieve a decisive victory. (50)

Activeness in combat operations presumes above all a seizing and holding of the initiative and imposing one's will on the enemy. This is achieved by application of the most diverse methods of combat operations, the basis of which must be anticipation of the enemy in fire destruction, in delivering forceful attacks, and in executing maneuver.

Anticipation in destruction by fire in a battle must be understood to mean not only anticipation in time - who is first to deliver a nuclear strike or to open fire - but chiefly anticipation in the result of nuclear strikes and fire - who is first to achieve decisive destruction of the enemy. (51)

As quoted in the 1975 edition of Marshal Grechko's book, "Hegemony in war belongs to the one who fights more energetically than all others and who uses any excuse to deliver an attack against the enemy." (52)

Having gained the initiative, it is most important to maintain it and resolutely carry the battle into the depth of the enemy's territory.

The high moral-combat qualities of personnel of the Soviet Army, the powerful means of warfare which they possess, as well as the advanced character of our military science ensure the Soviet troops a real opportunity to achieve the most decisive goals of combat operations. However, in order for these goals to be achieved, all personnel of our army must be imbued with a steadfast will to win, they must have an excellent knowledge of and skillfully employ the weapons entrusted to them, display high activeness, daring, persistence, and initiative, constantly strive to impose their will on the enemy, and, by keeping the initiative in their hands, destroy or capture him. (53)

The tempo of the attack should be maintained, day and night, until the goals are achieved.

The principle of combat activeness also demands effective use of successes achieved and the conduct of combat operations constantly day and night, under any weather conditions, with the total exertion of forces, until the final defeat of the enemy. (54)

Although the planning of the offensive is centralized at the top, it is essential for all forces to know the plan so that they can persist even when command/control is disrupted.

Understanding the goal of all the combat operations and the concept of the senior commander, as well as being oriented beforehand about their possible missions in the course of further actions, they will be able to make grounded decisions and persistently seek their accomplishment without ceasing active combat actions. (55)

This is the idea behind the concept of independence and initiative at lower command levels. As will be explained later, the units are to achieve their goals within the basic plan despite lack of support in firepower or even supplies from the high commands or rear areas.

While initiative and persistence in forming and carrying out the attack are crucial, the Soviets also recognize the need for constraints on these drives.   There are numerous checks and balances in Soviet military science.   In terms of the principle of combat activeness, the Soviets simultaneously stress the need to be realistic about the situation.

> The principle of combat activeness in this sense is closely interwoven with the principle of correspondence of the goal and concept of an operation or battle with conditions of the actual situation.   In setting forth the content of the latter, examples are cited where continuation of an attack would verge on an adventure and could involve a catastrophe. (56)

It is vital not to set the goals of the offensive too high and to make accurate prognoses of the capabilities of enemy forces and even of the capabilities of states or a coalition of states.

5. Preservation of the Combat Effectiveness of Friendly Troops

> In the course of an operation or battle the combat effectiveness of troops must be constantly maintained at the level which ensures successful accomplishment of assigned combat missions. (57)

This is probably the most obvious of the principles, for if troops lose their combat effectiveness, it is virtually inconceivable to apply any other principle of operational art and tactics. Because the principle is basic, however, considerable effort is devoted to its study and application.   The measures for preserving combat effectiveness are divided into four basic groups, the first of which is operational. Simply stated, the best way to limit damage is to destroy the enemy's nuclear weapons before they can be used: "Figuratively speaking, tearing the nuclear sting from the jaws of the enemy, means to ensure the chief condition for preserving the combat effectiveness of friendly troops." (58)   This increases the urgency of applying all means and methods to seize the initiative, strike first and destroy the enemy's nuclear forces completely before he launches a strike.

The second group relates to protection of the troops against weapons of mass destruction (nuclear and chemical).   The concept is, first, to conceal the location of one's troops from the enemy, and second, to limit damage by dispersal and protective measures.   Dispersal, concealment, periodic change of location, careful selection of routes for traversing contaminated areas, and prediction of contaminated areas are all undertaken to preserve combat effectiveness.   This principle becomes especially important in designing a conventional attack under threat of nuclear use.

The third group of measures involves the maintenance of a constant state of high combat readiness; that is, sustaining a high political-moral and physical state of the personnel, the combat capabilities of equipment and weapons, the combat coordination of force units and the provision of supplies - food, POL, and ammunition.

The most interesting aspect of this principle relative to Western practices is the emphasis the Soviets place on the moral, psychological and physical training and conditioning of the troops to fight and survive in both nuclear and chemical environments. The Soviets expend considerable effort to instill in their troops and civilian population a correct impression of the nature and effects of weapons of mass destruction and to insure a high degree of stability of personnel against the psychological effects of nuclear blasts and poison gas. Their people and equipment are prepared to an extent unmatched in the West, due to the Soviet philosophy that although such a war is not necessarily sane, preparations for it must nevertheless be made. The Soviets do whatever they can to brace their forces psychologically for the chaos of a nuclear battlefield, and to instill in them a determination to overcome panic, fear and the instinct to flee, so that they will continue to fight under the most unimaginable conditions.

The fourth group of measures deals with restoring combat effectiveness of troops after they have been hit with or otherwise encountered the effects of weapons of mass destruction. Measures include the forecasting, detection and identification of contaminated areas; identification of forces and means that are still usable; restoration of control, regrouping in designated areas, and resupply of the new or reformed units; decontamination of equipment and areas; and special treatment of exposed personnel. Some of the best examples of such capabilities include the antidote inoculants developed to counter the effect of nerve gas, the civil defense forces, the CBR (chemical, biological, radiological) defense troops, and the practice of reclaiming equipment and personnel from several damaged units and using them to create composite units on the spot.

6. Conformity of the Goals and Plan
to the Conditions of the Actual Situation

The goal of the operation or battle must fully conform to the conditions of the actual operational (combat) situation and be commensurate with the forces and means in their correlation with the enemy's forces and means and with consideration of the factors of space and time. (59)

This principle simply stresses the need to develop realistic plans. The enemy should not be underestimated, nor should the capability of friendly troops be overestimated. All estimates should be as realistic as possible and the goals of the battle should conform to the actual situation. If the goal is unrealistic, it must be changed.

The application of this principle is a major impetus for the heavy Soviet emphasis on modeling combat situations and operations. They work hard to improve their ability to estimate accurately the scope of action and the time and equipment required. This is a major effort in the field of military cybernetics and operations research. A particularly interesting activity is the calculation of realistic rates of advance, the manner in which they are achieved, and the extent of their delay as a result of the effects of weapons of mass destruction. While proper use of these weapons can speed the rate by reducing the opposition, their use must be carefully controlled because the resulting contamination, rubble, fires, and so forth, can have exactly the opposite (and undesired) effect of slowing drastically the rate of advance.

7. Coordination

The success of contemporary combat operations may be achieved only through the joint efforts of all forces and means participating in an operation or battle on the basis of their close and continuous interworking and fullest use of combat capabilities. (60)

The Soviets firmly believe in using all forces, each to its best advantage. In spite of the significant increases in the means of destruction, final success of combat operations can be achieved only through the combined efforts of all forces, with the decisive role played by nuclear weapons. (61) Certainly with regard to Europe, theirs is an offensive, not a defensive nor a retaliatory strategy. A nuclear strike by itself is not part of the Soviet strategy toward Europe. That strategy, in the event of war, is to seize and occupy Europe - a task which requires the ground forces for total victory.

If aggressive forces unleash a war, no one will take the place of the Ground Forces on future battlefields. They will determine the stability of the entire front of the armed struggle. They will have to solve the difficult tasks of defeating enemy groupings on the ground, occupying his territory and, in the final analysis, ensuring victory. (62)

The main purpose of military operations in land theaters is the decisive defeat of enemy units, the capture of vitally important regions and objectives and the occupation of his territory. (63)

Close coordination and joint operations are essential. Although the nuclear strike may be decisive, the grounds troops play the crucial political role of exploiting the strike and capturing the enemy's territory. It is vital for the forces - all forces - to use the nuclear strike as effectively as possible. All forces are to be carefully coordinated "according to a uniform plan and directed toward a single goal." (64) This is the basis for the Soviet combined arms approach to force organization, and the coordinated employment in time, space and objective of nuclear strikes followed up by ground and air force exploitation.

8. Simultaneous Action

Although the preceding principles are those most highlighted in the book, The Basic Principles of Operational Art and Tactics, special attention is drawn to a "new" principle that has become increasingly realistic as a result of the adoption of nuclear weapons - the principle of simultaneous action.   The range of nuclear missiles and their enormous destructive force permits the engagement of the enemy throughout the entire depth of his deployment and upon objectives of the deep rear.   While the importance of this tenet is identified, only limited space is provided for its examination as a "principle." This could be due to some disagreement surrounding the concept or to the inappropriateness of treating such a concept in an unclassified book. The more obvious reason is possible disagreement as to whether the strike should be "simultaneous" or "successive" - whether all targets should be struck in "one blow" during the first day or rather in a number of "waves" over several days, striking only the most important, time-urgent targets the first day while maintaining the option of terminating the nuclear attack at various stages on the following days.   The problems of conducting a simultaneous strike and the advantages of "successive launching of nuclear strikes as the offensive is developed" are discussed in The Offensive. (65) It is clearly stated there that a simultaneous strike at the outset of a war is extremely difficult if not impossible to achieve, and further, does not allow one to fully capitalize on the shock effect.   The use of successive rather than simultaneous strikes is both more realistic and beneficial.

The principles reviewed here are deserving of serious attention by Western strategic analysts - for more attention than they have hitherto received because they represent the foundation of Soviet military thought, and, as such, are crucial to the development and evaluation of Soviet strategy.

It is difficult to overestimate the significance of principles of operational art and tactics. In striving to attain victory in a battle or operation, one cannot act without proceeding from the principles of operational art and tactics.   Of great importance for the attainment of success is not only, or even not so much the knowledge of principles of operational art and tactics, as the ability to take advantage of them and make decisions based on the complex aggregate of demands of the principles and the concrete situation. The fuller that the demands of the principles are considered, the more correct is the decision of the commander, and the greater the chances for winning victory. Principles are starting points for the commander's decision, and not the decision itself. In the latter case they would be transformed into stereotype and unfounded recipes for victory. (66)

4 Forces and Primary Operational Concepts

This chapter focuses upon the application of the principles of military art to the deployments and operational concepts that underlie Soviet military strategy toward Europe. As we discuss these deployment and operational concepts, the principles will be clearly present and easily recognizable. This examination provides an initial view of Soviet operational concepts for war in Europe and indicates the basic role of the individual capabilities of forces, and, to a lesser extent, the manner in which they are combined.

PRINCIPAL FORCES

The basic Soviet approach to an offensive in Europe emphasizes an initial surprise nuclear-fire barrage or mass strike, followed by rapid exploitation by the tactical air and particularly the ground forces. The nuclear attack might conceivably be preceded by a nonnuclear phase. The major armed forces components that enter most prominently into this concept are the Strategic Missile Force, the Ground Force, the Air Force and the Navy. In the area of ground-based air defense, the Air Defense Troops of the Ground Force will be considered rather than the National Air Defense Force, which is a separate service.

The Strategic Missile Force (SMF) is perhaps the single most important and powerful component of the Soviet military organization. Among its inventory of weapons, stationed in the Soviet Union, are intercontinental ballistic missiles (ICBMs), intermediate-range ballistic missiles (IRBMs) and medium-range ballistic missiles (MRBMs). All these systems are expected to be used against Western Europe as part of an initial Soviet mass nuclear strike, with the major role played by the IR/MRBMs — the SS-4, SS-5, and the SS-20. There are reported to be approximately 600 SS-4 and SS-5 launchers in the western areas of the Soviet Union, some with refire capability, resulting in a minimum inventory of 1,000 missiles(1) and a possible maximum of 3,000 if a uniform refire capability of four missiles per launcher is assumed.(2) The nominal yield ascribed to these systems is one megaton (MT), (3) with individual warheads ranging from 0.5 to 3 megatons.(4) Given this capability, the resulting image involves the application of several thousand megatons on an extremely small geographical area. Hence, it is not unreasonable to conclude that such a war is unlikely because the surviving prize would hardly be worth the risk.

One of the most disquieting aspects of Soviet doctrine is its implication that something called "victory" could emerge from a full-scale theater nuclear war. The term presumably refers to the destruction of enemy forces and occupation of vital areas of territory. However, "mass employment of nuclear weapons" as the preferred means of realizing those objectives almost certainly would entail enormous civilian and military casualties as well as the utter ruin of much, if not most, of the territory to be occupied. Also not to be discounted is the probable transformation of large areas into radioactive "deserts" incapable of supporting human or plant life.

This judgment appears eminently realistic with respect to densely populated Europe, where an estimated 2,250 Soviet TNW confront a NATO deployment of some 7,000. Even a massive employment of Soviet TNW that did not provoke a nuclear response from NATO would deprive Europe of any industrial or agricultural value that would otherwise accrue to the USSR. Over two-thirds of Soviet TNW are believed to possess yields well in excess of the 13-kiloton Hiroshima bomb; more than 500 contain yields ranging from ½ to 3 megatons. (5) [Emphasis added.]

While it is true that the missiles may be capable of delivering maximum payload megaton warheads to targets in Europe, they are also capable of delivering smaller warheads. This point is crucial because the megaton warhead creates an image of massive destruction and suggests that the Soviets are self-deterred from employing this force. In considering warheads, it is useful to recognize that the missiles were developed and deployed in the 1950s and early 1960s, long before there were any so-called hard targets — such as the French IRBMs — in European NATO countries. Most targets were essentially soft and did not require high yields. The few that did may well have generated the larger missile size. It is, however, uncharacteristic of the Soviets to put maximum payload warheads on each missile for it would involve needless and inefficient expenditure of very expensive nuclear material. The Soviet approach is maximum cost-effective application of military resources, and in this case it would entail using the least amount of material – the smallest warhead – required to do the job. As one Soviet general officer put it:

Initial attention is given to the selection of those enemy targets against which strategic nuclear means could be best used. Depending on the features of the strike targets, a selection is made of the nuclear weapons carriers (strategic missiles, missile-armed aircraft, submarines or surface craft) which could best and most rapidly execute the assigned mission with minimum expenditure of explosive power. (6)

Although the Strategic Missile Force is designed as a long-range striking force, the likelihood of the Soviets placing maximum payload warheads on more than a few hundred of the several thousand IR/MRBMs and back-up bombers is a matter of conjecture. It is possible that our perception of the Soviet force was influenced in the past by considerations other than their military thinking, including Khruschev's bombast and rhetoric on massive damage; the large Soviet test series of 1961-1962 that emphasized multimegaton shots in a period of relative nuclear scarcity in the Soviet Union; the momentum of the dominant nuclear philosophy of the 1950s, the "bigger bang for the buck"; and a political climate that was not at all conducive to suggestions that nuclear weapons might be used to fight a war. It is possible that most of the several thousand warheads on the long-range systems assigned a European NATO area role are considerably below the megaton range, and that the average yield of weapons in a Soviet initial nuclear strike might be as much as an order of magnitude below the one-megaton level commonly ascribed to this force. In short, there is little basis for assigning any yield to these missiles. It is only possible to set an upper limit, and it should not be assumed that this limit can characterize the entire force.

The SS-20 is a new IRBM that deserves special mention. This system has been described as a mobile missile replacement for the SS-4 and SS-5. It is reported to have a range of 2,000 miles and an accuracy superior by an order of magnitude to the older SS-4 and SS-5 - specifically 440 yards at a 2,500-mile range, and hence even less at most theater ranges of interest. (7) It is also reported to carry three MIRVs - a capability that could treble the number of Soviet warheads over that available with the older MRBMs and IRBMs. As the older systems are reported to number at least 1,000, this translates to at least 3,000 highly accurate SS-20 warheads, assuming a one-for-one replacement. The shift need not imply more megatons; the higher accuracy of the SS-20 allows the Soviets to reduce the size of the yield required to perform a given task. Moreover, the SS-20 enables the Soviets to reduce the yield in attacking area targets, such as air bases, by using multiple small warheads rather than single large warheads. Therefore, while the total inventory may rise from 1,000 to 3,000 warheads, the total megatons in the force could conceivably decrease. This consideration of yield is most important in assessing collateral damage and Soviet political objectives relative to Europe.

The main ICBMs recognized to have a theater mission are the SS-11 and the SS-19. Designed for intercontinental use, these systems might be very accurate at the shorter theater ranges and therefore quite effective against the harder theater targets, such as French IRBMs and command/control bunkers. These ICBMs, together with the MRBMs and IRBMs and perhaps a few SLBMs, constitute the major Soviet long-range ballistic missile threat to Europe.

Closely related to this capability is that of the Soviet Air Force (VVS), (8) which has two major strike components - the long-range aviation (LRA) and the short-range, or tactical, frontal aviation (FA). These forces would be coordinated with the IR/MR/IC/SLBM strike. It appears doubtful that air-delivered nuclear strikes would be launched before the main ballistic missile strike because of the warning and reaction time this would provide NATO forces, particularly quick reaction alert (QRA) forces, and because the Soviets speak of the need first to neutralize the air defenses with ballistic missiles before sending in the aircraft. The LRA and FA do, however, play a major role in providing supplementary or back-up coverage, and would probably constitute the second salvo of the initial strike. Their primary mission would be strategic reconnaissance of the missile strike and attack of targets where the missile strike had been unsuccessful for one reason or another (e.g., missile guidance failure or warhead failure). Second, the Soviets have made the basic decision to use missiles to attack fixed targets and air power to attack mobile targets or targets requiring last-minute confirmation before being struck, and these latter categories of targets would constitute the object of the second salvo with LRA covering the deep targets and FA covering those targets in the tactical and operational-tactical area. For example:

> When the requirement is to destroy mobile or insufficiently reconnoitered ground and sea targets (for example, depots for nuclear weapons or missiles, missile-carrying submarines, etc.), strategic bombers are capable of fulfilling the mission more successfully than missile podrazdeldeniya [subunits] and chasti [units]. (9)

The LRA and FA would supplement the ballistic missile strike against the land theaters of operations and the LRA would also assist the naval forces in strikes against sea-based forces - the most important class of mobile targets. The number of nuclear-capable aircraft that must be included in the threat to Western Europe is at least comparable to the missile threat, and ranges from 2,000 to 4,000. Other components of the Soviet Air Forces, such as interceptor, reconnaissance, transport and air assault, also play key roles in the attack and will be discussed below.

The Soviet Navy includes submarines, surface ships, auxiliary vessels, naval infantry and naval aviation. (10) These forces play important roles, not only in regard to the war at sea but also in regard to that on land, particularly in the attack of important ports and harbor facilities. Their first major mission is to combat NATO nuclear forces at sea, of which the highest priority in time is assigned to the aircraft carriers, followed closely by SLBM and ASW capabilities. The carriers are of exceptional importance because of the threat each is seen to represent - several hundred nuclear strikes - and because of the relative ease with which they can be destroyed.

The second major naval mission is the destruction of NATO supply ships, thereby cutting off the land battle from any supplies delivered by sea. The Soviets intend to isolate the NATO battlefield thoroughly and completely. This is also one of the tasks the Soviets have in mind when they speak of striking important economic targets. Military supplies, including oil, and their carriers, are urgent economic targets and consequently must be destroyed.

The Ground Force (11) - the oldest component of the Soviet armed forces - includes motorized rifle and tank troops, missile and artillery troops, air defense troops, and special troops which support the actions of basic troops, such as signal, engineer, radio, motor transport, chemical defense and others. The bulk of the combat troops is composed of the motorized rifle and tank troops. These combine to form the core of the two types of major formations - the combined arms armies and the tank armies - that face Western Europe. The missile troops and the artillery include the FROG and SCUD nuclear and chemical missile weapons. These, together with tube and rocket artillery and frontal aviation, constitute the basis of the firepower that is directly available for front operations. A particularly crucial segment of the ground forces are the airborne troops which are specially trained for air drop and landing in the rear of the enemy to conduct combat operations, both independently and in coordination with the advancing regular frontline units. It is interesting to note the high value placed upon the airborne forces in The Officer's Handbook where they are treated virtually as a separate service.(12)

The Soviet Ground Force has undergone significant improvement since 1965. Its upgrading has been the subject of growing concern in the West, as indicated, for example, in the United States Secretary of Defense Annual Posture Statements during the last ten years. Although these forces are often discussed in the context of conventional operations, a dimension in which the Soviets have remarkabley enhanced their ability, one must not lose sight of the commensurately improved capability to conduct nuclear war that Soviet force modernization has been carefully calculated to provide. In the Soviet view, combined arms combat is first and foremost nuclear. It is the nuclear battle that is the more demanding and sets the basic requirement. While it is true that the Soviet Union has significantly improved its conventional force capabilities over the past ten years and that a major consideration in deploying these capabilities has been the clear objective of the Soviet Union to be both quantitatively and qualitatively superior to NATO in the conventional area, this is only the tip of the iceberg, as it were.

The overall Soviet approach is to achieve and maintain a superior capability to conduct war, be it conventional or nuclear. The so-called conventional improvements in Soviet forces, unlike those in their United States counterparts, are in the main designed not merely for conventional war but nuclear and chemical war as well. The ground forces are equally important in both conventional and nuclear conflict and have been trained and equipped for both. In a nuclear war the objectives of the Soviet ground forces are to complete the destruction of NATO forces and to seize and occupy territory. These missions cannot be accomplished with nuclear weapons alone. As the Soviets make quite explicit, they need strong conventional forces to exploit a nuclear strike quickly by seizing and occupying NATO territory.

Most of the Soviet "conventional" force improvements have been bought with this in mind. For example, Soviet tanks are equipped to operate in a chemical, biological and radiological (CBR) environment. Combat vehicles are designed for action without the soldiers having to disembark and, among other things, for the transport of troops across "contaminated areas." All Soviet forces are issued clothing and equipment designed for protection in a CBR environment. The major developments in self-propelled artillery, in surface-to-air missile (SAM) capabilities, and most vitally in command and control, are all explicitly seen as essential to the conduct of nuclear war. There is no indication in Soviet literature that these improvements were purchased primarily for conventional war alone. Most of them are associated with the nuclear revolution in military affairs and its demands for force development. In fact, very few systems can be said to have been purchased exclusively for conventional war, while several systems such as IRBMs and tactical ballistic missiles (TBMs) have been developed specifically for theater nuclear use. Soviet combined arms and tank armies should not be viewed as conventional forces. Rather they should be viewed as dual-purpose forces that are equipped and trained to fight both nuclear and conventional (including chemical) war. Western strategic forces have always encountered difficulty in the concept of dual-purpose forces. Apparently the Soviets have not.

Special consideration for the protection of Soviet ground forces against NATO tactical air has led to major air defense capabilities referred to as Voyska PVO forces. These forces have received enormous investments in high quality antiaircraft artillery guns such as the Quad 23s, surface-to-air missiles (SAMs) such as the SA-2, -3, -4, -6, -8 and -10, and associated command and control. Most of these capabilities are highly mobile and integrated throughout all Soviet ground force units. Their activities are complemented by and coordinated with strong fighter interceptor capabilities designed for air-to-air combat, with the ground-based capabilities generally responsible for air defense immediately above and in advance of the avenues of attack, and the air-based capabilities responsible for the flanks or boundaries and low-level penetration threats. Since World War II, the Soviets have been oriented strongly toward air defense - for purposes of both defense and offense support - and the enormous investment in these capabilities attests to that fact.

While the forces described above constitute the majority of the Warsaw Pact capability, there are two additional elements that are unique to the Warsaw Pact and deserve special attention. These are the chemical defense and civil defense forces. These are not trivial forces; they number in the hundreds of thousands of troops and are organized as separate branches headed by three- and four-star generals, respectively. The two forces are closely related; civil defense originally grew out of the chemical defense forces formed in World War I. These forces are highly specialized to combat the contamination associated with weapons of mass destruction - chemical, biological and nuclear. They are not just defensive forces, but form an essential and integrated part of the offense to ensure that Soviet troops survive the effects of their own weapons as well as those of NATO. They are responsible for identifying, marking and decontaminating contaminated areas and equipment. Together with the Engineering Troops, they also play an important role in selecting troop waiting areas and transportation routes. (13) Civil defense is not just civilian defense oriented, but provides important military offense support as well. For example:

> In a future war, transport will have enormous importance. Civil defense can render enormous aid to the military command, in this area. Damaged bridges, railroad centers, and other communication installations can be quickly restored by civil defense forces. All this will facilitate the successful movement of troops into designated areas and will make it possible for troops to implement the required maneuver. This does not exclude a circle of problems which can and must be implemented by the close, continuous coordination of civil defense with the armed forces. (14)

The chemical and civil defense troops highlight an essential difference between the Soviet approach to war and that of the West. Many people in the West, military as well as civilian, believe it is impossible to fight and win a nuclear or chemical war. The only possibility is to deter it: "...it is hard to find any way-stations between successful deterrence and doom." (15)

Under a doctrine which calls for a pre-emptive strike if war seems imminent, the Soviet approach is to prepare to fight using all means - nuclear, chemical and biological - each to its best advantage in a sudden, decisive, successful onslaught. Soviet military planners put major effort into coping with and operating in contaminated environments - both military and civilian. The chemical and civil defense forces are clear and unmistakable evidence of the serious Soviet attitude in this regard.

PREPOSITIONING AND MOBILIZATION

A surprise or a "standing start" attack by Warsaw Pact forces is an issue of growing importance in NATO discussions. The question, very simply, is whether the Warsaw Pact could attack NATO without telegraphing a significant warning, and thus gain the benefits of surprise, or would significant mobilization of resources be required prior to such an attack. Closely related to those are questions of supply logistics and prepositioning of equipment. How much military materiel is in place and how large a logistics problem will the Soviet forces face in a major European war? While these questions receive close attention in the Soviet literature, until recently they have been largely ignored in the Western debate on the subject.

The Need for Peacetime Preparation

The age-old problem of the sizing, positioning and posturing of forces in peacetime has never been addressed as seriously as it now is in contemporary Soviet military literature. Both the United States and the Soviet Union suffered major setbacks early in World War II - the United States in the attack on Pearl Harbor and the Soviet Union in the German Barbarossa campaign - because of surprise. Years of intensive war effort were required to recover from these attacks - time which most likely would not be available in a nuclear war. This problem receives significant attention in Soviet publications. In effect, they deplore the mistakes made at the beginning of World War II and recognize that a replay could spell defeat. This is a major impetus behind their concern over the initial period of war.

Traditionally, a nation preparing to attack would begin by mobilizing forces and then moving them to their waiting or concentration areas immediately prior to the planned time of attack. Sufficient defensive forces were required to hold off an attack until additional forces could be mobilized and moved to the front. At the same time, industry was mobilized to produce additional war materiel and ammunition. The war effort itself tended to be drawn out and required as much attention to production of goods and mobilization of reserves to the front as in actually fighting the war at the front line. This was the pattern in World War II, Korea, and Vietnam. The Middle East War in 1973 was also headed in this direction with resupply from allies, rather than production itself, receiving the emphasis.

In a nuclear war in Europe, this traditional approach is not judged by the Soviets to offer much probability of success. The major consideration in a nuclear war or in a war that might go nuclear is the effectiveness of nuclear weapons. These weapons enable the outcome of the war to be determined in the opening phase, and the war to be completed in a short period of time. That is, the beginning period of the war can be both short and decisive. There may not be sufficient time to undertake the mobilization of resources, and the anticipated destruction of transportation nets will make movement of forces and supplies most difficult, if not impossible. (16)

Therefore, it is especially important that preparation for a modern war be fully accomplished in "peacetime" before the war begins. The initial operations will be conducted with the means and forces on hand and with maximum intensity. Both sides tend to build in peacetime all the nuclear destructive power, including resupply and reserves, they think will be needed. As stated in Voyennaya mysl':

> During the preparation there takes place in good time an accumulation of various reserves: material and technical means, various weapons, ammunition, and in addition, trained military cadres. The composition and quality of these reserves must provide for the complete mobilization of new formations in short periods of time, and also thereafter, the timely replenishment of obeyedineniya [armies] and soyedineniya [divisions] which have suffered losses at the beginning of the war. (17)

The same principle applies to general war, as stated in Military Strategy:

> The nature of the initial phase of a modern war requires that the material means required for conducting the first operations not only be prepared in peacetime, but dispersed, taking into account the requirements of antiatomic defense. Moreover, in the interior of the country at the points of troop mobilization, the required reserves of material means should be created and also reserves for casualty replacements. (18)

The Soviet strategy for war in Europe requires a war-oriented defense management and production philosophy in peacetime. This is referred to as maintaining a state of high combat readiness, which encompasses people, training, posture and equipment. All items are to be ready and in place for war - not only initial supplies, but resupplies as well, and of particular importance, fuel. This effort does not downgrade the importance of economic mobilization of the country to support the war effort after the war begins. However, due to the potential decisiveness of the initial nuclear strikes, the first phase of modern war is particularly critical. In an era when only the forces in being at the outset might count, lack of preparation can spell defeat.

Mobilization

To better achieve surprise, it is essential to avoid actions that would warn the enemy. Forces in place would be gradually brought to a state of alert, but mass mobilization and, most importantly, visible movement into the theater of major operational units must be avoided or minimized. Any preparations required would be covert, concealed or camouflaged. Military Strategy puts it as follows:

> Concealed mobilization is possible even under present-day conditions, but it will be realized somewhat differently than previously. As the relations between the belligerents become increasingly strained, a part of the armed forces intended for the solution of the

problems of the initial phase of the war gradually will be brought into a state of complete combat readiness. However, it must be borne in mind that with present-day means of strategic reconnaissance, widespread mobilization measures, even though concealed, cannot go unnoticed. Therefore, all the leading countries of coalitions strive to keep their armed forces in a maximum state of readiness.

The solution to this problem would be to maintain in peacetime those armed forces which would be in a position to reach at least the nearest definite strategic war objectives before successive echelons are mobilized and put into action. (19)

If the Soviets were to mount an attack, one could infer with reason that they would do so with the forces in place, augmented by key planning and command elements that can be mobilized in a covert manner. The last thing they would wish to do would be to clarify the nature of their intention to attack by mobilizing or reinforcing the forces in place so that NATO, particularly Germany and the United States, might respond with their own mobilization prior to the conflict.

... With the mass introduction of nuclear missiles into the armed forces of imperialist states, Soviet military science arrived at the conclusion that war can be begun by available grouping of troops, and not by previously mobilized armed forces, and that the beginning of a war can have a decisive effect on the outcome. (20)

In examining the tradeoffs between mobilization and surprise attack, the Soviets appear to have reached the conclusion that more is to be gained from a surprise attack from an understrength posture than from a fully mobilized attack against a warned and prepared enemy. But, especially if the timing is up to the Soviets, they would be violating their own doctrine if they attacked sooner than they felt sufficiently prepared to move from a standing start, without tipping their hand in advance.

One might expect that the Soviet approach to force mobilization would be very similar to their approach to the conduct of the offensive - namely, the echeloning of mobilization capabilities. Prior to launching the initial strike, all possible efforts to mask their intentions would be undertaken.

Special attention is given to ... the preparatory period ... surprise action is of importance ... The concealed execution of all preparatory measures and the deeply planned, active supply of misinformation to the enemy side about the true plans may catch the enemy troops unaware...

The execution of strategic missions for the occupation of specific terrain areas in continental theaters of military operations and seizure and holding of enemy targets will require the concealed formation of groupings, primarily ground troops and air forces, well ahead of time. (21)

At the onset of the strike or during the night before, forward-positioned units would mobilize and, together with the forward elements, would constitute the first strategic echelon. These forces would be designed to be as independent of supply from the rear as possible, with critical supplies provided by air transport, both fixed and rotary wing, operating from air bases in NATO and neutral territories as soon as they were overrun.

During the initial phase of the war, which might involve one to two weeks at the most, mobilization of the second strategic echelon would be completed for the subsequent resupply and consolidation phase which might last from the end of the first phase to several months. In the meantime, a deeper mobilization of a third strategic echelon would be initiated for the support of a protracted conflict.

Prepositioning

While many Western analysts are concerned about the moving up of weapons and materiel for resupply from the rear, particularly from the Soviet Union, it appears from their writings that Soviet planners regard this as a World War II practice outdated in today's world:

> Now nuclear weapons and other enemy means of mass destruction can create great zones of destruction and radioactive contamination in the path of the moving troops resulting in great losses. All this complicates effecting the maneuvering of strategic reserves to a significant degree or even wrecks it altogether. Therefore, old methods of carrying out the maneuver of strategic reserves are now in many ways unsuitable, and new, more effective ways must be sought. (22)

The author continues, explaining that now reserves must be in the territories of the coalition states: ". . .the strength and equipment of strategic echelons and state reserves must now be examined not within the confines of one state but on the scale of a coalition of states." More specifically, reserves are located forward in the mobilization areas and, in echelon, in the depth of the theater of military operations (TMO).

> The most important elements of strategic reserves,which are subject to decisive action, are, in our opinion, first, combined arms and tank obeyedineniya [armies]and soyedineniya [divisions], rocket nuclear weapons, and chasti [regiments] and soyedineniya [divisions] of other arms located in mobilization areas, concentrated in the depth of a given TMO. (23) [Emphasis added.]

Storage sites containing supplies and reserve equipment must be hidden and secure from enemy detection and strike.

Another and no less important part of preparing the armed forces for war is their logistical support. The main concentration for the resolution of this problem is the advance (in peacetime conditions) creation of sufficient reserves of technical and material resources to enable the armed forces to conduct combat operations successfully. The distribution and protected storage of these reserves should preclude the possibility of their mass loss from enemy nuclear strikes. (24)

Pre-positioned stocks of equipment and supplies might easily be concealed in an extensive set of underground storage facilities throughout Eastern Europe. During World War II, the Germans embarked on a large-scale development of underground manufacturing, refining and storage facilities, which totaled about 20 million square feet of storage area at the end of the war. The potential of these facilities, many of which are located close to the East-West border, has been clearly recognized.

From the point of view of antinuclear defense the most important industrial enterprises should preferably be located underground in premises prepared beforehand for this purpose. During the last war the Germans planned to construct approximately 9 million square meters of underground premises for the concealment of industry. However. by the end of the war they had succeeded in constructing only 1.5 million square meters. Naturally, under present day conditions, the preparation of underground premises must be developed on a particularly large scale. (25)

It is also important to position these supplies forward in the theater so that the first-echelon forces are better able to conduct the war "continuously" and to "maintain the strategic initiative." In the past, it was possible for these supplies to be located in the depth of the theater at a distance of 600-1,000 kilometers or greater, requiring three or four days to move them and bring them into the battle.

During the last war the equipment for manning the units frequently had to be brought in from dozens of storehouses located hundreds and even thousands of kilometers from the mobilization points. In a future war such a situation will be intolerable, since it does not correspond to present-day mobilization time limits. (26)

This is no longer acceptable. Supplies should be stored where they will be needed.

Special attention belongs to the question of retaining the combat readiness of troops during their movement forward into a region of combat operations, when they must negotiate zones of radioactive contamination and destruction. To insure the maximum preservation of the troops and their fast movement forward, it is considered necessary to create a network of special routes which have protected points for supporting the march (control points, fuel supply and water supply points, etc.) duplicate river crossings, and also reconnoitered regions for a day's halt and for concentration. (27)

Along with equipment, one would expect all consumables such as ammunition and POL required for the opening phase to be prepositioned far forward to minimize any logistics problem associated with the attacking units. (28) Attacking units should be as independent and self-supporting as possible. This appears to be one of the meanings behind the discussion of unit independence - independence in the sense of minimizing their dependence on higher headquarters for service, resupply and support.

Independence in combat is achieved primarily by: reinforcing the advancing podrazdeleniya [subunits such as companies and battalions] with the necessary forces and means of the various combat arms and special troops, the subordinate commanders' knowledge of the concept of operations of the senior commander which will permit them to control their subordinates in combat constantly even with the disruption of communications with him; the presence of a sufficient quantity of material resources in the motorized rifle companies and battalion which assured the successful conduct of the attack in case supply is interrupted. (29)

Foraging

The Soviets have an additional approach to the problem of supply. As noted in Military Strategy, "We should particularly note the ever increasing need to utilize the local resources within enemy territory, something for which our rear units must be prepared." (30)

The Soviets intend to forage in Europe for whatever additional supplies are required and have taken this into account in designing their attack. The rationale and extent of their consideration of this is elaborated in a 1966 Voyennaya mysl' article:

The destructive nature of modern warfare, the difficulty of transporting material means from the depth of a country and the great vulnerabililty of rear area organs make it necessary to devote serious attention to a study of the possibilities for acquiring local resources in theaters of military operations. For this purpose, it is very important to determine which targets and enemy regions should be left intact or rapidly reconstructed and used in the interests of strengthening the economic potential of our own country and for supplying the troops. It is important to determine which, what, where and in what quantity the local resources can be stored and used in the interest of the troops. It is important also to determine what are the conditions for acquiring or using local resources (the presence of electric-power and transport means, manpower resources, transport capability, etc.). (31)

This type of thinking grows partly out of previous experience. A whole year after World War II ended, Red Army occupation units in Central and Eastern Europe still depended more on local foraging for sustenance than on any organized system of supply from the Soviet Union. The concept of foraging would be of special importance in the event of global nuclear war in which a primary strategic goal would be the seizure of Europe and its resources for rebuilding the Soviet Union.

Reserves

The availability of reserves is a closely related problem. The nature of contemporary war is such that it is not believed possible in general to accomplish all missions with the original operational formation. Instead, the potential success of the attack is expected to depend in part on the ability to regroup forces and material. (32)

The presence of large reserves during offensive operations facilitates the intensification of efforts, swift and deep penetration into a defensive formation, the defeat of its groupings, and the achievement of the objectives of the operation.

An important factor influencing the successful execution of strategic missions during armed conflict is the constant availability of various strategic reserves within the armed forces groupings. The need and frequent changes in the strategic situation, so characteristic of modern war, which may demand additional efforts through the commitment of a specific part of the reserves. (33)

Of further interest is the fact that this regrouping and resupply as well as the original mobilization may be controlled by the General Staff from Moscow. (34)
These reserves must be carefully concealed, yet readily available.

The dispersal and covered displacement of the reserves, their concealment, especially against aerial and space strikes, and their prompt and purposeful employment will ensure the successful execution of the missions. (35)

Concealment of the regrouping is effected by maintaining strict secrecy over the plans and times for effecting the maneuver of the strategic reserves and equipment and by well camouflaging the troops while in the areas in which they are deployed and while on the march. This is achieved by skillful utilization of the camouflaging characteristics of the terrain, efficient formation of march order, by the timely exploitation of limited visibility conditions, and by the application of diverse camouflaging means, in addition to carrying out radio deception, counter radar deception, and effectively combatting enemy air and ground reconnaissance. (36)

Forested and other natural terrain features may also play a critical role in a conventional phase by providing cover for units held back to exploit the nuclear phase that is expected to follow. As discussed in an article from a 1967 issue of Voyennaya mysl' on "Combat Operations Involving Conventional Means of Destruction," the threat of nuclear weapons requires that important second-echelon and reserve forces be held back and concealed so that they are not subject to decimation, but they must also be readily available should the war go nuclear. Their role in the nuclear phase is more important than their potential contribution to the conventional phase. It would seem logical to hold these troops in the same concealed areas designed for regrouping and resupply, particularly if such areas also contain natural underground sites for use in storing equipment and possibly for other purposes.

THE INITIAL NUCLEAR STRIKE

A major nuclear war in Europe will, in all likelihood, begin as or become a nuclear war. The most decisive aspect of such a war is the initial nuclear strike, which, if well planned and implemented, could determine the outcome in the first few hours of the war. Nuclear firepower is, therefore, the most critical aspect - or at least the first among equals in a theater war - at all levels: strategic, operational-tactical, and battlefield.

Under contemporary conditions, nuclear weapons are the primary means of delivering the main attack. (37)

It is believed that nuclear weapons, as the main means of destruction, should be employed in all cases for the destruction of the most important targets and objectives. These include, first of all, enemy means of nuclear attack, large concentrations of his troops and especially armored troops, reserves, in particular tank reserves, artillery in firing positions, bridges, crossings, control posts and communication centers, objects in the troop rear area, defensive structures, and others. (38)

The most important method of achieving success in an offensive is now by a maneuver of nuclear strikes. (39)

Offensive operations in a future war will be the basic means for solving the problems of armed conflict in land theaters of military operations. They will be conducted by fronts and by combined arms, tank, and air armies. The main role in solving the combat problems of an offensive operation will be played by operational-tactical rocket troops and frontal aviation using nuclear ammunition and also by tank, motorized infantry, and airborne troops.

> On the battlefields the decisive role will be played by fire of nuclear weapons; the other means of armed combat will utilize the results of nuclear attacks for the final defeat of the enemy. (40)

In any Soviet discussion of nuclear war, there is one word that dominates all others - "decisive." Although the war by definition would not be brought on by the socialist countries, they certainly intend to seize the initiative, strike preemptively if nuclear war appears immiment, and terminate the conflict in a decisive and triumphant manner. The desirability of decisiveness - and surprise - in the opening phase of the war is further intensified by Soviet interest in a short war (that is, one that is over before United States mobilization and logistic strength can be brought into play) and in avoidance of a massive NATO first use of nuclear weapons. The outcome is to be a decisive military and political victory, and the primary instrument to this end is the initial, mass, simultaneous, in-depth nuclear strike.

The emphasis on preemption through striking first in the Soviet literature goes considerably beyond military discussions in the West, where debates focus on tactical warning of an attack - that is, detecting the launch of missiles - and, ideally, arriving at the final decision to launch the missiles within a matter of minutes. The response here is known as a "launch-on-warning" response. This concept is not at the center of the Soviet dialogue insofar as Europe is concerned. Their focus is on anticipating - not merely detecting - the attack and striking first. This concept is consistent and pervasive throughout the Soviet literature.

> One of the decisive conditions for success in an operation is the anticipating of the enemy in making nuclear strikes, particularly against the enemy's nuclear missile weapons. (41)

> The importance of the principle of surprise increases as the means of warfare develop. Surprise permits anticipating the enemy in delivering strikes, catching him unawares, paralyzing his will, sharply reducing his combat effectiveness, disorganizing his control, and creating favorable conditions for defeating even superior forces. (42)

It is also referred to as foresight:

> The enormous value of the time factor in scientific foresight in military affairs is especially evident at present. In a new world war, if the imperialists succeed in unleashing it, one should foresee the possibility of utilization of nuclear weapons in wide scales. The timely foresight of pecularities and perspectives of the course of such a war and taking the appropriate practical measures are the factors which play a paramount role in the provision of victory. The timely disclosure of intentions of the aggressor about the time of inflicting and the objects of the first nuclear strike has especially important value. (43)

An excellent recent example of such anticipation was the Israeli attack in the Arab-Israeli War in 1967. The lesson learned in that engagement should be obvious, particularly when contrasted with the October War in 1973.

Because many Westerners regard nuclear war as impossible or unthinkable, political leaders are often characterized as agonizing over, and putting off as long as possible, a decision to use even a few nuclear weapons. This same condition is often imputed to the Soviets, but this is not borne out in Soviet literature. The issue is not whether the Soviets desire a nuclear war, but rather: Is the war likely to go nuclear? Is it a major war? What are the political goals of the war? If the analysis of all these considerations suggests that the war will probably go nuclear – an analysis that will consider SACEUR statements, NATO exercises, and rhetoric from Bonn, Paris, London, and Washington – and that a nuclear strike is to the Soviet advantage, perhaps in the sense that it would shorten the war and limit escalation, then the Soviet strategy is to strike first without warning and at the "most favorable time."

Anticipation increases in significance because the nuclear strike is not an isolated act in the Soviet approach to war in Europe. The goal of the attack lies in the total defeat of the enemy and capture of vital areas of his territory. (44) Because the ground, air and naval forces are required for this purpose, the nuclear strike must be coordinated in time, place and objectives with the maneuvering of these forces.

> The main purpose of offensive combat is the complete destruction of a defending enemy, and will now be achieved, first of all, by strikes of nuclear weapons and firepower of other means of destruction, and by the growing (in force) swift actions of the motorized infantry and tank troops coordinating with aviation and with paratroop drops. (45)

The time required for an integrated offensive movement naturally is much greater than that needed to launch a nuclear strike. While it may be possible to launch a nuclear strike within perhaps fifteen minutes, it may require upwards of several hours or a day to launch an integrated ground/air offensive; hence, the need to anticipate and select a favorable time to initiate the nuclear strike rather than simply to detect and react. This anticipation is required further to enable the Soviets to put into operation special activities that should precede the actual launch of the nuclear strike by several hours. These activities include military intelligence, sabotage and other diversionary activities whose objectives would be to disrupt and disorganize NATO political and military command and control, thus making it difficult if not impossible to detect the Soviet attack and institute counter actions and force movements.

Nuclear employment planning appears to be concentrated on three levels - tactical planning at Army level, operational-tactical planning at Front level, and strategic, or operational-strategic - planning in Moscow at the Supreme High Command level (summarized in Table 4.1). The

TABLE 4.1. Soviet Nuclear Strike Planning

	Tactical	Operational-Tactical	Operational-Strategic
Geography	0 to 50 km	20 to 350 km	Beyond 250 km
Key Command Level	Army	Front	Supreme High Command
Systems	FROG	SCUD, SCALEBOARD	IR/MR/IC/SLBMs
	Frontal aviation	Frontal aviation	Long and medium range aviation
	Artillery		
Targets	Nuclear artillery	Mobile missiles	Long range missiles
			Nuclear aircraft
			Naval aviation
	Command/Control division and below	Command/Control corps level	Command/Control nuclear air major NATO commands
	Main defense forces	Approaching reserves	Reserves
		Logistics	Logistics
			Military economic

most important of these is the strategic-level planning in Moscow, which entails the detailed planning of the initial mass nuclear strike and its coordination with the ground, air and naval forces that complete the destruction and seize the vital areas of NATO territory. While this initial strike would be based on the SMF and LRA forces, it would also include coordinated use of the Front subordinate weapons, SCUD/ SCALEBOARD missiles and frontal aviation. The key planning agency for this strike is the Soviet General Staff.

> The decisive means of achieving the goals of modern war are rocket and nuclear weapons, with their unlimited effective range and tremendous destructive capabilities. This requires maximum centralization of control of the principal nuclear-rocket weapons in the Supreme Command, particularly in the initial period of the war, for here and only here is it possible to decide correctly and most effectively questions concerning the objectives of nuclear strikes, targets for destruction, power of warheads, means for delivering them to the targets, type of explosive effect, time for delivery of strikes, and issue orders for signal dispatches. Only here can the authority be placed for "pressing the button" to activate the principal weapons of war. The Supreme Command has thus become not only a directing organ of supervision, but also the immediate executor of the principal mission of the armed conflict.

> The most important task of the General Staff in preparing for a modern war is the detailed planning of the employment of nuclear weapons by all services of the armed forces. (46)

For the purposes of establishing a base target list, several target categories or classifications are established. One approach (47) which is consistent with the bulk of Soviet literature is the following:

Group 1: Strategic nuclear: missile, submarines, theater aviation, naval bases, nuclear storehouses, associated command/control. (48)

Group 2: Operational and tactical nuclear: tactical and carrier aviation, cruise missiles, tactical missiles, airfield, nuclear storehouses, and associated command/control.

Group 3: Large ground troop formations: reserves, storehouses of arms, equipment and fuel, and naval bases.

Group 4: Air defense: interceptor airfields, anti-air rockets, associated command/control.

Group 5: Military industrial objectives: administrative, political centers, transportation centers and ports, centers of state administration.

Each target is ranked according to the degree of danger and time-urgency it poses for the attacker.

Besides this, the indicated objectives should be examined and classified by the degree of their danger for the attacker. Thus, the launch position, from which 10 minutes ago a strategic rocket was launched does not represent a threat in the immediate period of time, since the firing of another missile requires a certain period of time. And although strategic rockets are regarded as the most important objectives, in the given case the launch position will be less dangerous than other objectives which could inflict immediate strikes. An airfield of strategic aircraft with bombers which have just landed is just as important an objective for attack, but it is less dangerous than a similar airfield with aircraft ready to take off which are carrying nuclear arms. (49)

Having classified targets according to their importance, degree of danger and vulnerability, the priority targets are determined. The most dangerous objectives to the attacker - which apparently will receive multiple strikes - will be the first targets. "It is most desirable to double the destruction of the most important objectives using resources of either a single or various branches of the armed forces." (50)

The strikes are then assembled and selected in accordance with carefully selected and sequenced tasks and goals. For example, as explained in a Soviet paper concerned with deep strikes, their objectives and organization:

Deep attacks are not uncoordinated and chance attacks on separate objectives of the defender, but coordinated actions of various types of armed forces according to a single plan directed toward the solution of specific operational and strategic tasks within the limits of the theatre of military operations. But most important in understanding the content of the phenomenon being examined is the strategic result, that is, the achievement of the strategic goal. (51)

The opening phase of a nuclear war is viewed as the battle between the nuclear means - and thus aims at the destruction of the enemy's decisive, or nuclear, weapons. It is crucial to tilt the correlation of nuclear weapons at the outset to the overwhelming Soviet advantage so as to make the enemy for all practical purposes open to unavoidable defeat. Not only must these "active targets" be destroyed, but so must the "most important means which insure their effective application" - in particular their associated command and control, targeting (tactical intelligence and target acquisition means), and ground support means. (52)

Preparations for the nuclear strike involve not merely its strictly military aspect - that is, its impact on the course of the conflict - but also the broader political and economic implications of the strike on the entire life fabric of the country under attack.

In selecting any specific region as the target and determining the sequence of nuclear strikes against it, first and foremost it is necessary to determine the effect the strikes will have at a given

time, the influence of the target on the progress of armed combat
and on the functioning of the entire life of the country. (53)

This political analysis focuses on the long-range, postwar environment,
and the political objectives of the strike.   These objectives differ
according to the target area and thus lead to varying attacks on
different parts of the world.   This is the principal thrust of a 1964
Voyennaya mysl' article on the classification of theaters of military
operations.

Developing the principles for defining the concepts of subdivision
and classification of theaters of military operations is not only of
theoretical interest but of great practical importance. In peacetime
the probable theaters of war are carefully studied in order to be able
to use in one's own interests the military-political, military-
economic, military-geographic, and directly operational-strategic
elements characteristic of this or that theater. (54)

The Soviets express interest in using to their benefit the political,
economic and geographic components of the prize which Europe
represents. As indicated above, moreover, they would use Europe in an
operational-strategic sense - for example, by planning to use NATO
bases of operation in the war against NATO as well as in the war in the
ocean theater, and, possibly, in the intercontinental war.
    In planning for a war, the General Staff is to subdivide the world up
into strategic regions.

A "strategic region" is one in which there are objectives the defeat,
destruction, or capture of which may be the goal of a strategic
mission. Such objectives are groupings of the armed forces of the
enemy, including strategic nuclear armanent, and formations of
land, air, and air defense troops in continental TMO's, and naval
forces in ocean theaters, and also military-economic and administrative-political regions and centers. (55)

The attack on these regions may be governed by different objectives -
particularly, by military-economic objectives. In certain theaters it
may be desirable to seize them or merely render them ineffective for
the planned period of operations.

The role of military-economic objectives is determined by the
importance of economics in modern war, and accordingly, by the
missions for the seizing, destruction, or making ineffective the basic
elements of the military-economic potential of the enemy. Mili-
tary-industrial plants, arsenals, bases, and weapons and fuel depots
are now the most important targets for destruction and the blows
against these targets will be the more powerful, the more important
the place they occupy in providing the armed forces with modern
instruments of war. From this point of view, the various theaters of

military operations play by no means identical roles. And consequently there will be essential differences in the strategic mission, the forces, and the material brought into action in the various theaters, and in the ways in which they are used. (56) [Emphasis added.]

The foregoing mandate introduces a dilemma for the Soviet planners - namely, the problem of destroying the capability of Europe to resist the Soviet armed forces without destroying those prizes in Europe (political, economic, military, and geographic) that the Soviet Union wants to capture intact for its own purposes. All of the assets in Europe are important to the Soviet Union in the event of a war, and the General Staff is advised to recognize this in designing the nuclear forces of the future. This is essentially apt in view of the destruction anticipated from NATO nuclear weapons, and would be of particular importance in a world nuclear war.

This approach appears to have reached maturity in a 1968 Voyennaya mysl' article, "The Question of Influences on Military and Economic Potential of Warring States." Toward the beginning of this article is a very interesting paragraph which because it is not essential in terms of the analysis the article presents, may well be there to convey an important perspective to the reader.

In the past war if one of the warring countries, in planning military actions, counted upon quickly destroying the enemy army, seizing his vitally important areas and driving any particular state out of the war, it did not attempt to destroy the industrial installations. On the contrary, it was interested in preserving them for the support of its own troops and the entire country. In such case air attacks and other means of destruction were directed only against those targets which, during the planned period of military operations, provided the enemy with the greatest capability for active resistance. This proposition is confirmed by numerous examples. (57)

The objectives stated in the beginning of this paragraph are always crucial in any Soviet discussion of a war in Europe. The second sentence reiterates the rationale for avoiding the destruction of industrial regions, and preserving them for the use of the Soviet Union and Soviet troops. The final sentence indicates the need to direct early attacks only against those targets whose destruction will have the highest payoff during the initial period of military operations. Implicitly, strikes more pertinent to the conduct of a longer war can be withheld.

The remainder of the article is directed to an examination of World War II strategic bombing and the lessons to be drawn from it. The basic conclusion is that the mission of World War II strategic bombing was correct, but that its conduct was not overly effective, primarily because insufficient consideration had been given to critical and vulnerable areas. The article suggests that the key target areas -

power, fuel and transport - did not become targets until the very end of the war and, further, that the vital nerve center of German industry eventually was paralyzed only when the strikes were focused on key branches as opposed to the industry as a whole.   The article clearly states that the general attack of cities did not accomplish the strategic aims, and in a modern war the broad-scale nuclear attack of cities might well be counterproductive in terms of subsequent occupation of the territory. The Soviets do not want an alienated population on their hands if at all possible; it is far more rational to enter an area with the local populace on one's side, for it obviates tying up troops and other resources to keep it under control. Moreover, it is far better to capture cities with the ground forces than destroy them with nuclear weapons which will clearly render potential assets useless. As regards such issues as political targeting or nontargeting, the article states: "Political motives can force the abandonment of strikes against extremely important economic and military targets or their implementation with smaller forces and means and on a selective basis. [Emphasis added.]

On the other hand, a few cities might be struck for political effect, such as Hiroshima was in World War II: "In a number of cases it is possible that attacks will even be made against objectives which are not of great military and economic importance, but which are advantageous from a political viewpoint."(58) The overall philosophy is summed up in the article as follows:

It is obvious that the need for a thorough evaluation of the political situation when sapping the military and economic potential of warring states assumes incomparably greater importance under conditions of a nuclear war.

At present political conditions will be considered when selecting regions for delivering nuclear strikes on a country-wide scale and when determining the number of objectives, the priority of inflicting strikes, and the methods of destruction of industrial, administrative-political and other centers. (59)

While the initial nuclear strike would certainly be on a large scale, involving hundreds of warheads, its exact force is unknown. In the Soviet liteature, the initial strike is described as a mass strike, but just what does "mass" mean? This issue is rarely addressed in Western perceptions of the strike; instead, it is commonly assumed that mass means "all," "most" or at least "an awful lot." This is not how the Soviets define mass.

The Soviets distinguish between three types of nuclear strikes: individual, group and mass. The individual strike is exactly that - one nuclear round against an individual target. A group strike is carried out simultaneously with several nuclear rounds against one major objective such as troop concentrations, grouping of nuclear rocket means, or an airbase. Individual and group strikes will usually be carried out in the interests of individual operations (battles) and normally will be planned in direct support of Army or Front operations. A massed strike provides for the destruction of several of the most important troop groupings and major strategic and operational objectives, (60) and most likely would be planned by the General Staff. A mass strike would involve enough strikes to accomplish the objective - the strategic aim. It need not involve the whole force or even most of the force, but could involve scores, hundreds, or perhaps even thousands of strikes, or whatever would be necessary to accomplish the objectives or strategic aims. As a lower bound, "scores" of weapons have been identified as constituting a "mass" strike in several places in the Soviet literature.

Another common Western perception of the mass strike is one of colossal damage that would entail enormous casualties and the utter ruin of much if not most of European NATO territory. While the Soviets clearly have the capability to conduct a strike that would transform all of Western Europe's "industrial and administrative political centers into a heap of ruins, and the territory into a lifeless desert contaminated with deadly radioactive substances," (61) such a strike would not be in accord with their primary political objectives, nor would it appear to be consistent with their major interest in ground force operations in a nuclear war: "If the enemy, as the result of nuclear strikes, is completely destroyed and his territory becomes a massive zone of destruction and contamination, there is no need to consider offensive operations of ground troops in general." (62)

There are two radically different approaches to nuclear war. One looks to the traditional defeat of military forces; the other, to annihilation and destruction. The first is primarily a war-fighting approach, while the second pertains more to a deterrence or retaliation approach. Both have their roles and rationales, and the Soviets state that they considered and decided to prepare for both. (63) However, most of the West's attention has been concentrated on the deterrence portion of the Soviet capability, and has tended to ignore the other perhaps more significant portion. In examining Soviet strategy for war in Europe, it is important to distinguish both simultaneously. In examining their literature and capabilities, it appears that their clear preference and majority of their effort is for the war-fighting capability and strategy.

GROUND FORCE OPERATIONS

The real heart of the Soviet threat to Europe has been, and remains, the ground forces, particularly the tank and combined arms armies. The nuclear capability, although it triggered a revolution in the organization and operations of the ground forces, does not detract from the importance of that fundamental threat. The nuclear strike may decide the war, but the ground forces secure the ultimate victory - the building of worldwide communism or the "establishment of peaceful order and control." A detailed appreciation of this component of the combined nuclear-conventional threat is essential to any analysis of Soviet military strategy in Europe.

Beginning of the Combined Arms Concept

The watershed year for the combined arms concept appears to have been around 1964 when the basic notions were first presented for distribution to officers and generals via the restricted-level version of Voyennaya mysl'. The article that is credited as having "for the first time examined jointly the fundamental characteristics of preparing for and conducting combined-arms combat when nuclear weapons are employed by one or both sides, and when they are not used," (64) is by the Soviet dean of tactics, Major General V. Reznichenko, which appeared in March 1964.

Before that time, questions concerning the organization and conduct of combat were examined with respect to two different and independent positions. These were situations involving the use or nonuse of nuclear weapons. (65) General Reznichenko's article initiated the development of combined operations in which both nuclear weapons and "conventional" forces work together in an integrated and complementary fashion.

In considering this process of thought development, it is useful to recognize the NATO threat as perceived by the Soviets at that time. In 1954 the United States began deploying nuclear weapons throughout NATO Europe, and adopted a policy whereby nuclear weapons would be considered like any other weapons for use immediately in any war. The rearmament of Germany and its integration into NATO defense plans also commenced at this time. In 1957 nuclear weapons were officially integrated into NATO policy with the adoption of the NATO strategic doctrine. Forces began to reorganize and train for nuclear fighting. The Pentomic division concept was developed and widely discussed. At congressional hearings in the mid-1950s, public attention was focused on the effects of nuclear weapons and their employment in war; tactical nuclear warfare became a major topic of discussion. Although the brakes were applied to this process when President Kennedy took office in 1961, the deployments of nuclear weapons in Europe continued to increase, reaching a peak, according to the United States secretary of defense, of some 7,000 weapons in the mid-1960s. It was against this backdrop that the Soviets began in earnest to study theater nuclear war and learn how to organize and equip to fight it. The result was the modern combined arms concept.

The Need to Achieve High Rates of Advance

One of the principal characteristics of the combined arms concept is the emphasis on rates of advance or very simply, speed. This is not a new characteristic - but one whose importance becomes greatly magnified in nuclear operations.   Immediately following the main nuclear strike, the primary mission of the attacking forces becomes the rapid exploitation of that strike to complete the smashing of surviving enemy forces and to seize specific positions, areas and objectives. The actions of the troops on the battlefield are coordinated first, with the nuclear strikes and are directed toward the exploitation of their results. Swift, highly maneuverable actions to exploit gaps, breaches and intervals ·in the enemy combat formation left by the nuclear strikes form the basis of the attack of the motorized rifle and tank battalions in modern battle.

> The combat formation must ensure swift use of results of nuclear strikes and destruction by fire of the enemy so that he has no time to collect himself, execute a maneuver, close the breaches, restore his system of fire and control, and conduct other measures to eliminate the after effects of nuclear strikes and the effects of fire.

> A sudden and swift attack from various directions will lead to the rapid dismemberment of the enemy forces into parts and to their demoralization and destruction. (66)

There appear to be four primary rationales - consistent throughout the Soviet military literature - underlying the emphasis on rapid and immediate exploitation. The first is to capitalize on the shock effect of the initial strike. It is recognized that even in conventional attack, the more quickly one can attack following the lifting of these fires, the better use one can make of the confusion and initial psychological shock that results from massive fire barrage.   Exploitation of this shock effect appears to be given much greater prominence in Soviet doctrine than in that of the United States - perhaps because the United States is not on the offense - particularly in the case of nuclear weapons, where the Soviets recognize that the shock or psychological effect may extend far beyond the immediate lethal area of blast or radiation.

> M.V. Frunze, in speaking of the psychological effect of any nuclear weapon wrote: "The extent of the psychological loss cannot be calculated and under certain conditions it can exceed by many times the material damage which is caused by these weapons of destruction."

> The possibilities of such a loss from nuclear weapons is immeasurably greater than that observed with the appearance of a new means of destruction in the past. The sudden launching of nuclear strikes may cause panic and confusion in the ranks of the defenders. A portion of the personnel, even if it has not landed in the sphere of immediate destruction, may be stunned, disorganized, and lose its self control. (67)

The second rationale behind the importance of rapid exploitation is a simple question of survival: ". . . such a character of the attack creates unfavorable conditions for enemy employment of weapons of mass destruction. He cannot precisely determine the targets for delivery of nuclear strikes and is forced to move his means of tactical nuclear attack often." (68) As was stated in the 1960s:

> In nuclear war, the combat activities of the troops will inevitably be distinguished by great activity, swiftness, and exceptionally high maneuverability, for only in such conditions will the results of their own nuclear strikes be used in full measure on one hand; on the other, the carrying out of similar strikes by the enemy will be made difficult.(69)

> It follows that speed of action is one of the main conditions for defeating the enemy and for preserving one's own forces. (70)

> Daring and decisive attack and swift and skillful maneuver will not only assure the defeat of the enemy but will be the best means of protection from his nuclear strikes. (71)

This approach, in conjunction with surprise and deception, appears to constitute the major Soviet counter to the United States/NATO use of battlefield nuclear weapons (primarily artillery, but also HONEST JOHN and LANCE). These weapons pose a very special problem. When on alert in firing position, they are difficult to target because their reaction time is short. Moreover, when deployed in a waiting role, they are difficult to find and constitute a hard target. The first solution to this problem is to exacerbate the United States/NATO target acquisition problem by executing swift and skillful maneuvers. The second - and particularly important answer - is immediately to pin down a detected United States/NATO target with conventional or chemical fire until nuclear fire can be brought to bear. Conventional artillery fire does not usually kill or destroy - it merely suppresses. Only nuclear fire destroys.   In combating NATO nuclear means, the goal must be destruction or seizure. Suppressing, putting out of action, or pinning down are only temporary or holding actions pending the final resolution of destruction or capture.

Speed and coordination in the attack are essential for a third and perhaps less obvious reason. The Soviets recognize that they cannot depend on the complete success of their initial strike. Hence, the first priority for all forces - conventional as well as nuclear - is to find and destroy the nuclear weapons that might be used against the Soviet force. The attack is a combined strike plus exploitation, with common objectives, the most important of which is destruction of the nuclear weapons. The purpose of exploitation is not only to build on the nuclear strike in taking land, but also to find and destroy the remaining nuclear means of attack.   The faster that is accomplished, the fewer the weapons that can be used against them.

A final corollary advantage to rapid movement is the reduced time of exposure to radiation when transiting contaminated areas: "The importance of high tempos of attack under modern conditions rises still more because now a very important factor of the situation is radioactive contamination of the terrain. The higher the rate of attack, the less that troop personnel receive radiation." (72)

The Soviets recognize full well the potential destructive nature of the battlefield.

> ... armed conflict in theaters of military operations will be characterized by great violence, the mass destruction of troops, colossal destruction, and the formation of broad zones with a high level of radioactive contamination. (73)

> Under the influence of nuclear strikes, the nature of a locale sharply changes. On the ground and underground explosions will form great craters, piles of dirt and also high levels of radiation on large areas. In wood and population points fires and dense debris will arise. As a result of destroyed bridges and hydroelectric equipment, inundated regions will be formed. All this will not only significantly hamper but in some cases for some time the possibility of waging active combat operations in the regions of nuclear strikes will be completely excluded. (74)

> A new characteristic feature of the offensive in nuclear war is the conduct of combat actions under conditions of the presence of vast zones of contamination, destruction, fires, and floods. (75)

Once again, the implied destruction pertains more to NATO weapons than Soviet ones, and this explains the associated emphasis on mobility, cover, deception, and timing. Of further importance is the psychological training of the troops. The impact of the battlefield environment on personnel during the war is very skillfully woven throughout the Soviet literature. In fact, it often appears that the material might well have been written by a psychologist preparing the troops for what might easily be regarded as their last battle. For example, in The Philosophical Heritage of V.I. Lenin and Problems of Contemporary War:

> The highest form of heroism is self-sacrifice. Its significance consists in the fact that such a step usually becomes a source, an initiation of a mass movement, making the unusual usual, as it were. The history of our army and navy is rich in examples of conscious self-sacrifice. We all remember the deeds of thousands of Soviet fighting men who, clutching grenades, flung themselves under enemy tanks, pilots who rammed the enemy, and men who blocked with their bodies the death-spewing ports of enemy pillboxes.

> Deeply-conscious self-sacrifice will be required to an even greater degree in a nuclear-missile war. For example, it will frequently be necessary not only to cross but also to fight on ground with a high radiation level. Certain units may be assigned the mission of destroying a hostile missile launcher, missile storage site, etc. All this will demand of our fighting men an extreme degree of self-

sacrifice and the willigness to achieve the goal even at the cost of
their lives. (76)

The psychological training of troops parallels the use of psychological
preparation in the larger strategic sense.

In sum, the Soviet views relative to fighting a nuclear war appear to
be in complete consonance with preparing the USSR both psychologically and physically for such risk taking as may be necessary in
consequence of the stated Soviet purpose of continuing to strive for
a further and ever more decisive shift in the balance of world forces
in their favor. (77)

The psychological preparedness of troops receives considerable attention throughout the Soviet literature, with particular emphasis on
problems of nuclear war. This problem is widely recognized and may be
one of the greatest uncertainties associated with the unknown dangers
and conduct of a nuclear war. In The Offensive, the psychological
aspect is inextricably linked to the revolution in warfare and to the
importance of the nuclear strike supported by all the forces whose only
chance of survival lies in the very rapid exploitation of that strike. The
message that comes through is that if one expects to survive, one had
better "go like hell."

A corollary thought is that if one does not succeed early in the
game, he may be faced with mass desertion and associated disciplinary
problems. Operations designed to bring about the rapid demoralization
of enemy forces and to counter it in the Warsaw Pact forces also
constitute a major area of attention throughout the Soviet literature.

To assist in the rapid exploitation, special emphasis is given to the
use of artillery to suppress antitank capabilities. (78) Swiftness of the
attack is ensured by reliable suppression of the enemy, by rapid
organization of passages through obstacles, and by the resolute and
continuous advance of battalions directly behind the bursts of shells
from their own artillery. Guns and tanks are assigned to conduct direct
fire and to destroy enemy weapons the moment their location becomes
known, particularly antitank means, and defensive structures on the
forward edge and in the immediate depth of the enemy.

The Soviets view high rates of advance at least as important in an
initial conventional phase as they are in a nuclear conflict and for many
of the same reasons. First, such a war is conducted under the ever-
present threat that it will go nuclear and hence there is the continuous
need to avoid presenting lucrative targets to the enemy. Second, a
swift advance into the rear to destroy or capture NATO nuclear
capabilities before they can be used is the best means to limit damage.
Third, a rapid advance decreases the effectiveness with which NATO
can employ nuclear weapons to stop the Soviet offensive. Fourth, speed
is necessary for the piecemeal destruction of NATO forces before they
can be mobilized into an effective combat-ready defense force. Over
the past decade, the rates of advance as discussed in the Soviet

literature for nuclear and conventional combat gradually have been approaching each other.

Complementary Role of Forces and
Weapons of Mass Destruction

The most obvious major change in combat operations is in the mission of the troops: "Employment of nuclear weapons on the battlefield, the increased fire and maneuver capabilities of troops, and a change in the character of the offensive led to a substantial change in the content, depth and form of assignment of the combat missions." (79) As stated by Marshal Grechko: "The appearance of qualitatively new and more powerful types of weapons and their mass adoption by the troops predetermine changes in troop combat formations, depth of missions, forms of maneuver, nature of defense and other forms of combat activity." (80)

The major revolution lies in the approach to defeating enemy forces. In World War II, forces were used to defeat, destroy or capture forces. The typical operation was a broad, massed frontal assault - force against force. In a nuclear environment or in a conventional environment under threat of nuclear weapons use, a massed frontal assault would merely create a good target for the enemy. Further, such an assault does not allow for high rates of advance, but simply slows the attacker. It is better to avoid such confrontations and move directly into the enemy's rear. This is one of the most important aspects of the new Soviet approach. The main mission of the ground forces is not the destruction of the opposing forces. Weapons of mass destruction, chemical and nuclear, with air support playing a major role, are used to destroy major troop groupings.

In the past encirclement and annihiliation or capture of opposing groups was a major mission or objective of the attacking forces. Under modern conditions, however, there is no time for such a task to be executed. An encircled grouping is capable of quickly organizing a strong defense; nuclear weapons and high mobility enable it to break out and withdraw its main forces before the encirclement is completed.(81) This does not mean that under modern conditions such enemy groupings cannot be encircled and destroyed; rather, it implies that attacking troops must take measures to prevent the enemy from employing nuclear weapons and putting up an organized resistance which would slow the attacker's advance.

Encirclement and annihilation of groupings must proceed rapidly so as to leave the attacking forces free to accomplish the advance in depth and capture their main objectives.

The basis of actions for the encirclement and annihilation of defending groupings is the use of nuclear weapons and a swift attack from several directions. These actions will be organized in a way that will deprive the enemy of opportunities to use nuclear weapons, that will not give it time to prepare organized resistance, and that will not slow down the execution of the main missions of the offensive operations. (82)

As regards combat operations by tank units against operational defense reserves:

> Even if the defending forces have been able to deploy and simultaneously bring large reserves into action, it will of course not be advisable to employ against these reserves the entire force of the tank group, thus creating the threat of becoming involved in a protracted engagement. To take care of such forces it is desirable to use primarily mass destruction weapons and minimum forces from the tank group, using the rest of the tank forces to advance deep into enemy lines. In order quickly to complete the elimination of enemy reserves, sometimes part of the forces from the second echelon or senior command reserves can be moved up. Thus in order to wipe out defense force reserves joined into various groupings, under modern conditions as a rule one should not employ the main forces of the tank groups operating out in front. These groups should push their rapid advance deep into enemy lines in the interests of carrying out their main assignment - rapid attainment of the objectives of the operations. (83)

The Soviet plan is to avoid engaging in a major World War II-type battles. Rather than meet major forces, the Soviets would bypass them, move into the rear and capture important objectives such as nuclear means, airbases, important bridges and road junctions, and generally complete the work of the nuclear strikes. This strategy also applies to the conduct of conventional operations. In that case, it is also considered expedient

> . . . to seek methods of overcoming a defense which are carried out with the least expenditure of forces and means. In this regard, decisive importance is acquired by a penetration into the depth of defense through sectors which are unoccupied or are lightly occupied by troops, the infliction of strikes in zones where the defending large units have not yet become consolidated, and also in a turning movement of open or poorly defended flanks. (84)

In both the nuclear and conventional cases, this strategy is critically dependent on good intelligence about the location of opposition forces. One of the major potential contributions of satellites and other high-altitude reconnaissance (e.g., FOXBAT) capabilities is exactly in this area. A 1978 Polish article, "Penetration of the Enemy Defense: A Form of Offensive Operation," discussed these new possibilities.

> An extremely important role in present and future combat conditions is played by a new branch of reconnaissance, satellite reconnaissance. Effective instantaneous operations will be

impossible if accurate data from this form of reconnaissance cannot be used for tactical purposes. It is a question of reducing the information and reaction time to a minimum. For example, it would not have been possible (for Israeli forces in 1973, October War) to penetrate to a great depth into the defenses of the Egyptian 2nd and 3rd Armies in a short time using limited tank forces without accurate information concerning the gap that had opened between the two armies. It is possible to penetrate the enemy defense when a large amount of reliable data about it is available. (85)

The extent to which the Soviets are able to use these national intelligence resources in the type of tactical and operational-tactical maneuver suggested by the above passages is not known. However, there is little question that the awareness of the need for such a capability is implicit in their discussion of maneuver, that the technology is probably well in hand, and that their expertise in cybernetics, combat modeling and troop control should enable them to make efficient and effective use of the data. To the extent that this is an accurate inference regarding Soviet capabilities, its potential impact on combat operations might be as dramatic in a future large-scale war in Europe as ULTRA was in World War II.

Operational-Tactical Nuclear Strikes

The initial massive nuclear strike is planned and directed from the top, the Supreme Command Headquarters. Such a strike would also include missions in support of Front interests, and might be followed by group and individual strikes planned and directed from the Front command headquarters. The Front objectives fall into four main categories:

1. Destroy the means of nuclear attack.
2. Destroy the main groupings of combat forces and their command/ control.
3. Isolate the battlefield.
4. Breach the main line of defense and define the main attack corridors.

Only highly significant targets are to be attacked in the Front nuclear strikes; nuclear weapons are not to be used against "conventional" targets.

It is believed that nuclear weapons, as the main means of destruction, will be employed only for the destruction of the most important objectives; all other targets are neutralized and destroyed by the artillery, aviation and the fire of tanks and other weapons. In other words, nuclear weapons are employed in combination with other means in accordance with the concept of the battle. (86)

Use of nuclear weapons against insignificant, secondary objectives contradicts the very nature of this weapon. (87)

From the point of view of achieving the greatest results and inflicting of damage on the enemy, nuclear weapons should be used on his most important concentrations in order, first of all, to break his main center of resistance. (88)

The use of nuclear weapons against important force concentrations brings about a major change in troop operational concepts. In World War II conventional operations, the offensive shock forces were assembled in a departure area some 25 to 30 kilometers from the forward edge of the battle area (FEBA) and were moved out of that area over a period of several nights. Their disposition close to the enemy was comparatively safe because the defender was not employing the powerful means of destruction which could frustrate the effort if it were detected.

The requirement of massing forces for conventional attack has not changed; a favorable correlation of forces is definitely required. On the other hand, the traditional approach to concentrating for attack is exceedingly dangerous when the defender possesses nuclear weapons: first, because it warns the enemy and affords him the opportunity to undertake defensive measures, which, in turn, deny the attacker the benefits of surprise; and second, because the attacker is very vulnerable to nuclear weapon strikes and the defender is afforded the opportunity to destroy efficiently and easily the main attacking forces.

The problem is how to achieve the necessary correlation of forces on the main avenues of attack at the right time in the face of a possible nuclear defense. This issue was clearly stated in 1974 congressional hearings by the Supreme Allied Commander Europe (SACEUR), General Goodpaster:

This presents a dilemma to them. From our standpoint, it is a dilemma that has considerable value. That is, if they are under a threat of weapons of this kind, it denies them the ability freely to mass without consideration of what the consequences would be. If they were to mass in order to achieve the kind of local superiority conventionally that would allow them to rupture our position or, as you say, to resort to other means to try to overlap it, then if they were to try that kind of massing, they would become extremely vulnerable to these weapons. They are inhibited against that kind of massing.

This, in itself, then, becomes an assistance to us, a great assistance in terms of the conventional posture on their side that we have to deal with.

I have to say that in my best judgment, and this is a matter to which I assure you I give the very deepest consideration, the presence of those weapons, both as a deterrent and in terms of the potential warfighting use to which they could be put, has a very beneficial effect from our side in our objectives of deterrence and the defense pattern that we are able to follow. (89)

This, as mentioned earlier, was one of the principal objectives of the initial United States tactical nuclear deployments to Europe. The manner in which to attack - to achieve the local force concentrations required to develop a breakthrough - when the defense was a nuclear one, was a recognized problem. The Soviet solution when the war begins in a nuclear mode comes in three parts: first, use nuclear weapons to develop the "required" breakthrough conditions; second, change the qualitative approach to concentration so that timing is its most important feature; and third, interdict the movement of enemy reinforcements to maintain the favorable correlation of forces developed by the nuclear strikes.

Of paramount importance is the opening nuclear fire barrage. Traditional concentration of forces if the attack is to be made nuclear is both unnecessary and undesirable.

It became clear in the fifties that for a decisive defeat of the enemy in the chosen area it is not obligatory at all to concentrate on a limited space a large number of forces and means. For this purpose it is sufficient to concentrate the fire of powerful weapons disposed over a large area. This is even more beneficial in that the concentration of forces has become very dangerous due to the presence of the same powerful weapons in the enemy arsenal. . . . A large concentration of troops will most often create a lucrative target for the enemy and may sooner lead to failure. (90)

With the appearance of nuclear weapons, the capability arose to neutralize dependably and smash the enemy defense in short times without the preliminary concentration of large masses of artillery close to the enemy. (91)

Nuclear weapons are now to be used to define the main avenues of attack.

. . . the main efforts of the advancing troops should be concentrated in basic decisive directions. The direction of the main efforts under modern conditions will be determined by the regions against which the main nuclear rocket strikes are concentrated and also by the lines of advance of the main groups of troops. (92)

Under conditions where nuclear weapons are employed, the breakthrough as a method for smashing the defending enemy and overcoming his defense will no longer have such decisive significance as formerly. The primary method of attack will be the launching of nuclear strikes and the swift advance of tank and motorized rifle podrazeleniya [battalions] into the depth of the enemy's defense through the breaches formed by nuclear weapons. (93)

The targets of this strike are first, NATO nuclear weapons, and second, main groupings of combat forces and operational reserves - avoiding simultaneously radioactive contamination that may impede or otherwise constrain the exploitation of the strike by troops. (94)   The nuclear strike and its exploitation are part of a single integrated concept – the concept of an operation. It is generally conceived at the highest level and worked out by the various subordinate commands.

> The basis of the concept of an offensive operation, carried out by ground troops, consists of the use of nuclear weapons by operational units, primarily in the first attack, and the effective use of its consequences by motorized infantry, tank and airborne troops. Because of this, in determining methods of defeating the enemy in the concept of an operation the following must be indicated: how many nuclear rounds and of what strength to use in the first nuclear attack; what enemy targets and groupings to destroy to a specified extent; where, in what sequence, and in cooperation with whom to complete the defeat of these groupings by forces of   attacking troops; and what targets and troop areas must be captured in order to promptly exploit the results of nuclear attacks and to implement the next task; how to conceive the use of nuclear weapons and troops during the development of an operation. (95)

In considering the use of nuclear weapons and troops during the development of the operation, it is important to recognize the particularly acute tactical problem of target uncertainty and as-sociated limitations on the ability at the operational-tactical level to conduct a simultaneous strike - a strike which, realistically, may be impossible. As explained in The Offensive, simultaneous launching of nuclear strikes is

> . . . possible only with the presence of the corresponding quantity of nuclear ammunition and means for its delivery to the target as well as complete and reliable data on the enemy objectives throughout the entire depth of his defense. But the attacker will not always have such capabilities and data.   It is considered difficult to determine the location of all objectives reliably and accurately for the launching of a simultaneous nuclear strike against them even with the presence of modern means of reconnaissance. And before destroying such objectives, final reconnaissance is required to refine their location.   A portion of the objectives may be in motion or appear anew. Hence, the conclusion is drawn that one can hardly count on the fact that the attacker will succeed in destroying all important objectives with one simultaneous nuclear strike. In the course of the offensive it will often be necessary to launch nuclear strikes as the attacking troops advance and targets are disclosed for destruction by nuclear weapons. (96)

This is equally true when the war begins conventionally, although in a different manner. In that case, which weapons are employed, when and for what missions, depends upon the time of transition.

Forward Detachments and Attack from the March

The emphasis in troop actions is on speed and agility. Large massive assaults are replaced by the use of nuclear weapons. Rather than concentrate the troops in a fixed position for an attack, they now attack from the march.

> The complete motorization of the troops permitted moving the podrazdeleniya [companies, battalions] out quickly, launching an assault from the march, and exploiting the results of nuclear strikes swiftly. In addition, when the defender has nuclear weapons available the prolonged stay of the attacking troops at a short distance from the enemy became extremely dangerous. All this also became an objective precondition for the appearance of a fundamentally new method for the troops to launch an attack of a prepared defense-from the march by moving out from a waiting area.

> The launching of an offensive from the march with the movement of the podrazdeleniya [companies, battalions] out from a waiting area is a fundamentally new method because it is employed at the very start of the offensive in the breakthrough of the enemy's prepared defense, which did not occur formerly. (97)

To the extent that some troop concentration is required, the effectiveness of an operation becomes largely a question of timing:

> Consequently, a concentration of effort on the most important axis under the new conditions is achieved by different means and methods (employment of nuclear weapons) than was done before.

> In addition to this, the concentration of forces and means has taken on immeasurably greater importance in time than in space. Moreover, concentration in space now represents a great danger and can be done only for a short time, quickly, and resolutely. (98)

Timing is a major ingredient of success, highlighted throughout the Soviet literature. It enters into the attack disposition, development of concentrations, strike coordination and exploitation. Its effective application has the further benefit of concealing the main avenues of attack. Presumably, the forces prior to attack would be well dispersed along the entire border. Concentration would occur only at the last moment as the forces depart from their individual waiting areas and merge at the FEBA for the attack. The main avenues of attack would need to be known sufficiently in advance to ensure that the approach march routes are well marked, but this would require only a few hours and should be easy to accomplish in a covert manner. However, this method of attack creates problems of operating under great stress and confusion.

> At the same time, such a method for the launching of an attack by the battalion requires precise organization of the movements of the podrazdeleniya [companies] toward the FEBA and strict time co-ordination of the deployment for the attack of the enemy right behind nuclear strikes and the fire of conventional weapons. What has been said is unthinkable without the comprehensive preparation of the routes of march and their marking, which assures timely arrival at the indicated positions day and night, and without the careful study by the commanders at all echelons of the terrain on which it is intended to move out and then to conduct the battle. (99)

The forces moving out for the attack are different from the conventional ones of World War II in that they are smaller and more self-contained. They are, in effect, forward detachments of battalion-, regiment-, and division-size units that are expected to outrun their second-echelon and reserve forces as they proceed into NATO's depth. While the division and corps were the major force units in World War II, the regiment and division appear to be the major force units today. The regiment has been regarded as the primary ground force unit and is the key forward detachment. (100)

Of particular interest was an article which appeared in the November 1964 Voyennaya mysl', "Operations of Tank Armies in Operational Depth." (101) The author, Army General P. Kurochkin, examined World War II experiences and singled out examples and lessons relevant to modern combined arms operations. A discussion of highspeed pursuit by armies and mobile forces is worth quoting in detail:

> The speed of advance of troops, especially of tank groups, will be still higher under modern conditions. In this connection, there arises especially sharply the problem of the uninterrupted action of troops, day and night, despite their having to pass through zones of destruction and areas of radioactive contamination. It must be expected that the highest speeds of advance will be in sectors where the enemy is being subjected to nuclear blows, including some from the very beginning of the operation.

> It is noteworthy that tank armies, depending on circumstances, more often carried out parallel - less often, frontal - pursuit, or both in combination. In many cases the pursuit was carried out by combined-arms armies from the front, and by mobile forces by routes parallel to the retreat of the enemy. Parallel pursuit was the most decisive and advantageous. In this the tank armies made a headlong rush, prevented the enemy from moving into prepared zones of defense in his depth, intercepted communication lines, struck blows on his flank and the rear, defeated his operational

reserves piecemeal (as they moved up from depth), and from the march broke through operational defense zones and forced water barriers.

Especially instructive, it seems to us, is the fact that in most cases the tank armies pursued the enemy in dispersed formations and even in columns of the march, deploying in combat formations only on meeting the enemy. The strong advance detachments played a great role in this. They were selected from the tank and mechanized corps. In many cases they had a greater complement than usual, and were assigned missions of operational importance. (In the composition of such an advance detachment most often there operated a tank brigade, reinforced by a self-propelled artillery regiment, one or two battalions of artillery and up to (one) engineers battalion, and sometimes infantry podrazdeleniya [companies].These detachments, operating ahead of the main forces at a distance of up to 40 kilometers and more, did not become involved in protracted battles with the enemy, but bypassed his centers of resistance and hastened on to objectives subject to capture. First among such objectives were still undestroyed bridges, especially across large rivers, fords, and bridgeheads. There is no doubt that the role and importance of the advance detachments now will not only persist, but become still greater, with their being called on to execute missions taking advantage of the results of nuclear strikes, in cooperation with airborne troops, making possible the swift advance of their own forces. (102)

This passage lays out the basic concept which involves the use of strong forward detachments advancing along numerous axes into NATO depth, bypassing strong points of resistance, with the objective of disrupting NATO mobilization, and seizing critical targets and terrain features. This subject was more thoroughly addressed in March 1965 in "Forward Detachments in Offensive Operations and Battles." (103) The thrust of this article is similarly the increased importance of forward detachments under modern conditions. The stated missions of continued importance include the timely capture of bridges, road junctions, mountain passes and defiles. These will contain NATO maneuver, hamper NATO's employment of nuclear weapons, undermine its defense stability and help the attacking forces achieve a high rate of advance. (104)

Forward detachments of varying size will be used - the smallest of which could be considered the lead reconnaissance companies. The next larger, and smallest "strong" detachment capable of taking on concrete tasks, appear to be of battalion size, referred to as tactical detachments. These forces are strictly conventional and have as their tasks, in addition to the seizure of areas, the destruction of NATO nuclear capability. In reference to these detachments:

By rapidly penetrating into the depth, they may fairly inconspicuously and safely (because of the large "dead zone" of rockets) reach the immediate positional areas of rocket units (airfields for missile-bearing aircraft) and destroy or capture them. The detachments could be extremely effective against rocket units on the march while they change their positions. Execution of these tasks is facilitated by the fact that rocket launchers are very vulnerable to fire from artillery, tanks, and even rifle fire, as reported by the foreign press.(105)

The special role of these advance detachments in so-called raiding operations is also examined. These operations consist of several hit-and-run objectives, located at various depths, according to each detachment's capability.(106)

There are also large forward detachments that have their own nuclear weapons. It is proposed that these be called operational forward detachments. These are used not only to capture and hold objectives, but also to destroy individual, small, advancing NATO reserve groupings, and large control points and communication centers. Additional significant objectives are PVO (air defense) groupings - including SAM and AAA sites and control and guidance points, (107) which also appear to be excellent candidates for the previously mentioned raiding operations -warehouses and bases of material, (108) and, of particular importance, airbases. ". . .[V]ery great importance is attached to the seizure of airfields by the advancing troops, providing assistance in the restoration of such airfields, and in the rapid movement forward of aviation logistical support."(109)

These detachments generally appear to be of regiment size, but can be of larger, division size, as well. They, too, are commonly employed along numerous axes. "Thus it may be assumed that under modern conditions the overall number of forward detachments will be increased. It is believed that they will be employed simultaneously or consecutively, but with various targets, tasks, and along various axes of the troop offensive." (110)

Thus, the Soviet operational strategy is to use smaller, albeit firepower-strong, forces as forward detachments to advance quickly into NATO's rear along numerous axes. This leads to another major change in troop operations - the complete concept of a front and, in particular, the FEBA. The FEBA is the line of demarcation and the transition between friendly and enemy forces or the area between the territory occupied by the opposing forces. The point is that it is drawn as a line - straight, curved, with bulges but still a line. This is still the way the confrontation of forces is portrayed in the vast majority of Western studies and war games concerned with war in Europe. It is, however, not the way the Soviets perceive things. In the Soviet viewpoint, there will be no well-defined FEBA. (111) The Soviet forces are instructed to prepare for operations in what is variously referred to as the broken front, porous war, uneven development of the front, or simply the absence of a well-defined FEBA. A more realistic concept than that of the FEBA will be that of a zone, quite wide in some areas, of mutual interpenetration.

A characteristic feature of military operations in land theaters in a future war will be the absence of linear troops actions, the absence of solid fronts. Military operations simultaneously will be extended for great distances along the front and to the rear; they will be, to a certain extent, of a focal nature. (112)

Under contemporary conditions combat actions will unfold from the very beginning not on a solid front but in all directions. This is due on the one hand to the possibilities developed in connection with the use of nuclear weapons and on the other to requirements for protection of troops - the desire to avoid unnecessary losses in case of enemy attack.

Application of nuclear weapons and airborne landings, the absence of a solid front, conducting battle in (all) directions, and differences in the degree of enemy resistance in different sectors will lead to extremely nonuniform development of combat actions along front and in depth.

In some areas subunits and units, using the results of nuclear and fire strikes, will swiftly advance in depth; in others, where limited use will be made of nuclear weapons, they will conduct a persistent fight with the resisting enemy; in still others they will be forced to slow the advance or to stop it temporarily to liquidate the consequences of enemy nuclear attack, to switch to the defensive to repulse his blows, or ever retreat. (113)

The offensive on directions of attack also created certain difficulties. The flanks of the forces attacking on directions of attack will be open, which requires their dependable support. . . .

The conduct of the offensive on directions of attack and the different degree of destruction of the enemy and of his resistance in different sectors cause the <u>unevenness of development of the offensive</u> even when overcoming the tactical depth of the defense...

All this will lead to the absence of a clearly determined front line in its former meaning when combat actions developed from line to line and the troops attacked with the presence of close lateral contact with adjacent units. Now the front line, obviously will have a broken, meandering interrupted outline, and its configuration will change quickly. Considering this, some military theorists even propose abandoning the very concept of "front line" and using in its place one which corresponds more to a contemporary condition — "Line of combat contact of the troops."(114)

All of the units are not expected to achieve success, but those that do are to be reinforced. Therefore, there will be a need to be able to shift efforts between axes to support those actions - which serve to define the main avenues of attack. (115) This is further evidence of the requirement for and impact of flexibility in the Soviet approach to command control.

Air Assault

The uneven development of the front and the need for a forward detachment approach are intensified by use of airborne assault forces.(116) These air assault and airborne operations – which receive almost as much attention in the Soviet literature as that accorded to tanks – are doubly important because of the minor importance generally attached to them in the Western literature, where they are often ignored completely.

> The main role in solving the combat problems of an offensive operation will be played by operational-tactical rocket troops and frontal aviation using nuclear ammunition and also by tank, motorized infantry, and airborne troops. (117)

> The use of aeromobile and airborne forces is an important direction in improving the methods of an offensive under present conditions. Being used in massed numbers after nuclear strikes, these forces are capable of playing the role of a unique echelon for developing the success, however, with the essential difference that they will carry out these missions simultaneously with completing the defeat of the first enemy operational echelon. (118)

> The armed helicopter may turn out to be a means of fundamental change in the nature of ground combat.

> In a war involving the wide employment of nuclear weapons, airborne landings will play a very important role in the form of "airborne infantry."

> Tank troops, with their high tactical mobility on the battlefield, and airborne landing parties, possessing operational mobility in the air, supplement each other well. (119)

These landings are part of the first wave and are designed to take place covertly, under widely varying weather conditions, and at night.

> The experience of troop exercises has shown that such landing operations are employed most often during critical and dynamic period of combat operations. (120)

> Movement by air transport will permit small units to arrive relatively covertly in the assigned area in a state of combat readiness, bypassing zones of radioactive contamination and devastation, in periods of time which none of the other methods of movement can achieve. (121)

> . . . special importance is attached to ensuring that constant and secret control is exercised over the landing operations. . . .

The secrecy of control is determined to a considerable degree by the secrecy of communications. If special measures are not undertaken in this regard, the enemy may detect the preparations for the landing and if therafter he does not succeed in disrupting of the tasks altogether, he will at least be able to make them more complicated. (122)

The organization of troops is being perfected on the basis of the new combat equipment and the system of training and educating the personnel is being improved. In a series of exercises in the last few years, large landings have been made in which they were dropped at great depth, in complicated meteorological conditions at diverse points both during the day and at night. (123)

Three types of airborne operations are envisaged - helicopter assault, paratroop assault and transport landings deep into NATO territory, with the main emphasis placed on helicopter and transport landings. Helicopters will be used as the principal means of dropping tactical airborne troops. Transport planes will also be used for operational landings. (124) Civil aviation is considered a "powerful reserve" of the pool of military transport aircraft for this operation. (125)

These forces will have the task of making the most effective use of the results attained by a massed nuclear strike - capture of the region where nuclear weapons are located, important objectives, river crossings, bridgeheads, mountain passes, defiles, and the annihilation of strategic objectives which cannot be put out of commission by any other means.

Several major rationales for these assault operations are discussed in the Soviet literature. The first is to make maximum use of the nuclear strikes.

The role of the <u>airborne troops</u> increased greatly with the appearance of nuclear missile weapons. This is determined first by the fact that they can quickly exploit the results of nuclear strikes by landing in the depth of the enemy dispositions. (126)

By their swift action they promote the reduction to a minimum of breaks in time between the moment of delivery of a nuclear strike and the exit of troops into the destruction area. Besides the former missions regarding the capture of separate objects in enemy territory, they can be assigned such complicated missions as combat with enemy nuclear attack means, destruction of antiaircraft defense forces, control centers and communication units, i.e., more active and independent missions. (127)

Under present conditions there are expanded capabilities for building up efforts through employment of airborne landings. Landed from helicopters in the depth of the enemy's defense right after nuclear strikes, they can make more rapid use of their results than ground troops, and can capture important areas, junctions of lines of communication, and crossing over water obstacles. They can hinder the approach of reserves and thus facilitate an increase in rates of attack.(128)

The second rationale, closely related to the first, is to help achieve high rates of advance.

Offensive operations of a future war will be distinguished by high tempos.

An offensive should be mounted primarily on tanks, armored personnel carriers, and helicopters. (129)

There is no doubt that the use of airborne landings for purposes of consolidating results of the employment of nuclear weapons is one of the main ways to increase rates of advance. (130)

High rates of advance, exceeding 2-3 times the rates of operation of past war, and caused primarily by the unprecedented power of attack achievable by nuclear strikes, by complete motorization and mechanizations of land troops, by powerful support of their jet supersonic aviation, and by wide utilization of air landings. (131)

The third reason is to capture enemy nuclear weapons or otherwise prevent their employment: "There should be wide employment of airborne landings, the chief mission of which will be seizure and destruction of enemy nuclear means in the tactical and operational depth." (132)

While the above tasks are discussed in a nuclear context, they are all equally important in a nonnuclear phase. In this case, there would be be a massive insertion of airborne units into NATO's rear at the very start of the war or perhaps on the eve of war under cover of night. Their missions would include the seizure of key transportation points to forestall NATO mobilization and force deployment; massive sabotage of installations, particularly command/control/communication facilities; identification and reporting of NATO nuclear means and where possible their destruction; and of special importance, seizure of NATO airbases for subsequent Warsaw Pact use in inserting large airborne units (transport-landings) in NATO's rear. These missions are not, however, strictly military. A most important task involves the use of assault units - possibly special military intelligence units, or as the Soviets usually put it, "divisionary forces" (133) to seize immediately important political administration centers and take control of individual governments. This would probably be a major military intelligence or KGB activity that would make maximum use of various in-place internal agents, the indigenous Communist party elements, and left-wing organizations. One of the major advantages to the Soviets of an initial conventional phase of a war in Europe is that it would provide the time and cover to insert all these units and enable them to begin performing their tasks.

A fourth task of the assault operations, more restricted to the nuclear phase, is to facilitate crossing zones of radiation and destruction. This applies to all forms of supply and force movement and is a major reason behind the interest in seizing NATO airbases for subsequent Warsaw Pact use.

Considerable concern has been voiced in Western literature about the vulnerability of forward-deployed nuclear weapons to attacking Soviet forces.   To judge from this examination of Soviet military literature, the capture of United States/NATO nuclear weapons is certainly a top-priority objective of the Soviet attack and a serious threat to NATO capability. However, the main form of the threat may not be the attacking tank armies as much as sabotage units and airborne assault battalions. Consequently, whether the NATO nuclear deployments are forward or rearward may be a less important variable in determining their vulnerability than, for example, NATO capabilities to counter agent activities on the eve of the war and to detect and engage airborne assault groups before they have landed and secured their position.

Meeting Engagements and Battles

As the forward detachments proceed into the enemy's rear, they will encounter opposition. This encounter is the meeting engagement or battle. The Soviets view the meeting engagement as the main form of force-on-force combat in a future ground war. It takes place when two opposing units on the march run into one another. After the initial nuclear strike, the meeting engagement is the main situation in which the use of nuclear weapons is expected. It is also the scene of the most prominent "tactical" use of nuclear weapons in the Soviet literature. The problem is to identify the advancing enemy - preferably before he becomes aware of the location of the attacker's forces to locate his nuclear support means, main groupings and control points, and to destroy these before the two forces meet. As discussed early in 1964 by a Soviet general officer of the tank troops:

> It must be assumed that such meeting engagements will begin with nuclear strikes, rocket troops and aviation and will have a purely tank character and large scope. They will usually evolve on a wide front and to a great depth under complex, rapidly changing situations, and will be distinguished by exceptional intensity, dynamism, and varied operations of tank troops. (134)

The strikes will occur on an individual and group scale, and will be concentrated against the group of forces most heavily equipped with nuclear weapons. If these forces are fixed, missiles will be used; if mobile, air strikes will be used, with air support playing an extremely strong role both in identifying and striking the advancing units. (135)

The outcome of meeting engagements will also largely depend on the effectiveness of anticipatory nuclear and air strikes. Under these conditions aviation is called upon to play an exceptionally large role. It can quickly and accurately detect an enemy grouping on the march and determine its main forces and main missile means by establishing continuous surveillance over them. This enables it and the tank forces to subsequently deliver effective anticipatory strikes against these forces. (136)

The use of air to support the ground forces, particularly the forward detachments, is vital and differs fundamentally from World War II support operations. As will be discussed in the subsequent section, the air operations support the ground offensive in reconnaissance and in providing firepower to destroy enemy forces in large groupings and in reserve units advancing to the attack. Once again, weapons rather than forces are to be used to destroy enemy forces whenever possible. The task of forces is to capture critical facilities, terrain and other rear objectives.

AIR OPERATIONS

The role of airpower in Soviet strategy also underwent several changes in the recent past. In the early and mid-1950s, the Soviet air forces provided the main nuclear strike arm. In the late 1950s, that role was gradually taken over by the long-range missile units. The change, coupled with the rising expectations for air defense missile (SAM) capabilities, apparently led to a temporary decrease in the importance of airpower. The nuclear missile received the main attention of Soviet strategy and resources. However, with the development around 1964 of the combined arms approach to fighting war in continental theaters of operations, the importance of airpower also grew - although in a slightly altered form. The main missions worked out for air in a nuclear war were reviewed in a 1967 Voyennaya mysl' article by Marshal of Aviation, General S. Krasovkiy.

In a nuclear war, aircraft are capable of carrying out successfully the following basic missions: carrying out aerial reconnaissance at any theater of military operations in the interests of all branches of the armed forces and of the war on the whole; destroying the means of nuclear attack of the enemy on land, in the sea, and in the air; destroying objectives which have strategic and operational-tactical importance; jointly with the forces and means of air defense protecting the troops, fleet, and rear objectives from strikes from the air; protecting the ground troops; combatting the transfer of the enemy in air, sea, and ground routes of transport; and landing airborne troops and supporting completely their operations in the rear area of the enemy.

Besides the above, aircraft have a large number of other missions involving the destruction of nuclear-rocket means of attack of the enemy and its mobile objectives the number of which now, as is known, has increased by several times. We can include in such missions, for example, target designation for ground troops, submarines, and surface ships which use rockets against mobile objectives, guidance of the strike forces against mobile objectives, guidance of the strike forces against mobile targets, control of the results of the strike, execution of the functions of communication, etc. (137)

Recently, a major change in the nature of frontal aviation has been observed. Traditionally, this force has been a short-range force with a heavy emphasis on its air defense (interceptor) mission. In the 1970s, with the development of newer aircraft, this range has been greatly extended to give it a significant ground attack capability. This change may well have been forecast (or explained) in a 1969 Voyennaya mysl' article discussing the battle for air superiority and recent trends.

Some aspects of past experience in regard to methods of fighting for air superiority have also not lost their current nature. Thus in organizing a nuclear attack the prime targets of an aggressor's strikes are airfields and the aircraft thereon, launchers, takeoff strips, stores of nuclear weapons and radio-technical means. Returning to the experience of World War II, we invariably arrive at the conclusion that even at that time strikes against airfields in the beginning of the war occupied one of the chief places in the overall system of struggle for air superiority.

In addition, analysis of past experience shows a gradual reduction in the role and importance of actions against airfields in the battle against hostile aviation in the further course of the war and an increase in the proportion of aerial combat and engagements. This was caused by dispersal of aviation with the beginning of the war to operational airfields, an increase in the combat readiness of units and large units. PVO reinforcements of bases and improvement of the entire VNOS system, which made it more difficult to deliver a surprise attack against airfields, complicated the very organization of raids and required a great expenditure of aviation forces. Moreover, the results of actions against airfields also dropped sharply. Simultaneously the ground force requirements for air support continuously grew and the opposing sides were forced to concentrate the main efforts of the VVS primarily on accomplishing missions, even though very important ones, moved to the background. As noted earlier, the mutual concentration of aviation in limited regions led to intensification of the air struggle, as a result of which aerial combat acquired greater significance than strikes against airfields.

At the present time this situation has undergone considerable change. Judging from everything, strikes against airfields will now play a greater role than aerial combat, not only at the beginning of a war, but in its subsequent course. The increase in importance of actions against airfields is connected with the fact that they represent fixed targets of large area. This is a direct result of qualitative changes in aviation equipment. New supersonic aircraft at present require landing and takeoff strips which are two or three times larger and which usually have artificial hard coverings. The complexity of special equipment and armaments of modern aircraft requires long periods of time in preparing them for repeated sorties. All this has increased the attachment of aircraft to airfields and reduced the possibilities for their dispersal and camouflage.(138)

It must be stressed that even in Israel's aggressive war against the Arab countries the outcome of the struggle for air superiority was decided by a massive surprise attack against airfields. Aerial combat was extremely rare and did not have very much influence on the air struggle of the combatants. (139)

Therefore, the shift in the nature of FA, while almost invariably explained in a conventional context, may be more complex - involving the vulnerability of current airbases and the growth in effectiveness of forward missile air defenses and associated interaction problems (i.e., difficulties involved in operating ground-based and air-based air defenses in the same air space). While this would also make the conventional-phase air superiority mission of FA not only necessary, but practicable, it should be pointed out that this article was written in a nuclear context as well, with the air superiority mission shared by both the missile troops and the aviation. (The missile troops were to destroy the air defense belts and both would then be available for attack of airbases.) A likely scenario might involve a missile strike to neutralize air defenses and simultaneously attack the highest risk nuclear capable airbases. The aircraft would then attack the lesser risk airbases, because they are "large area targets" that are more effectively attacked (i.e., lower collateral damage) with a smaller yield and more accurate aircraft delivery, where no nuclear yield is desirable - by conventional or chemical munitions - because in many cases final confirmation of the target may be required to account for possible NATO dispersal actions.

The principal advantages of airpower in Soviet strategy are the presence of a pilot (eyes), the mobility of the plane and its relatively large payload. The most important of these is the ability of the pilot to conduct reconnaissance and detect targets. The principal missions of air are reconnaissance, the attack of mobile targets - which depends on tightly integrated target detection and attack capability - and the transport of people and material in both an assault and supply mode. The transport and assault missions were discussed in the previous section and will not be considered further, except to reemphasize their importance and their use of NATO airbases. The remaining missions - reconnaissance, attack of mobile targets and ground support - will be examined in this section.

Reconnaissance

The point has already been emphasized that the most important universal mission for all forces is to destroy the enemy nuclear means of attack. This mission has two important components: attack of fixed targets and attack of mobile targets. Airpower has the important mission of conducting reconnaissance of the former and detecting and attacking the latter.

In the period of time immediately preceding the initial strike, many targets such as airbases and troop concentrations must be kept under surveillance and their existence as real targets confirmed. This is a major task for frontal and long-range reconnaissance assets.

> Military thought began to be directed at working out questions of using aviation as a reconnaissance and transport means. An analysis of the conditions of waging armed struggle in nuclear rocket war showed that all services of the Armed Forces to one degree or another needed data of air reconnaissance, which remained the basic source of rapidly receiving authentic information of the intentions and actions of the enemy in his rear areas, on the approaches to the front and directly in the pre-frontal area. The volume of air reconnaissance significantly increased. This is explained by the great concentration of groupings of enemy ground troops in deploying them in place and in movement, the presence of new objectives of reconnaissance - missile means, which are constantly changing their place of location. Moreover a new consumer of reconnaissance data has now appeared - the rocket troops, for whom aviation must systematically carry out intensive air reconnaissance. Modern aviation equipment permits the airplane-reconnoiterer to penetrate deep into enemy territory and discover the location of his nuclear means and other objectives, and swiftly transmit data about them to the command points.(140)

> Aircraft have the important mission of aerial reconnaissance for all services of the Armed Forces, especially Rocket Troops. Hence, means of reconnaissance aviation are continually being improved in the directions of increasing their capacity to detect enemy targets at high speeds and altitudes at any time of day and in any weather and automatically transmit the reconnaissance data directly from the plane to the appropriate headquarters over great distances. (141)

Air reconnaissance operates in two modes: 1) as targets are identified, this information is immediately radioed back; and 2) pictures are taken for subsequent processing and target confirmation upon return.

> On one of the exercises, it became known to the command that the "enemy" was concentrating weapons for a nuclear missile attack. ... Reconnaissance aircraft . . . by Guards Major V. Shchukin, and Guards Captains V. Sedov and . . . immediately took

off upon command. . . . The pilots had to investigate the assigned search areas, locate the disposition of the "enemy" targets in his tactical interior and transmit the information to the command. Each of them had his own route and area of operation. . . .

In a short time, they detected, identified and photographed the major objectives, and after executing evasive maneuvers, took the course to their base. The laconic and accurate reports on the reconnaissance results were radioed through the ether.

After landing, the airmen reported in detail on the course of the fulfillment of the mission and pointed out the disposition of the targets on maps. The aerial photography was soon processed and it confirmed the accuracy of the reports of the reconnaissance crews. (142)

In this same article, all-weather capabilities to perform this mission are claimed: "Reconnaissance aircraft are now equipped with the most complex automated systems which assure detection of objectives and determination of their coordinates during day or night, in any weather, from maximum low or high altitude." (143)   Side-looking radar, permitting standoff surveillance, appears to be highly regarded: "We should distinguish in particular the high degree of effectiveness of using for aerial reconnaissance side-looking radar. The crew of a reconnaissance aircraft equipped with such a set can obtain data on a particular objective of the enemy without entering the zones of his air defense." (144)

Further, the strong possibility of real-time video information being transmitted back for targeting purposes has been indentified. For example, "Being introduced and utilized more and more broadly here are various technical means designed for speeding up the processing and transmission of reconnaissance information to the interested parties directly from on board, the aircraft and flight." (145)

Initial Attack Phase

Once the attack is under way, reconnaissance is pursued with increasing vigor. To enable this reconnaissance to be carried out, NATO air defenses are to be neutralized using all possible direct and indirect means. These air defenses in at least the main air penetration corridors are targeted by the Strategic Missile Force and attacked in the first strike. Air operations are designed to follow close on the heels of this strike and exploit it by penetrating through the NATO air defense belts.

The actions of the air forces are planned in such a manner so that they too can use the results of strategic nuclear strikes, especially those delivered by rocket troops. Aircraft flights to targets of destruction and strikes against those targets are carried out with the minimum possible break in time after the strikes of rocket troops, in the course of which the enemy will not be able to repair the damage caused by the latter to his air defense system. (146)

Other actions designed against NATO air defenses are radio-electronic jamming, ground force assault, and in a conventional phase, air strikes and artillery barrages as well. The ground force assault is particularly important. Air penetration corridors should coincide with avenues of attack so that the forward detachments are provided with air cover. Thus, the main attacks will naturally be directed to overrun the NATO air defense installations as touch-and-go or raiding objectives for the forward detachments.

The fight against NATO air is also an important mission early in the attack.   The Soviets see tactical aviation as the chief means of delivering nuclear weapons, as does the American command - a fact which is confirmed in exercises where 70 to 80 percent of the NATO nuclear strikes are air delivered. (147)   While the missile troops are primarily responsible for strikes on NATO airbases, Soviet airpower also plays a role. The use of air is highly dependent on the means for controlling aircraft, including, for example, ground control radar and navigation signals, all of which are important targets for Soviet air strikes with conventional or chemical munitions. As it is unclear which airbases NATO will be using, the Soviet air forces also have a mission to identify and strike newly activated airbases, as well as to conduct secondary strikes against airbases previously hit by the Strategic Missile Force.

After the war starts, frontal aviation takes on a new reconnaissance mission in support of the ground forces - damage and radioactivity reconnaissance.

Data on the size, system and nature of obstacles and destructions can be obtained ahead of time with great reliability by means of aerial photography of the terrain in the area of advance.   It is believed that the degree of radioactive contamination and the general boundaries of the contaminated region can be most quickly established by an aerial radiation survey. (148)

Chemical and bacteriological reconnaissance, as a rule, is conducted by ground methods; but the use of air methods are, in principle, not excluded.   Special instruments and devices are needed for this; for example, intake devices for sampling the air. Planes and helicopters will be useful also for the quick transfer of ground-reconnaissance subunits to their area of operations. (149)

While of general interest, this mission is also specifically tied to the support of the advancing tank units.

Continuous aerial reconnaissance plays a large role throughout the pursuit. In addition to accomplishing ordinary missions, it is capable of detecting probable avenues of troop withdrawal, reconnoitering roads and setting up zones of destruction, inundation and radioactive contamination of terrain. Timely information on all this is greatly needed by tank forces. (150)

Attack of Mobile Targets

The major mission of the air force is the detection and attack of small and mobile targets.

> Aircraft of all arms and branches will be used to destroy those objectives which cannot be destroyed by various surface-to-surface rockets, and above all for operation against small and mobile targets. Such objectives on the ground can include mobile or newly equipped multi-purpose rocket launchers, control and guidance posts, etc. (151)

There are two basic categories of mobile targets - land based and sea based. The single most important mobile targets are those at sea, and in particular the United States carrier forces and the SLBM forces. Most long-range air reconnaissance and attack forces will be employed primarily in this area and secondarily as back up to the missile forces in the attack of fixed, deep land-based targets. (152)

> Long-range bomber craft, armed with long-range missiles, retain the capacity of delivering independent blows to enemy targets, especially at sea and in the ocean, but also on the coast and in the deep areas of the enemy territory. (153)

> One of the tasks of long-range aviation is the destruction, together with naval aviation, of means of nuclear attack at sea, especially attack aircraft carriers.)154)

> Naval aviation must be able to attack enemy warships at sea at a distance at which they will not be able to use their aircraft-carrier forces and missiles for attacking targets in the socialist countries. In addition, naval aviation will be called upon to destroy enemy transportation at sea and at their bases (155)

The secondary mobile targets are the land-based mobile targets and in particular mobile nuclear missiles, troop concentrations and moving forces, and control points.

> An important quality of aviation is its capability to discover independently and immediately destroy enemy means of nuclear attack. (156)

> The air forces can successfully combine the search for means of nuclear attack with their swift destruction. In connection with this, actions for destroying missiles on launch positions and in movement, which are small-sized and moveable targets, and also stores of nuclear weapons, organs of aviation and missile guidance have become most characteristic for piloted aircraft. (157)

Aviation can locate the target rapidly and strike it directly. It is especially necessary for strikes on mobile and small-size targets in the depth of the enemy's location, which can be an important element of his combat power. (158)

A question that arises in examining these missions of frontal aviation is whether they are to be nuclear or conventional. The answer is clearly both - although when nuclear, such missions are not to be conducted too close to Soviet ground forces.

. . . the use of nuclear weapons is limited by a number of conditions. They can be used only in the presence of a considerable interval between combat formations of advancing groups. Therefore, along with this, an important role in the defeat of cutoff groupings will be played by aircraft and artillery fire. Aircraft strikes will be inflicted mainly by means of nuclear attack on the enemy and his reserves which can render aid to cutoff troops. (159)

A second question concerns Soviet faith in nuclear armed strike reconnaissance: Would the Soviets "trust" a pilot to locate a target and strike it on his own initiative with a nuclear weapon? Although direct statements on this subject are seldom encountered, there are enough indirect statements to indicate that the Soviets probably do plan to employ nuclear armed strike reconnaissance missions, although by groups of aircraft specifically assigned for the purpose rather than by individuals. (160)

For example, as stated in a discussion on combat against tanks in modern conditions:

It is considered expedient to use nuclear-warhead missiles against tanks in concentration areas and nuclear air strikes against tank columns on the road. This guarantees effective and efficient utilization of nuclear weapons and affords the opportunity to strike at the most appropriate spot at the proper time. (161)

Ground Support Operations

The use of air force in support of ground operations can be divided into two groups of tasks. The first group includes general, front-line tasks of reconnaissance, destroying nuclear weapons, combating enemy aviation and deep reserves, and so forth. The second group of tasks is carried out in operational or tactical coordination with ground troops, supporting them during combat when they are in immediate contact with the enemy. This includes the destruction of nuclear weapons in tactical and immediate operational depth, combating immediate enemy reserves, destruction of radio technical equipment and control points, as well as continuous reconnaissance. (162) This role is considered particularly important in providing support to the forward detachments, which are expected to outrun the main force support, e.g., artillery and reserves.

> I want to especially emphasize the role of aviation which, just as in the past, is the most important and frequently the only means capable of supporting forward detachments. Aviation is called upon to conduct reconnaissance to discover the nature of defense of the objectives to be seized, to carry out strikes against advancing reserves of the defender and his nuclear systems which might be used against the forward detachments, as well as to cover the detachments from the air. To maintain uninterrupted cooperation with aviation, it is desirable that the forward detachment command have the constant services of an air force representative equipped with communication means. (163)

The following refers to the coordination of tanks and air support:

> Aviation can first strike the most distant and important objectives, primarily the mobile ones, of advancing enemy forces. These objectives may be operational and tactical missiles on the move, tank columns on the march, and major points for control of troops and enemy tactical aviation. Fighter-bombers can deliver very effective assault strikes against these objectives, employing conventional and nuclear weapons. (164)

Nuclear weapons are the preferred form of attack against tanks, either in concentration areas or on the march. This requires careful coordination and it appears that the commander of the unit being supported has his own organic means for accomplishing this. (165) To a certain extent, it also appears that this support is planned in advance - a view which is reflected in both the ground and air operational plans. (166)

In reviewing the evolution of tactical aviation, two basic changes are noted in the Soviet literature. First, while in the past, bomber aviation was employed quite frequently directly against objectives on the field of battle, now its basic targets have been shifted to the operational depth when the principal objectives become the enemy's means of nuclear attack and its reserves. (167) Second, the concept of "aviation escort of ground troops" does not imply continuous patrol of the air over the battlefield, but rather the response to ground troops' requests at a given time, under conditions when the ground troops are advancing rapidly and may be separated from the main forces of the front. (168)

NAVAL OPERATIONS

The Soviet Navy has six significant Europe-oriented strategic missions. The first, the SLBM component of the strategic nuclear strike, was covered within the first strike discussion, although the SLBMs might well be held in reserve for follow-on use after the initial period of the war because of their presumed inherently high survivability.

The second, the attack by naval air and long-range aviation of sea-based mobile nuclear targets, NATO SLBMs and carrier task forces was addressed under the discussion of air operations. The Soviets view the carrier task force as representing a potential of several hundred nuclear strikes against Warsaw Pact territory and have attached appropriate importance to its destruction.

There is little discussion in the unclassified Soviet literature about the counter-SLBM task or antisubmarine warfare (ASW) except to stress their importance. ASW appears to be the most important Soviet naval mission - as nearly all Soviet ships are cast in this category - to the extent that many other tasks and forces can be considered subsumed within it.

The fourth task, the attack on selected rear area targets, is of lesser importance and is encompassed within the first two tasks.

The remaining two tasks are to isolate the battlefield and to assist in the seizure of important islands and straits. The former is particularly important in that it may impact on NATO plans for resupply and support from the sea, and destroy NATO shipping in the process. NATO stores of military supplies at sea are regarded as economic targets of priority importance because they contribute to NATO requirements for the early period of the war.

The final naval task, which involves the transport of armored troops and amphibious landings, is coupled with ground force and air assault operations. It is directed at the seizure of critical islands and terrain such as those that control the straits that are important to the passage of Soviet naval vessels, particularly ASW and SLBM forces. The immediate goal is to ensure the secure dispersal of Soviet strategic naval forces from harbors, inland seas and Soviet territorial waters to the broad ocean area.

An examination of naval operations brings to light a critical issue involving the possibility of nuclear war at sea while the land battle remains conventional. Nothing has been found in the Soviet literature that would deny this possibility.

CONVENTIONAL WAR CONSIDERATIONS

In the mid-1960s, the possibility of an initial conventional (nonnuclear) phase received serious consideration in the Soviet military literature. This conventional phase is, however, quite different from a World War II type of conventional war; the Soviets recognize that the transition to a nuclear war can come at any time. Because of that awareness, and because the decisive element is the nuclear offensive, the conventional phase is designed with this transition as the most important considera-tion.

To appreciate the problem involved and the Soviet solution to it, it is useful to review what is often referred to as the dual capability dilemma. Simply stated, the problem is that large-scale conventional wars - such as World War II and Korea - and nuclear wars are believed to require very different and basically incompatible force postures and plans. These differences are widely perceived to be so extreme as to make it impossible to posture or design a force that is prepared to fight both types of war. In a nuclear war, the anticipated environment calls for a dispersed posture and in a conventional war, a concentrated posture. Therefore, the modern-day commander faces a considerable dilemma in deciding how to posture his forces, for in choosing a posture for one means of war, he leaves his troops vulnerable to attack by the other. This problem is also present in the use of weapons systems. If planes are loaded for nuclear attack, then they cannot contribute generally to any initial conventional phase; conversely, if configured for conventional attack, they would be unable to respond quickly to a surprise nuclear attack because of the several hours required to change bomb loadings.

One of the most descriptive Soviet statements on the problem of transitioning was identified by John Erickson in his analysis of Soviet military power:

> One must suppose that in conducting combat actions with conventional weapons it is also necessary to increase their spatial range and dynamism, as well as increasing the speed of the attack. But the chief influence on the methods of actions undertaken by troops in any given situation is the constant threat of the use of nuclear weapons. From this comes the main task - to train troops to operate both with the use and without the use of nuclear weapons, to achieve rapid transition from one mode to another, from fighting with conventional weapons to operations waged with nuclear weapons. Here there is a problem: how to combine the separate and simultaneous use of nuclear and conventional weapons in a common decision and one common plan for carrying out the same operation. The complexity lies in the fact that it is difficult to foresee at which stage of the operation nuclear weapons may be used. All this makes it necessary to train men for the successful execution of combat operation in all conditions. (169)

The Soviet approach to solving this dilemma, based on analysis of their literature, appears to be quite different from that taken by the Western nations. The Western approach, largely conditioned by the hope that the war will begin "conventionally," has been to stress the conventional defense - thus raising the nuclear threshold. Western forces are conventional forces, postured to fight a conventional war. Nuclear weapons are to be employed by these forces as a last resort should the NATO conventional defense fail to stop the Soviet advance and to deter Soviet use of nuclear weapons. The transition from conventional to nuclear war thus involves mainly the introduction of nuclear weapons into a conventional battle without significant changes in the concept of fighting or the force posture itself, which remains basically conventional in character.

The Soviet approach is based on two major assumptions: first, that the decisive element in a war in Europe (or in peace, for that matter) is believed to be the nuclear element; and second, that the war is likely to go nuclear. Therefore, the Soviet force posture devised for the conventional phase must have the constant threat of nuclear use as its initial premise. The Soviets do not think that the conventional phase of the attack can last very long, since Soviet forces would be overrunning, capturing or destroying United States/NATO tactical nuclear weapons, thereby increasing the pressure upon the United States, rather than tolerate the degrading of its TNW capabilities, to opt for the introduction of nuclear weapons.

In effect, the Soviet approach can be viewed as learning how to fight a conventional war from a nuclear war posture, in contrast to the Western approach of fighting an initial phase of a nuclear war from a conventional posture. As might be expected, this has led to differences in forces, which, in turn, has exacerbated the problem of assessing the Soviet forces. Even Soviet studies of World War II cannot be fully appreciated without recognizing the distinction between the two types of war. The lessons to be learned from studies of the first type of conventional war are valid only insofar as they relate to the second, or modern type; when they do not, they must be altered in order to apply them to the modern environment. This may be why in much of the current Soviet literature, it is often difficult to distinguish the type of war under consideration and why much of their recent literature reads like the literature of the late 1950s to mid-1960s when the threat was clearly nuclear. This may also explain why many people discount Soviet books such as The Offensive, believing it to provide an outdated description of nuclear war only. The opposite, in fact, is probably closer to the truth: The Offensive is strongly in the "initial conventional phase" camp.

In the Soviet approach to a conventional phase, the emphasis is on mobility and maneuver. As in nuclear war, the advance forward detachments are small and fast moving and concentration is a question of timing and rapid dispersal. To achieve the necessary correlation of forces, surprise becomes a most important factor - especially, perhaps, for the attacker. For that purpose, the attack might well be initiated directly from garrison without prior assembly in waiting areas. The rationale for this is very clear.

> Of immense importance in achieving victory is the art of employing one's forces. If a commander has at his disposal a sufficient number of troops to ensure superiority over the enemy, war experience demonstrates that this facilitates the attainment of victory, but does not guarantee it, as testified to persuasively by the victories of gifted field generals over a more powerful opponent. A more important condition for achieving victory than overall superiority in weapons and manpower is the ability to use concealment in

preparing one's main forces for a major strike and the element of surprise in launching an attack against important enemy targets. Defeat of the enemy under these conditions would be inevitable, assuming availability of sufficient reserves to maintain and increase the momentum of the offensive, as well as if the defending force has spent more time on maneuvering for the purpose of closing a breach than was required by the advancing forces to put second echelons and reserves into the battle. (170)

This is further acomplished by rapid advance into NATO rear areas before its forces are organized as coherent fighting units, and by defeating sequentially those forces that would remain following an effective surprise assault. Surprise, therefore, is critical to the success of the initial operation. Further, as observed in Voyennaya mysl',

. . . attack from the march is considered the main method of offensive troop operations when nuclear weapons are employed. But will this be the main method of troop operations when nuclear weapons are not employed? In discussing an attack against an enemy who has hastily assumed the defense the answer to this question is affirmative.(171)

The individual units are not to be bogged down fighting NATO units, but proceed rapidly into the rear.

Large units of the first echelon carrying out the encirclement and destruction will boldly and daringly penetrate through gaps and holes deep into the enemy operational formations, split and quickly crush isolated enemy troops unit by unit, and destroy nuclear weapons, reserves, and control points. For the most rapid completion of the rout it is necessary that strikes for the purpose of splitting and destroying encircled enemy groupings be delivered even as early as during the process of encirclement maneuvers, not waiting until basic routes of withdrawal are seized. (172)

It is advantageous that attacks for the purposes of splintering the enemy be delivered in the shortest directions and in those sectors where the enemy cannot use previously prepared lines and where he does not have strong reserves. (173)

Second-echelon armies may not immediately proceed to support the first strategic echelon forces because to do so would make them highly vulnerable to NATO nuclear strikes and, further, because they must be available to exploit Soviet nuclear strikes when the war goes nuclear. (174) The commitment of these second-echelon and reserve armies is a major decision in the offensive operation and, as such, a consideration in the nuclear transition decision.

As in nuclear war, the conventional phase will be highly porous with numerous advance detachments striving to get into NATO's rear. The primary targets of the advancing detachments are NATO command/control, nuclear means and critical areas whose capture can disrupt mobilization of NATO reserves. As noted above, it is expected that these advancing units will outrun most of their organic fire support - providing tactical air with the opportunity to move out in front of these units to strike at approaching reserves, command/control facilities and nuclear means. These units are to advance along independent axes, with the second echelon and reserves of the first strategic echelon used to exploit successes or capitalize on breakthrough corridors rather than reinforce units that get bogged down or meet resistance. Units that meet such resistance will either redouble their efforts (by using new weapons such as chemical) or assume the defense and in so doing, tie down NATO forces. The main target objectives in designing the attack are NATO antitank defenses that could hold up advancing ground units, air defenses that could hinder Soviet reconnaissance and air support of advancing troops, NATO tactical air that could slow up the advance and inhibit Soviet air support of advancing troops, and NATO nuclear means that could destroy the Soviet offensive. Insofar as command/control is a vital aspect of all these objectives - particularly air defense, tactical air and nuclear means - it becomes probably the single most important target class.

Because the short war remains a priority objective and because conventional munitions are still quite limited in their effectiveness, the Soviets have strong incentives to make full use of chemical weapons against all the priority targets. These weapons are seen by the Soviets as particularly effective in the conventional phase; moreover, the use of chemical weapons in a substitute nuclear role enables the Soviets to fight the conventional war from a nuclear operations concept and posture. This employment of chemical weapons may be the implication in several Soviet discussions of the role of artillery and air for destroying, as opposed to harassing or suppressing, ground forces in a conventional war. (175) This may also be what is meant in a 1969 Voyennaya mysl' article that makes special reference to a statement made in 1963 by Harold Brown that chemical weapons are intermediate weapons between conventional and nuclear. (176)

In assessing the differences between a "conventional" and a nuclear attack, the main focus is placed on the mission of frontal aviation. In a conventional phase, aviation is seen as providing a significant role in the attack of fixed targets that are out of reach of artillery - particularly, air defense sites, airbases themselves, and command/control/communication centers.

A special role belongs to aviation, which will be the main long-range means in these conditions. Aircraft are capable of destroying operational-tactical type missiles, as well as aircraft on the airfields and in the air. However, in order to carry out these missions the aircraft must overcome very strong air defense of the opposing side. To suppress it in conditions when nuclear weapons are not used, the aircraft must allocate a large portion of their forces. (177)

Under such conditions, some tasks may be relegated to second place - in particular, as in the United States, those in support of ground force operations.

> The use of air power is somewhat different in those areas where military operations will employ only conventional weapons. If the ground forces launch the main attack primarily against a weak spot in the enemy's operational formation air power must be brought to bear not only against the enemy force in that area but also against enemy nuclear weapon-carrying aircraft and missiles. Neutralization of enemy nuclear-weapon carrying aircraft and missiles will constitute the major task, which will require a large number of aircraft. Therefore only limited air power can be assigned to support ground operations. The requisite degree of massed air power employment in the area of the main ground force thrust is achieved primarily by reducing the width and depth of combat operations. This in turn conditions the character of the process of overwhelming the opposing ground force based on sequential thrusts aimed at deep penetration. (178)

If, however, a nuclear attack is contemplated, the use of airpower in the attack of fixed, well-known targets is expensive and ineffective when compared to that of surface-to-surface missiles with nuclear warheads. Moreover, standdown of air and logistics movement, and warning to forward detachments appear to be the major problems in transitioning from the conventional attack to the nuclear strike.

The Soviet approach to planning for a porous war-plans which involve numerous axes of advance and the ability to shift efforts between them, the achievement of the required force concentration by timed force movements, and the utilization of cybernetic techniques and, in particular, network planning and PERT techniques to prepare their force movements - may provide the Soviets with a unique attack flexibility. That flexibility is the capacity to plan their offensive and optimize it according to NATO's posture immediately prior to the attack (i.e., the night before). The placement of the principal forces depends upon NATO's defense positions, which could run the gamut from in garrison to on alert in one of several prepared or hastily assumed emergency defense positions. If the Soviet system becomes operational (that is, recognizing that the foregoing descriptions are focused on their literature, not on their actual capabilities), it should be possible for them to update constantly their attack plans - both conventional and nuclear and on a daily if not hourly basis - to optimize their position relative to that of NATO, whose time constant at present appears to be measured in several days, at best.

CRITICAL ASPECTS OF THE OPERATIONAL CONCEPTS

In reviewing the material in this chapter, several aspects of Soviet operational concepts stand out - some because of their importance in the Soviet literature, others because of their role in assisting in our understanding of the Soviet approach and still others because of their importance in assessing NATO strategy and posture.

The most fundamental aspect of the modern Soviet combined arms concept is that it provides for the conduct of both nuclear war fighting and conventional war fighting under threat of nuclear use. This has been the intent from its beginning in the mid- 1960s, and subsequent force developments in the late 1960s and 1970s attest to that fact.

The Soviet approach to combined arms operations, with its emphasis on "conventional" abilities within an overall nuclear posture, may have resolved or vastly facilitated the problem of transitioning. The transition from conventional to nuclear war is seen to be best accomplished by the air force because of its relatively quick response and high mobility.

The element of suprise is crucial to the success of the concept for it allows the Soviets to move in and attack NATO forces piecemeal before they can be mobilized and assembled into significant fighting units. In this regard, the recent (1974) Soviet text on The Initial Period of the War, bears careful analysis.

Mobility is also of vital importance. The Soviets have turned to smaller force units, the most critical of which is probably the regiment. Regiments will operate along numerous axes as forward detachments, often well in advance of main second-echelon and reserve forces. These larger forces will shift to follow the most successful forward detachments in consolidating their advance.

The larger forces, unlike their World War II counterparts, do not have the opposing forces as their immediate objective. Rather, they are to bypass NATO strong points in proceeding to the contemporary objectives which include critical terrain features and military capabilities such as nuclear means, control points, transportation choke points, warehouses and airbases.

The war will be extremely porous, with airborne and airmobile units playing a major role behind the lines. The Soviet command/control is designed to handle this type of war from Moscow, exercising tight and direct control down as low as regimental level.

The air force has a key role in supporting the advance of the forward detachments; it detects and destroys advancing enemy units before they reach those detachments. The role of the air force in an initial conventional phase is very different from its role in the later phases or in a nuclear war. In the former, the air force must give first priority to those missions which in a nuclear war would have been accomplished by the Strategic Missile Force. Those missions must be accomplished quickly in order for the air force to be available to provide the required support to the forward detachments.

The transition from conventional to nuclear operations is primarily a question of standing down the air operation and adjusting the nuclear strike to take account of the progress already made by the advancing ground force units - an action which requires the same detailed knowledge of all unit locations that is necessary for their centralized control.

The principal means to be used against enemy forces are nuclear and chemical munitions, with chemical weapons almost certainly having a major role in a nonnuclear phase. All forces and weapons are to be employed in the first-priority mission – combating NATO nuclear means, and most importantly, the aircraft carriers.

Of perhaps the greatest importance is the fact that all of the above are critically dependent on command/control. Command/control must be highly survivable, flexible, responsive and dynamic. In light of these requirements, the Soviet emphasis on cybernetics and automation takes on increased significance and provides a reason why it is regarded as the third phase of the revolution - a phase that stands nearly equal in importance to the nuclear warhead and the long-range means of delivery.

An added advantage of the Soviets' approach may consist in their ability to tailor their offense to the NATO posture at the last minute. This capability is a two-edged sword for not only does success of the Soviets' concept hinge on the quality of their command/control, but also on their ability to destroy that of NATO. As a major objective of Soviet strategy, all forces and means will be employed in that effort. The destruction of NATO command/control - as important an objective as surprise - would place NATO forces in all likelihood into the very disarray for which the Soviet operational concept is designed, and may even cause their immobilization. The vital issue of command and control is the subject of the following chapter.

5 Command and Control

In the Soviet Union, command and control receive as much attention as any major weapon system. Following the nuclear warhead, long-range means of delivery, and the troops themselves, it is viewed as the single most important aspect of the Soviet military forces.

Under modern combat conditions where weapon effectiveness indices are exceptionally high, the Soviets recognize that the outcome of combat activities "will only depend on the quality of the control system and troop morale." (1) Accordingly, the quality of the command and control is an important factor in Soviet calculations of the correlation of forces (2) and, consequently, is a principal target complex to forestall NATO from mobilizing and launching forces.

While more difficult and time consuming to analyze than the delivery systems portion of weapons systems - which are the central preoccupation of the West - command and control may nevertheless be one of the most accurate perspectives from which to assess enemy capabilities and intentions. For this reason, the Soviet command and control deserves at least as much attention in the West as it receives in the Soviet Union in order to assess their interest and capability for conventional war, nuclear war fighting and nuclear retaliation.

The goals of Soviet command and control are a product of those qualities required to <u>fight</u> a nuclear war. Soviet literature is unambiguous on this point and the capabilities that are emerging appear to bear this out. At the same time, because of many similarities in the use of ground forces in a conventional phase and in a nuclear conflict, the demands on command/control for the use of these forces are not particularly different. Therefore, the system undergoing evolution in the Soviet Union should be more than adequate to handle a dynamic conventional conflict.

The developing Soviet command and control system represents an enormous investment in resources - an investment that emphasizes speed, accuracy, flexibility, and survivability, far beyond that required for either conventional war or mere nuclear retaliation. Moreover, this development in the Soviet Union represents a very steady and long-term effort. In the 1950s, the unique importance of command and control in the nuclear age was recognized, design criteria were set, and the organization and top-level attention necessary to address the problem as a matter of highest priority were established. In the first half of the 1960s, people were trained, command and control was modeled and analyzed, and hardware requirements were established. The entire decade, but particularly the latter half of the 1960s, saw the advancement of technology to meet these requirements and the deployment of initial high-priority portions of the system. In the early 1970s, its implementation was extended to the principal operational command levels. Advanced hardware was incorporated, and major hardened facilities became operational. The latter half of the 1970s, with Marshal Ogarkov as head of the General Staff, may well witness the system's extension into the lowest combined arms command levels - such as regiments - which would make the whole system operational and combat ready.

METHODOLOGICAL APPROACH AND DESIGN CRITERIA

In the Soviet literature, command/control - or more correctly, troop control - begins with the commander's decision. The support, development, and implementation of troop control is focused on that decision. While the importance of the decision is certainly not unique to the Soviets, their approach appears to differ from that of the West because of the unique thrust which it is given. In the West, the literature of command and control is often dominated by discussions of staff operations, procedures, and, most noticeably, hardware. These considerations are certainly not neglected in the Soviet literature, but do not share the central importance of the initial decision. In the Soviet Union, all aspects are analyzed insofar as they contribute to the decision process itself.

Command post exercises (CPXs) provide an excellent example of this difference. In the United States these are "procedural exercises," particularly at the higher command levels. Their objective is to identify problems related to staff, hardware or procedural shortcomings that require solutions in order to insure operability in the event of an actual conflict.

In contrast, it appears in exercises in the Soviet Union that it is the decisions that are on trial - the ability of the commander to reach the correct decision in a hypothetical test situation. Procedures, hardware and staff operations are on trial only insofar as they support or fail to support the commander in assessing the situations, considering the various options, reaching a decision and communicating the decision to the appropriate subordinates.

For example, the following statement of the Soviet exercise director's activity typifies the emphasis on the decision:

The important item in the director's activity is to teach commanders of all levels expedient methods of quick and well-founded decision-making under complicated situational conditions, the ability to present a plan and to assign tasks to the troops under their command clearly and concisely; also, to exercise continuous control and direction of these troops during the course of combat operations, and to direct the operations of their staffs, arms and service chiefs. (3)

Further, as regards the staff activity:

The personnel of participating staffs must master the skills of rapid collection and processing of situational data, precise operation and battle planning in a limited time, with requisite operational-tactical calculations, creative, maximum-effective utilization of men and equipment, utilization of control process automation and mechanization equipment, observance of the rules of coded control, plus organization of coordinated action, and comprehensive support of the battle and operation. Staffs must acquire the ability for precise elaboration and fast preparation of battle documents, including in "express form" tirelessly working for operational smoothness in performing all duties involved in troop direction and control. (4)

It is the people, particularly the commanders, more than the staff, who are on trial, not simply impersonal procedures or pieces of hardware. Further evidence of this is found in Soviet postexercise critiques which explicitly identify commanders by name who either did or did not perform well. Rank provides no immunity to this process; general officers as well as those of lower rank are severely redressed by name in print. This concept is totally alien to Western exercise critiques.

The focus on the decision, moreover, permeates Soviet analyses of command and control which make wide use of the mathematics of the decision process including decision theory, operations research and cybernetics - the theory of information and control. These are used to analyze the entire decision process, including the commander's assessment of the situation which is seen as the most time-consuming activity in the process.

The criteria on which the Soviets have based their operations research and cybernetics in design of their troop control system are clear and simple. The first criterion is speed; the command and control system must operate rapidly. The time delays experienced in World War II in analyzing the situation, making decisions and issuing appropriate directives are no longer acceptable.

The time factor has always played an extremely important role in combat operations. Now, in connection with the spread of nuclear missile weapons and the revolutionary transformations which have occurred in the structure of armed forces, in the methods for conducting armed conflict, and in military theory, this factor has begun to play, not simply an important role, but the decisive role in the development and outcome of combat operations. (5)

As stated in 1975 by then Minister of Defense Marshal A.A. Grechko, "The fight to win time is the primary problem in the process of command and control." (6) Time is critical because the main effect of nuclear weapons is to speed up the whole process of war. The difference between survival and destruction of a target is measured in terms of the time required to deliver the warhead - minutes. Consider, for example, the following discussion:

> Let us assume that in the course of an attack a commander has obtained reconnaissance information about an enemy launcher which has occupied a launch position, and that it is possible to have the launch of a nuclear missile from it within 18 minutes from the time the reconnaissance data was received. This launcher can be destroyed by the fire of one of the artillery battalions, but they are moving and are able to open fire, let us say, in 20 minutes. It can be destroyed by the strikes of several fighter-bombers, but according to the conditions of combat readiness, and the distance of the airfield at the given moment, they can deliver a strike in 22 minutes. It can be destroyed by a missile with a large-yield nuclear warhead from a launcher. In the given situation, let us assume its readiness for launch is in 16 minutes, but a small-yield nuclear burst is sufficient to destroy the enemy launcher. There is also a missile with such a warhead, but its launch is possible, let us assume, in 27 minutes. Let us assume that it takes one hour for a special detachment to move to the area of the enemy launch position to destroy the launcher, and that it takes two hours to drop an airborne team for the very same purpose. At the given time the commander has no other men or weapons to destroy the enemy launcher. The commander's decision to destroy the enemy launcher with a nuclear missile by means of a strike by our large-yield nuclear missile in 16 minutes in this situation, would be economically ineffective, but fully expedient, since the enemy missile could be destroyed before its launch only by our nuclear strike, albeit of excess yield. (7)

In a more general vein: "Time has always played an important role in combat. At present, due to the development of new weapons, time has come to play not simply an important but rather a decisive role in the development and outcome of combat." (8)

The Soviets recognize simultaneously that mere time reduction is insufficient because of the modern requirement for accuracy: "Adoption of a decision in the shortest time constitutes a very important condition of victory. However, a still more important factor is its conformity with the situation, its truth, and its validity." (9)

The second important quality, therefore, is accuracy. In nuclear war, mistakes are costly for they can result in the destruction of friendly rather than enemy units. The consequences of decisions in a nuclear war are incomparably greater than those in a World War II-type of war and it is thus essential that the quality of the information - timeliness, comprehensiveness and accuracy - be the best possible.

One of the key technical directors of the cybernetic revolution and of the redesign of the command/control system appears to have been Col. P.N. Tkachenko. In his 1969 book <u>Mathematical Models of Combat Operations</u>, he reviews the results of Soviet combat modeling and the importance of the control system. The latter has several effects on combat: first, in time lost obtaining data; second, in the lag in the decision process relative to the actual state of the war; and third, in relation to accuracy.

The need for timeliness, comprehensiveness, and accuracy coupled with the availability of data, provided the impetus for the cybernetic revolution. That required combination represents a dominant theme throughout the Soviet literature on command and control. The features of command and control in modern war, writes Tkachenko:

> ...are determined primarily by the significant amount of information which each staff should collect, transmit and process. This applies to the information concerning the position, grouping and state of one's troops and the enemy troops, the technical specifications of weapons and equipment used by the sides, the state and equipment of the theaters of military actions, the terrain and hydrometerological conditions, the radiation situation, and so forth.

> The necessity of carrying out a large number of diverse calculations in the process of processing the obtained information is the next feature in troop control under modern conditions. These calculations are essential for a correct assessment of the situation, for correctly determining combat capabilities of the forces and means and for using specific types of weapons, for forecasting the possible results of combat and for taking optimum decisions, as well as for organizing all types of combat, material, technical, medical, and other types of supply. (10)

> The rapidity of those processes which must be controlled by military bodies has caused the exceptionally acute nature of the struggle by both sides to gain time. For precisely this reason, in the process of training military personnel, a conviction is instilled that success comes to the side which is able to collect the necessary information and take the decision in the shorter time, to set the mission and organize the actions of troops, to prepare and make strikes against targets, and to promptly bring up and commit the reserves to combat. (11)

> Due to the high speed of modern weapons, the increased maneuverability of troops and abrupt changes in the situation, critical time shows a tendency to be reduced. In other words, the obtained information concerning the situation is rapidly obsolete. For this reason, for a prompt response to a change in the situation, it is essential to reduce the time of action of the troops (for example, by raising their combat readiness) and reduce the time expenditures on the control cycle.(12)

The reduction of time is especially important as it affects the command planning process. Many people in the West perceive the Soviet system to be highly preplanned, and therefore, highly inflexible. The Soviets do believe in preplanning for the simple reason that they view the command and control apparatus as a most important target and therefore likely to be temporarily disrupted or even destroyed in nuclear war.   This was particularly true in the 1960s.   Hence, considerable preplanning was required in order to prepare the lower commands for any eventuality - even the total disruption of command and control. Because the Soviet command and control system has been improved to survive in a nuclear war, however, the principal emphasis is no longer on preplanning per se, but on the ability to conduct planning in a minimum amount of time.

The Soviets have designed a command/control system to cope with the fast-paced and highly dynamic nature of a nuclear war. It not only enables planning to be conducted in a short period of time, but allows for replanning as well; in fact, a major focus of the Soviet attention has been to design a command/control system that has the capability to "abandon quickly and decisively the previously adopted plan," (13) and generate a new one.

Implementation of coordination organized between obeyedineniya [major field formations] branches of the armed forces during an operation consist primarily in strict and accurate fulfillment by each of the assigned missions. But the situation right at the very start of an operation can change to such an extent (in comparison with the assumptions), that literally in the first minutes and hours of an operation it will be necessary to make substantial revisions in the planned procedure of actions by branches of the armed forces to include also the organized coordination between them. (14)

The Soviets recognize that:

In the process of implementing a previously adopted decision, various unexpected phenomena and processes can arise which are connected with sudden operations of the enemy, with the conditions of the terrain, with the weather, and with other circumstances. This hinders to some extent or prevents fulfillment of a previously adopted decision.   All of this makes it necessary to constantly change the decision. Change in or adoption of new decisions in the course of a battle and operation constitute a more complex and difficult matter than during the period of preparation for military operations, because a change in a situation in the course of a battle occurs much faster than before it begins.   There will be an especially fast change in the situation in the course of a battle or operation in a nuclear war, when the development of combat operations are combined with the broadest use of various methods of armed struggle and types of maneuvers. (15)

Soviet literature stresses the need to consider variants and to have the capability to shift to a new set of plans with the development of a new situation. (16)   In brief, Soviet command and control is designed to operate in the highly dynamic environment that is believed will be characteristic of a nuclear war.

CENTRALIZATION

The dominant requirement of the Soviet command and control structure is its rigid, absolute or maximum centralization of control. One man at the top is to have complete control and that individual is the Supreme High Commander. In World War II, his headquarters was referred to as the STAVKA of the Supreme High Command. The origins, applications and justifications of this centralized control have been described in Voyennaya mysl':

> For direct supervision of the armed forces the STAVKA of the Supreme Command was formed, headed by the chairman of the State Defense Committee, who was at the same time the leader of the party and government, and Supreme Commander of the Armed Forces. In comparison with the past, this arrangement of higher organs of control represented increased centralization, or merger, of general governmental and military leadership and, despite the known mistakes of Stalin, proved justified. It made possible the conversion of the country into a unified fighting camp and the attainment of victory over the enemy. (17)

The strategic leadership of the armed forces in World War II was exercised by the State Defense Committee (GKO) through the STAVKA of the Supreme High Command. (18)   In effect, the many tasks with which the STAVKA became involved could be considered "strategic" to the war effort. In World War II, the STAVKA was headed by Stalin. It is believed that its modern counterpart most likely would be headed by General Secretary Brezhnev, who recently has been identified as both the Head of the State Defense Committee and as the Supreme Commander. (19)

The principal executing agent for the STAVKA in World War II was the Soviet General Staff. It was responsible for the detailed planning of the war effort.

> The principal working organ of the STAVKA was the General Staff. The most important functions of the STAVKA and the General Staff included the formulation of concepts of strategic operations, general support for these operations, the organization and implementation of coordinated action among branches of the armed forces and commands, the readying of reserves, the operational and strategic movement and regrouping of troops, the supervision of combat forces during operations, and the analysis of results of combat operations. (20)

While the General Staff was the working organ of the STAVKA, it is important to recognize that it was not subordinate to the STAVKA. Rather, the General Staff reported directly to the Supreme Commander.

In addition to planning, the General Staff was also involved in operational supervision of the fronts.

> In addition, the STAVKA and the General Staff were concretely involved in matters of operational supervision. In the planning of many operations the front headquarters were not only informed of the concept and mission of the operations, but were instructed as to the directions of main effort; the composition and missions of striking forces, and their formations; the sequence in which tank armies, cavalry and mechanized groups, and second echelon forces were to be committed; the employment of air forces; the types of coordination between neighboring units and between branches of the armed forces; and supply and equipment measures. On this basis the front headquarters planned operations in detail and submitted views on forthcoming operations to the STAVKA. To assist front headquarters in the planning of operations and for organizing coordinated action between fronts, representatives of the STAVKA were often detached to them along with small operational groups which then maintained control over the progress of combat operations. (21)

We should not lose sight of the Soviets' approach to and experience in detailed control at the top when we assess their command and control capabilities under conditions of nuclear war. The Soviet system is designed to be controlled operationally from the top, which leads to what Western strategists may regard as excessively rigid or absolute centralization.(22) As an example of the extent of this control, three times a day during World War II, Stalin received briefings in the form of detailed layouts of 1:200,000 scale maps for each of the thirteen fronts. The information presented included the disposition, conditions and mission objectives for each of the armies, corps, divisions and even critical regiments at each front. Plans extending to the lowest levels were formulated at the top and approved by Stalin.(23) The key executive agent for this operation was the General Staff,(24) possibly patterned after (25) and remarkably similar to the highly efficient German General Staff. There is no counterpart of the Soviet General Staff in the United States.(26)

This basic approach is perhaps more important under contemporary conditions where control and flexibility at the top could be vital to the success of a war. In the Soviet view, the revolution in military affairs has put in the hands of the strategic leadership the means for accomplishing strategic missions independent of the outcome of individual battles. (27) The Soviet practice in the Great Patriotic War, which they won, is particularly relevant because the basic approach to centralized control has been carried over into the nuclear revolution. The transmittal of the centralized Soviet system of World War II into the nuclear age enabled the Soviets to centralize control of nuclear weapons <u>and</u> permitted the development of the "unified plan" at the top for operational coordination and tactics.   As described in a 1969 <u>Voyennaya mysl'</u> article, "Scientific-Technical Progress and Some Questions of Strategy," this rigid centralization of control applies to the "very process of waging war." Western strategists may be appalled at the apparent stifling of "on-the-scene" creative initiative. The Soviets, nevertheless, seem convinced of its necessity.

This centralization takes on even greater significance in terms of the Soviet objective in war which is the seizure and occupation of territory as well as the destruction of targets. The nuclear weapon may be decisive but it cannot achieve total victory alone. The ground forces are essential to ensure the final complete control of the territory and its defeated inhabitants. The strike and its exploitation by the ground and air forces must be carefully coordinated and thus, centrally planned.

> In the main nuclear warfare operations have a different character. The major strategic scale of the operation, carried out in the continental theater of military actions, is primarily a "nuclear" operation in which the main role is played by strategic nuclear forces. Other branches of the armed forces whose role in the operation changes substantially use their nuclear weapons and operate on the whole to accord strictly with the strikes of the strategic forces. (28)

This coordination of all aspects of the attack is essential to ensure that the nuclear strikes do not preclude or interfere with planned operations of the other branches of the armed forces. (29) Thus:

> ...effective solution of strategic and operational missions by the combined efforts of <u>obeyedineniya</u> [armies] and <u>soyedineniya</u> [divisions] of various branches of the armed forces requires unification of their actions with <u>the single concept and plan</u> as well as organization and constant maintenance of coordination. (30)

More recently, it was stated that:

> The principle of centralism is becoming increasingly important in guiding and directing troop combat activities in modern warfare. The potential use of nuclear weapons will require careful coordination of the operations of the different branches and arms. Success in a future war can be achieved only if all strategic actions and all operations are rigorously coordinated on the basis of a unified strategic plan with unified, centralized direction, and if they are purposefully directed toward carrying out the common missions of armed conflict. (31)

The centralized approach to command and control (in Soviet terms) is inherently adaptable to the use of automation or cybernetics, which, as indicated earlier, has been embraced by the top Soviet leadership to improve significantly their command and control and staff operations.

Western experience suggests that centralizing control at the top, however desirable from a political point of view, leads to inflexibility; capability is limited, etc. The Soviets, on the other hand, having long made use of that concept, may have effectively worked out procedures and tools to make it responsive, rapid, effective, and in that sense, flexible. Western deficiencies in capabilities, skepticism about Soviet "flexibility," and belief in the impossibility of nuclear war have contributed to beclouded thinking about Soviet intentions and capabilities. The Soviets assess their system as placing flexibility in the hands of the political-military strategic leadership in time of war. As stated by Marshal of the Soviet Union, V.D. Sokolovskiy, in Military Strategy:

> Victorious conduct of a modern war is possible through the coordinated use of all types of strategic operations. Through the purposeful conduct of the operations, battles and engagements by a carefully centralized, specific, and flexible leadership of the armed forces. (32)

At the same time, many people in the West argue that decentralization is required in nuclear war because command/control lines will be cut, leaving front troops without direction. This problem is clearly recognized by the Soviets: "Under conditions of nuclear-missile war the achievement of continuity of control is greatly hampered. However, in spite of this, the commander and the staff cannot permit even brief interruptions in the leadership of the troops." (33) Both the problem and the Soviet solution to it are detailed in the following quotation:

> It is possible to unite the actions of a large number of troops with diverse combat equipment and weapons and direct them to the accomplishment of a common mission only with centralized troop control. Under contemporary conditions a rigid centralization of control permits the senior commander to determine the outcome of the battle as a whole at the necessary moment by concentrating the fire of nuclear weapons as well as that of other forces and means.
>
> However, the experience of the Great Patriotic War shows that centralization of troop control provides positive results only in the struggle for the tactical zone of defense, but with the move into the operational depth it binds the initiative of lower commanders.
>
> The highly maneuverable character of contemporary combat operations, the swift and abrupt changes in the situation, and great dispersion of troops demand that all officers and generals display broad initiative, independently make bold decisions in the spirit of the senior commander's concept which are appropriate to the situation at hand and which facilitate the quickest attainment of the common goal.
>
> The best results can be obtained by centralization of control within strictly requisite limits, by broader decentralization, and by increasing the autonomy and independence of podrazdeleniya [battalions] and chasti [regiments]. However, there must always be

assurance of the possibility of establishing a rigidly centralized troop control in the hands of the senior commander at critical moments of battle. (34)

The solution developed by the Soviets is what might be called "top-down" planning: "Consequently, our command cadres have a superior capability for insuring the stable and flexible control of troops from top to bottom." (35)

A single strategic concept is developed at the top by the General Staff and is used to coordinate all actions. Immediate and short-term goals of all units are carefully delineated. The strategic goals and missions for major operational units are developed in conjunction with the theater-strategic nuclear fire plan. That plan, which involves the principal nuclear weapons in the strike, is the responsibility of the General Staff. Strategic planning involves the precise coordination of the goals, timing and placement of all branches of the armed forces and all means with those of the main nuclear strike. (36)

As further elaborated in Voyennaya mysl':

Strategic coordination between major units of branches of the armed forces is attained by the coordination of their efforts during accomplishment of common strategic missions. Its organization consists of, firstly, the coordination of efforts of all other branches of the armed forces with the nuclear attacks of strategic rocket troops and, secondly, in the coordination of operations of ground troops, the air forces, the navy and combat actions of PVO strany troops among themselves.

It provides for coordination in the actions of strategic groupings of branches of armed forces primarily in regard to the objective and to a lesser degree in regard to time and place. Strategic coordination is organized by the highest command planning the major operation and supervising its conduct. (37)

Strategic missions for major troop groupings are in all likelihood transmitted simultaneously to Front, Army and division levels (and possibly even to regiments having critical missions). Front and Army levels, where representatives of the STAVKA of the Supreme Command may be present to assist as was the case in World War II, (38) have primary responsibility for operational coordination and probably operational-tactical nuclear weapons employment. (39) The division level then has the task of combat mission planning. (40)

The critical combat levels are the regiment and battalion. (41) These are the units the Soviets appear to have in mind when they refer to the need for the lower echelons to accomplish their missions with initiative and independence - or rather, "self-reliance."

An increase in the role of initiative in the control of troops stems also from such a specific phenomenon of contemporary operations as the possibility of totally disrupting the system of troop control by simultaneous or consecutive disabling of a number of control points and the communications centers of varying levels. This possibility did not exist in the past, inasmuch as it was not ensured by the use of conventional weapons. Now, however, many chasti [regiments] and podrazdeleniya [battalions] can be left in a short time without control by a superior instance with simultaneous disruption of communications with adjacent units as a result of enemy nuclear strikes. Development of means of fighting radio-electronic means increases this possibility to a significant extent. Under these conditions the surviving control of organs and points will have to display a maximum of initiative and independence in troop control. Understanding the goal of the combat operations and the concept of the senior commander, as well as being oriented beforehand about their possible missions in the course of further actions, they will be able to make grounded decisions and persistently seek their accomplishment without ceasing active combat actions. (42)

Considerable care is required in interpreting the meaning of "independence." It does not mean undertaking "new" initiatives as it would in the Western literature. Insofar as "understanding the goal of combat operations" is concerned, consider the following example of what is meant by this concept as explained in "Independence - A Commander's Most Important Attribute":

Initiative presupposes boldness of thought and action and concern for the creative implementation of plans. But on the training field this is not always the case, and not always for everyone. At one command analysis session, for instance, a demonstration tactical exercise was conducted. The exercise itself proceeded well, but the battalion commander did not have the boldness to carry out certain missions. He tried to adhere strictly to his plan. And this was what let him down. In particular, smoke cover was supposed to be used to blind the "enemy" on the main line of resistance. But at the start of the attack the wind direction changed and the commander failed to take this into account. Instead of blinding the "enemy" the smokescreen only impeded the actions of his own podrazdeleniye [companies]. Hence, initiative must be intelligent and correspond to the situation which has taken shape in battle.

...every commander must creatively apply statutory provisions and display a maximum of initiative in such a way as to make efficient use of any favorable situation without awaiting instructions from above. Of course, no independent action should be at odds with the general plans and design of a senior commander. (43)   [Emphasis added.]

Initiative may be appropriately exercised if the action becomes inconsistent with the objective, but only within the limits of the basic plan. Initiative presupposes the existence of a specific plan and is directed strictly to its accomplishment. It does not extend beyond the plan or the individual's understanding of it, which tends to be highly channeled to preserve secrecy and central control. (44)

COORDINATION

...nuclear strikes do not represent some kind of isolated act, but a component of combat. The operations of tank and motorized rifle podrazdeleniya [battalions] and chasti [regiments] are closely coordinated with them. Nuclear strikes and troop operations represent a uniform and inseparable process, joined by a common concept. (45)

As indicated above, coordination is essential for these operations. Nuclear strikes must be coordinated with each other and with the exploitation forces. For these and other forms of coordination – such as ground air defense and air interceptor operations, (46) forward detachments and air support strike operations – the primary mechanism is one of space and time assignments to prevent potentially dangerous conflicts between nuclear and conventional operations. Such assignments appear to be developed as part of the unified plan at the outset of the war. The nuclear forces are allocated time and space for their strike and the conventional forces are warned not to penetrate until after H-hour.

Podrazdeleniya [companies, battalions] usually move up at night or under other conditions of limited visibility with observance of light, sound, and radio discipline and at prescribed speeds. In order to ensure unhindered movement, podrazdeleniya of engineer troops are sent out ahead of time to difficult sectors. As they approach the enemy defense during preparatory fire, podrazdeleniya deploy in turn into approach march and combat formation at their designated lines, to which they move at a precisely established time. [Emphasis added.]

The nuclear safety line (rubezh bezopasnogo udaleniya) is crossed by attacking troops at a precisely designated time. On approaching it, personnel of motorized rifle podrazdeleniya [battalions] take cover in APCs, drivers close viewing slits, and the tank crews close hatches and observation instruments.

...and at a designated time ("H") they break into the forward edge of the enemy's defense. (47)

This use of H-hour is not confined to the work just quoted.

The battalion commander, after making sure that the information about the enemy had been confirmed, ordered the chief of staff to calculate time expressed in terms of H-hour to celestial time and inform podrazdeleniye [company] commander of the time of attack, time of delivery of nuclear strike, and time for passing the initial points.(48)

H-hour is used primarily to coordinate the strike's exploitation and not, in general, merely to "warn" the nearby troops.

The assignment of time and space does not relate merely to the FEBA at the start of the war, but also to the nuclear strikes targeted against each strategic region into which NATO is divided. Force assignments are preplanned as objectives and tasks for all major units in branches of the armed forces are determined.

> In general, coordination by branches of the armed forces can be defined as the coordination of objective, place, time and methods of operations and the application of their efforts for accomplishment of missions assigned to them and for achieving common objectives of the operation. (49)

As noted, such coordination is particularly critical for airborne and air strike operations, as well as for individual aircraft.

> Firm control based on rigid centralization and accurate coordination of a place and time of nuclear-rocket strikes of small groups and even of single aircraft flying along various courses will ensure a high degree of concentration of forces of aircraft, as well as success of their operations. (50)

One of the few situations in which troop warnings, as opposed to space and time assignments, are important as a coordinating mechanism is that in which the attack is at night and the luminary effects of nuclear detonations which can lead to temporary blindness or dazzle are expected to extend to much greater distances. Efforts must be made to maximize the effectiveness of the casualty radius of light radiation at night while providing protection to their own troops. "There is an especially precise organization of troop warning about time of delivery of nuclear strikes in order to take timely steps necessary for protection against the blinding action of light radiation." (51) Considering the possible use of night attack to achieve surprise, this could be important.

> Nighttime facilitates secrecy in moving troops up to the forward edge and shifting into the attack, and it thus makes it easier to achieve surprise of attack, which in turn deprives the enemy of the possibility of orienting himself correctly and in a timely manner in the situation of night combat. (52)

Of critical importance is the danger such strikes would pose to pilots of both fixed and rotary wing aircraft. Nighttime missions of reconnaissance, long-range patrol and other behind-the-lines assault force penetrations are important in the Soviet approach to war in Europe and great care must be exercised to insure that these units are appropriately warned.

Thus, with this type of exception, coordination between nuclear strikes and the conventional forces is almost wholly a question of space and time assignments designed to facilitate the ground forces' role in exploiting the effects of the nuclear weapon and to maximize the speed with which the exploitation can occur throughout the operational depth of the enemy's territory.   Real-time coordination appears to be the exception rather than the rule.   This may explain the role of the operational (coordinating) commands - rather than the tactical level commands - as the decision authority on operational employments. The role of the new Soviet nuclear artillery, however, raises several questions in this regard.

COMBAT MODELING*

The Soviets see computers and cybernetic techniques as indispensable to the success of the war-winning effort in that they significantly increase the combat capability of all forces and all levels of command.   The manner in which the Soviets appear to be applying computer techniques and using computers in the field to assist the command decision process is impressive.   The basic command organization is indicated on a simplified schematic shown in Figure 5.1.   The basic on-line algorithms have been grouped in six categories: 1) fire planning, 2) troop maneuver, 3) reconnaissance, 4) supply, 5) air defense, and 6) engagement.

The limiting factor in computer utilization for troop control is the extent to which these activities can be modeled with appropriate algorithms.

> The preparation of the troop control process or an individual problem from the process for machine solution can be called the formalization of the control process or problem.   The formalization of the problem provides for its tactical (or operational) decision, development of the algorithm and program writing.

> From what has been said it follows that algorithm theory is an exceptionally important decision of cybernetics, the use of whose tenets make it possible to prepare the necessary store of military problems for the automation of labor-consuming troop control processes. (53)

Table 5.1 presents several examples of the types of detailed algorithms that have been developed for combat use and are described in the Soviet military literature.   From Col. Tkachenko's book on combat modeling and other sources, it appears that most of these fundamental algorithms had been developed prior to 1969 and that the task of the 1970s has been to make them operable in complex situations which arise in full-strength combat. In this process, the Soviets recognize that one of the important problems of modeling is the evaluation of the accuracy of the results. For this purpose, they set up special field exercises and compare the model results with the experimental data. Field exercises appear to be used to evaluate the free parameters, test the modeling, verify the results, and gain confidence in using the capabilities. This is

*Based on research conducted jointly with Mr. John A. Shannon.

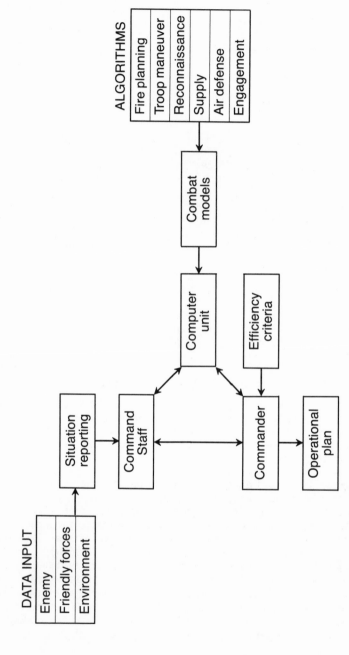

Fig. 5.1. Soviet command organization showing the application of computers to the command process.

one aspect of Soviet field exercises that has become prominent in the 1970s, but is rarely recognized — namely, their use for purposes of research, experimentation and testing in addition and in contrast to their use for training and exercise of maneuvers and plans. An excellent description of this use of exercises was provided in a 1976 article in Red Star by Colonel General M. Kozlov, then deputy chief of the General Staff.

> In planning military-scientific work it is necessary to make bolder use of those forms and methods of scientific investigation which insure the greatest effect. Naturally, the main emphasis must be placed on research during relevant exercises. It is precisely at these exercises that the correctness of theoretical conclusions is tested and that the operational introduction into practice of everything positive occurs. (54)

General Kozlov points out that Soviet military science must be a pioneer of practice, revealing possible paths for new development. Any evaluation of Soviet exercises should distinguish between practice and research -a distinction that is particularly important in the analysis of Soviet interest in such topics as conventional attack, selective nuclear attack, and limited nuclear war.

Four final points should be recognized with regard to the entire preceding discussion of the use of modeling, analysis and computers in solving troop control problems. First, the Soviet effort is focused primarily on combat - not on the requirements and force structure applications that receive so much attention in the United States. The models developed for use in combat then appear to be used to assess new capabilities under consideration and to establish requirements.

Second, considerable effort is made to insure that the computers serve the commander, not vice versa.

> It is now generally recognized that any mathematically described formalized human activity can, in principle, be turned over to a machine.

> However, it cannot be forgotten that troop control does not amount to simply controlling weapons systems. At all levels it is always control of the men, of the military collectives.

> Therefore, automated systems of control over troop combat actions are not designed for fully automatic, that is independent of the human being, control of troop combat actions. No one has posed and no one is posing such a task for full automation of troop control.

> Adopting the plan for battle is the highest stage of the commander's activity. This work cannot be reduced to a simple thinking operation, to considering the variants and selecting the best one. (55)

References to full automation of control (56) always include the commander as part of the system.

TABLE 5.1. Selected Soviet Combat Modeling Described in Open Literature

Fire Preparation and Delivery	Troop Maneuver	Reconnaissance and Intelligence Processing
Weapon effectiveness against point, area, and group targets considering weapon system reliability and enemy countermeasure and mobility	Movement of troops; on foot, by truck or aircraft	Determination of requirements for reconnaissance patrols
Comparative evaluation of different types of armament	Optimization of speed of movement	Determination of patrol routes for maximum probability of enemy encounter
Optimization of the target allocation process	Selection of optimal space-time troop formations	Optimum routes for reconnaissance aircraft to minimize losses
Determination of optimum ratio of costs of weapons and control systems	Determination of friendly troop casualties	Evaluation of effectiveness of various detection means
Planning a missile attack for maximum enemy losses	Planning the march of a tank battalion	Optimum distribution of search units with respect to search zones
Optimization of the size of firing units as a function of weapon type	Selection of optimum reserves	Determination of target detection probability by radar
Optimization of weapon system firing distance	Optimum distribution of forces for combat and reserve	Determination of accuracy of target coordinate estimates
Determination of required ammunition caliber to fulfill a mission at least cost	Enemy target damage estimates	Processing of target coordinate data
Tank/antitank weapon effectiveness	Selection of axes of advance	Communications processing requirements for target damage estimates
Determination of target damage probability	Optimum ordering for a river crossing	Assessment of enemy troop strength

TABLE 5.1. (Continued)

Supply	Air Defense	Battlefield Engagement
Quantity of supplies for a mission	Optimum number of echelons in an air defense and their composition	Mixed model of Chast (Soyedineniye) combat operations
Ammunition and fuel supply requirements	Selectio of optimum flight ranges for antiaircraft rockets	Combat model of groups of homogeneous means
Optimum storage facility assignment to units and subunits	Evaluation of antiaircraft system firing effectiveness	Combat models of nonhomogeneous linear groups
Ammunition transport and delivery	Optimum trajectory for pursuit rockets and maneuver trajectories for pursued rockets	Model of tank podrazdeleniye tactical combat operations
Optimum supplies for minimum expenditures		
Optimum number and handling capacity of repair shops	Evaluation of combat efficiency of antiaircraft defense groups	Model for determining requirements to repel a tank attack
Optimum time for equipment replacement	Evaluation of guidance system effectiveness	Model for optimum combat versions for repulsing attacks
Optimum regimes for preventative maintenance operations	Evaluation of the effectiveness of firing at targets as they appear	Model for determining the effects of nuclear weapons on the course and outcome of armed combat
Optimum distribution of personnel for a battalion to service tanks, artillery and firearms	Evaluation of the effectiveness of antiaircraft armament against group targets	
Transportation requirements for equipment and materiel		

135

Third, the Soviets design from the top down. The first part of their system is implemented and perfected at the top - the General Staff level - and then extended down. At the present time, this effort has reached down through the "entire chain of command" to include the lowest level teaching in the service academies. The General Staff level has probably employed a completed, tested, automated system for perhaps ten years - a system which may in fact have been used to plan the Czech invasion in 1968 and the Egyptian river crossing in 1973. The current effort is now directed to complete and test battle engagement capabilities at the division and regiment levels.

Finally, while the use of computers increases the speed with which data can be assimilated and plans can be formulated and adapted to the situation, its impact in terms of vulnerabilities remains somewhat ambiguous. Although this capability may increase the flexibility of the force, it could also lead to great inflexibility and problems because, for example, the data base and algorithms are based on conventional experience, and because bugs in programs have a habit of appearing at the least opportune time. This problem, however, may not be too severe in the Soviet system because much of their work began prior to the development of computers. Their initial effort was to develop nomographs for use in the various calculations - nomographs which were subsequently computerized, but not discarded. Their retention is to ensure that the command system does not stop if the computer shuts down. (57)

SURVIVABILITY

Due to the critical importance of command and control in the Soviet system, great efforts are made to assess its vulnerability and ensure its survival. (58)

The basic components analyzed in Soviet vulnerability assessments are the commander himself, various command and data centers where information is processed and plans are developed, and the communication links, including the communication (propagation) paths. All components are thoroughly examined in regard to possible attack by NATO with conventional munitions, special agent teams, electronic warfare capabilities, such as jamming and interference, nuclear weapons, including the use of high-altitude electromagnetic pulse (EMP), and in the event of unintentional interference by their own systems - self-interference resulting from their use of electronic countermeasures (ECMs) against NATO command/control/communication links.

The major Soviet approaches to survivability appear to focus upon redundancy, hardening, hiding, self-healing and finally, plans and training designed to accommodate temporary loss of command and control.

The principal Soviet criterion is to avoid reliance upon a single indispensable element, and to provide for alternatives through redundancy. Thus, depending upon the importance of the function, two or three alternative centers, commanders, and communication channels are available, each designed to be complementary and distinct so that it would be most unusual for all to fail in any situation. A greater degree of duplication is simply not cost effective.

> Duplication - the creation of certain interchangeable elements of the operational organization of troops and other combat formations - is carried out jointly with dispersion and constitutes one of the effective and obligatory ways of increasing the protection of troops both on the offensive and on defense. It is necessary, for example, for control organs.

> It is extremely important here to determine the degree of duplication. The greatest increase in viability is insured with the presence of 2-3 duplicating elements. A further increase in the number of them does not produce a significant increase in the level of viability. Thus, if there are two duplicating points in the organ, the level of its viability is increased by about 1.3 times, if there are three duplicating points, it is increased by about 1.6 times, and if there are four points, it is increased by only 1.7 times. (59)

Individual components are then hardened to insure their survival in a particular hostile environment - conventional, chemical, nuclear, or electronic warfare. Large, fixed facilities are built underground in hardened concrete bunkers. Antennas are specially designed and constructed to be equally hard.

The Soviets recognize that mobile targets are difficult to locate and, if found, hard to hit before they move again. Accordingly, mobile facilities are used where possible to complicate NATO targeting.

The most elusive target of all, of course, is one that cannot be found. As expected, hiding and secrecy are integral to the Soviet approach to command and control - not merely for survivability of the system itself, but also for security of the process and product (e.g., plans and decisions). Simple communications discipline is vital in this regard; there must be no message transmitted if someone is listening. Hard wire communication links are desirable when possible because they can rarely be intercepted using remote listening devices. Of further importance are hidden or camouflaged command post facilities and constant shifting of position.

> Special significance is acquired by the selection of terrain which assures the concealed disposition of the post and which does not require a large expenditure of forces and means on the engineer improvement of the area. Also completely justifying themselves are such measures as reducing to a minimum the stay time of the posts at one place and their rapid change of areas, careful camouflage against the ground and aerial enemy, and dependable cover by PVO (air defense) means. (60)

Third, the Soviets are well aware of several approaches to covert communication and will doubtless employ such capabilities in operations; the use of burst transmission, laser, millimeter wave, and spread spectrum techniques both to achieve covertness and to harden against electronic jamming was recognized as early as 1964 in <u>Voyennaya mysl'</u>.

Since the nuclear revolution, a central aspect of the Soviet approach has been to expect disruptions in command and control; accordingly, they have built into their system the capability to cope with such disruption and even with the loss of important command and control elements. As part of the basic operations plan, expected communications losses are calculated and forecast. Based on these calculations, forces and means of communications are distributed throughout the depth of the offensive operation and reserves are stored and camouflaged in such a manner as to minimize the mathematical expectation of communication outage. (61)

There are at least two basic means by which the Soviets deal with disruption. The most important is in understanding the basic plan. The Soviets do not appear to be too concerned about a NATO out-of-the-blue surprise attack. They believe in a period of warning, a buildup in tensions - one that causes both sides to increase their readiness, although they would like to minimize any such NATO actions and intend to undertake their own as covertly as possible. Under such conditions and where they see the situation leading to war, they intend to seize the initiative and preempt. In doing so, the concept of actions will be promulgated by the Supreme Command and detailed plans will be distributed to all levels. The concept of action is to be sufficiently laid out and understood by all so that if command and control is disrupted, unit commanders can continue to operate in accordance with the general plan. This basic approach is often ritualistically described in a surprise attack context and couched in terms of preplanning.

> Since a surprise attack is considered to be the most probable method for commencing military operations by the aggressor, consequently, the time for carrying out control measures (the time for readying the troops for combat) will be greatly limited.

> From this follows the indisputable conclusion that for the troops which are destined for combat immediately after the enemy attack, all control measures should be prepared ahead of time. Under this condition troop control with the onset of combat can be successfully carried out with brief signals. In the event of a break in communications with the superior chief, the subordinate commanders can begin to carry out the mission upon their own initiative, since they will be informed as to the overall purpose of the battle or operation. (62)

Once command/control breaks down, the highest priority is attached to its reconstitution. In this process the second approach to dealing with disruptions comes into play. Each command post is to be able to assume the duties of command posts immediately below or preferably, above it.

Obviously, the best variant is the designation of one of the control posts of subordinate troops as the alternate post. They are similar in content of work and therefore may begin more rapidly to perform the new duties which, in this case, will differ only in scale and not in specifics. (63)

Furthermore, the chain of command does not consist merely of serial links, but is designed to be able to bypass or "skip" echelons that for one reason or another may be out of the net. While in the field armies, these capabilities relate only to bypassing the most immediate higher or lower echelon, the top leaders have the further capability to skip all intervening levels and go directly to critical commanders such as those of divisions, regiments and nuclear delivery units.

This concept, too, appears to have had its origins in World War II. Stalin ran the war from the top, as indicated earlier, and conducted most of the critical planning down to division and even regiment level. Representatives from the Supreme Headquarters were detailed to the front to ensure that the actions were carried out in accordance with those plans and to provide a Supreme Headquarters decision authority at the front. Stalin would routinely reach down to whatever command level he desired to obtain information and issue instructions. In contrast, the operational commands (Front and Army level) were instructed not to meddle in the affairs of their subordinates. In a sense, it appears that Stalin may have had little faith in the operational commands and thus built a system of command which habitually skipped over them. (64)

ATTACK OF NATO COMMAND AND CONTROL

One of the most striking impressions provided by the Soviet military literature is the importance attached to the attack of NATO command and control. Based on the analysis of this material, it is believed that a Soviet attack on NATO will begin against all elements of the NATO C^3I (command, control, communications and intelligence) systems from top to bottom, that it will be as important and intense as the attack on NATO nuclear means, and that it will involve all Soviet forces and means.

In the West, this battle is most commonly referred to as electronic warfare (EW) or more recently, radioelectronic combat (REC). As such, the tendency has been to consider it as an electronic battle involving electronic countermeasures (ECMs) or means directed against electronic targets, which in turn are forced to adopt electronic counter-countermeasures (ECCMs) for self-protection. This Western electronic view of the battle, however, is woefully incomplete and hence misleading. While the Soviets use the same term, REC, their threat to NATO C^3I is not merely an electronic threat; rather, it involves the use of all forces and means, both active and passive, including nuclear, conventional, air strike, air assault, ground assault, chemical, and electronic; not only ECM such as jamming, but deception and false target generation as well; and is directed against NATO personnel, facilities, electronics and propagation mediums associated with NATO command and control.

The importance of the strike against command and control in a modern war was recognized very early by the Soviets.

> There is very solid ground for asserting that the outcome of many operations, given present day conditions, will be determined by the relationship between the possibility of neutralizing electronic installations and keeping them operable in the face of enemy action. (65)

The rationale is very clear:

> The importance of radioelectronics as a means of control of combat operations and a means of directing combat training and ensuring high combat readiness of troops is so great that it is hard to overestimate. For example, combat actions under modern conditions with the use of rockets and nuclear weapons cannot be conducted successfully without the use of radioelectronics, or with its inadequate use as a science. Every officer, no matter what branch of the armed services he represents, is well aware to what extent the different military units are now equipped with means of radio communications and automation, based on radioelectronics and radar. Let us just imagine a situation where, for some reason, the means of control of troops, equipment and weapons based on radioelectronics should suddenly be "inactive" and eliminated from the combat activities of the troops. What would happen in such a case?

> The airplanes would not take off, or even if they do take off they would not find their targets; the radar devices would "go blind," and the mobile systems would be ineffective; the troops would lose their combat efficiency, and control would be disrupted. (66)

The Soviets view command and control as uniquely important to both sides in a modern war. The Soviets put considerable effort into assuring the survivability of their own command and control and equivalent effort into assuring the destruction of that of NATO. They analyze carefully NATO command and control - both political and military - identify vulnerable points, and plan the integrated application of all forces and means to bring about its rapid destruction.

The Soviet examination of NATO command and control takes into account all its facets, including all radioelectronic capabilities - command center computers, antennas, data links, air defense radars, missile guidance and control, target acquisition means, radio navigation grids and direction beacons, and so forth.

> Under conditions of a nuclear war, the system for controlling forces and weapons, especially strategic weapons, acquires exceptionally

great significance. A disruption of the control over a country and its troops in a theater of military operations can seriously affect the course of events, and in difficult circumstances, can even lead to defeat in a war. Thus, areas deserving special attention are the following: knowing the coordinates of stationary operations control centers and the extent of their ability to survive; the presence of mobile command posts and automatic information processing centers; the communication lines; level of development and, first of all, that of underground and underwater cable, radio-relay, ionospheric and tropospheric communication lines; field communication networks and duplicate communication lines; communication centers and the extent of their facilities, dispersion and vulnerability. (67)

In the fight for air supremacy, the battle against NATO radioelectronics is viewed as one of the highest priority. The principal task is the destruction or suppression of radar stations for aerial observation. The reason is simple.

By depriving the enemy of means of observing air space or creating conditions for him which do not permit normal utilization of these means, he is placed in a position where he is unable to repulse promptly and in an organized manner aerial strikes or provide his own aircraft with the conditions for the most effective overcoming of the countermeasures of the forces and means of air defense. (68)

A mission of "no less importance" is the destruction of control posts (both ground- and air-based) and the means for insuring accurate navigation.

Without these means, at modern flight speeds it is extremely difficult to utilize aircraft successfully, especially during their operations at night and in difficult meteorological conditions during the day against such small objectives as ground rocket launchers, command posts, etc. (69)

This also applies to the mission of isolating the battlefield and disrupting transportation.

However, in the struggle against air transportation, important results can be achieved through the intensive infliction of nuclear-rocket strikes against the airports, bases, and storage areas, as well as by suppressing radio technical means of control of aircraft in the air and means of navigation support to the flights. (70)

These techniques are effective in disrupting air transport supply of material or reinforcements because these operations are difficult, if not impossible, without radio-technical means of control and navigation.

While radio jamming is one approach to this suppression, there are limitations on its use because it also interferes with one's own communications. Consequently, other methods - particularly attack and seizure with conventional weapons - come into play.

To disorganize the control system of the aircraft (including the navigation systems) and the air-defense means, the combatants will strive to employ broadly and are employing (as is indicated by postwar events and conflicts) along with the aircraft the services of radio-technical troops, airborne troops, naval forces, and diversionary and other detachments. Experience shows that detachments even consisting of several men which are landed from submarines or dropped from aircraft can destroy or put out of commission for a long time radar stations, control towers, long-range and short-range homing airport stations, glide-path and approach beacons, equipment for instrument landing, etc. All these operations are usually complemented broadly by false orders and misinformation capable of leading the flight personnel and crews of the control posts into error and leading to confusion and error of judgment. (71)

Nuclear weapons would probably be used on the most urgent targets such as theater level fixed command posts.

Control points and means of communication have become the most important objectives of nuclear strikes. Unbelievable difficulties arise in restoring destroyed communications since the performance of work in setting up new and restoring damaged communications lines and communications centers on terrain with high radiation levels and in zones of fire and rubble turns out to be practically impossible. (72)

The seizure of guidance and control posts are singled out as decisive operations of the attacking advance detachments in a conventional phase:

Strong and maneuverable advance detachments which have a high degree of independence are very broadly used in the combat structure of formations and large units of attacking troops in order to carry out very quickly, many important issues. The absence of a solid front, the presence of great gaps and intervals in the formation of the enemy and the increased maneuvering capabilities of tanks are creating favorable conditions for their fast penetration in depth and the conduct of active, decisive operations for the purpose of carrying out such missions as the destruction or seizure of enemy missile units and guidance and control posts. (73)

Poorly defended forward control posts could be regarded as intermediate missions for smaller raiding operations by independent battalions. Particularly lucrative targets of such raids would be NATO air defense radars and control points. Such missions reveal the combined and integrated nature of the air and ground threat to NATO air defense in the opening phase of the war. This combined approach is especially important should the war begin without the use of nuclear weapons. The composite of these techniques - jamming in conjunction with air and artillery strikes - is cited as the means to neutralize NATO air defense in a nonnuclear war.

> While in a nuclear war, the fight against air defense installations is facilitated by delivering nuclear strikes against the most important ones, the overcoming of air defense during the stage of transition to defense, without the use of nuclear weapons, will be one of the complex problems. It will, evidently, be solved by neutralizing the radio electronic systems of surface-to-air units by creating strong interference, by strikes of long-range artillery, as well as by air attacks from low altitudes. (74)

Further, conventional air-delivered ordinance is considered particularly effective against certain NATO command and control targets.

> The most effective means for the destruction of radio-technical equipment is the use of conventional (nonnuclear) weapons by fighter-bombers. The armament of a modern fighter-bomber, its guns, and especially its rockets, can destroy any radiotechnical station. (75)

One important question is whether or not the Soviets might employ high-altitude nuclear burst to generate large electromagnetic pulses (EMPs). These signals can cause massive communication failures over a large territory. Such blackout effects and their military applications are well understood by the Soviets. If the tactic could be employed without causing the Soviets as many problems as it does NATO, they might well employ nuclear weapons in this mode. Judging from the emphasis accorded the concept in the Soviet literature, the use of EMPs should be expected. Indications are that the Soviets will do everything possible to be prepared to operate under the conditions of communications chaos which they will deliberately help to create. As explained in a discussion on creating interference to assist achieving surprise:

> To achieve surprise in a modern war, an aggressor on the eve of war and in the course of it, increasing the activities of his reconnaissance, will, evidently, take active measures to suppress and blind reconnaissance forces and means of the enemy by creating strong interference against radio and radiotechnical means.

> For this purpose, high-altitude nuclear explosions can be carried out in the beginning and in the course of the war to destroy the system of control and communications and to suppress the antimissile and anti-air defense radar system and the aircraft control systems. (76)

A reference suggesting that this type of attack might be a rationale for the very high yield Soviet warheads is contained in the following statement from Voyennaya mysl' in 1966:

> For example, a nuclear explosion in the 50 MT range of force at an altitude of 80 km can lead to a complete loss of ordinary ionospheric radio communications over an area radius of 4,000 km in the course of a day due to the influence of the radiation effects of a nuclear explosion. (77)

Radioelectronics are not only critical to the direct aspects of NATO command and control, but also indirectly through those systems that provide NATO with intelligence on enemy activity, force disposition and target acquisition. While these intelligence systems are to be directly attacked, Soviet war plans also include spoofing, misleading and otherwise deceiving NATO in the attack on NATO radioelectronics.

> Without well-organized camouflaging and successful counter-operations against enemy reconnaissance and intelligence it is impossible to keep one's nuclear weapons intact. Only with superior intelligence, reconnaissance, camouflaging and superiority in suppressing enemy intelligence and reconnaissance is it possible to gain advantage in a battle and combat operation, in directing nuclear and conventional strikes against enemy nuclear weapons. (78)

In a discussion couched in terms of NATO intentions:

> The bourgeois military press recommends that radio be used more extensively for misleading information, for radio can be used to create the apparent existence of command posts, nonexistent airfields, to demonstrate supposed preparations for an operation by increasing radio communications volume, and to simulate the deployment of fighter planes and guided missiles. It is considered that radio misinformation should be conducted together with other measures intended to mislead the enemy. Other measures include the following: rumors to incite confusion, the semblance of shifting troops and equipment, simulated heavy use of roads, and fictitious offensive operations. It is recommended to build decoy missile launching pads and mock-ups of nuclear warhead storage areas, to effect decoy transfers of nuclear weapons under heavy guard, to limit the movements of military personnel and totally prohibit civilians from areas simulating deployment of nuclear weapons. (79)

The following considers the tricky problems of river-crossing operations and associated camouflage and decoy activities:

> The setting up of a dummy bridge requires the development of standard designs and the creation of the simplest means to set it up - inflatable rubber boats or collapsible wooden boats with an upper

structure and angular reflectors.   Sets of such designs and equipment, together with trunks to carry them, should be available in the pontoon units. (80)

The use of corner or angular reflectors is a particularly important aspect of the Soviet passive countering of NATO electronic intelligence assets. Many NATO target acquisition systems are based on radar or on the energy reflected by the target and detected by appropriate apparatus, and in the case of cruise missile guidance and aircraft controls, on energy reflected by the terrain or key features of it. A corner reflector is made up of three mutually perpendicular metal surfaces forming a three-faced corner. These reflect radio waves and send a strong return to the radar detector in order to confuse the radar picture of the target area or terrain. They are relatively inexpensive and easy to employ in mass as the Soviets indicate they will do. The examples identified in the Soviet literature include such diverse uses as in the single bridge decoy cited above, their use to simulate troops (i.e., tanks and other vehicles) moving on the road, to simulate fixed targets such as artillery and missiles in deployment areas, and even to change the perceived shape (radar signature) of the terrain and its key features that automatic radar control or guidance devices may depend on for their successful operation.

These activities are not limited to the postattack situation. Many would be employed before the war actually becomes "hot" for the purpose of rendering NATO sensors useless on the eve of war and to better achieve tactical surprise. In a discussion of attack on C^3I capabilities,

> We should also consider the circumstances whereby for the purpose of deception, an aggressor might resort to the use of such methods of operations which do not produce the end result (that is, destruction) in complete form, but insure a higher level of probability of achievement of surprise. (81)

In addition to the expected uses of such measures in the war itself, particular attention is directed to the problem of transitioning to nuclear operations if the war begins with a conventional phase.

> To achieve surprise of nuclear attack in the course of nonnuclear operations, it is necessary to insure not only secrecy in bringing nuclear means to the regions of combat operations, but also constant protection of them from enemy strikes and secrecy and maximum speed in direct preparation of the first strike from any previously unprepared region. A skillfully organized struggle against reconnaissance, the suppression of his radioelectronic means, especially early detection systems, false and deceptive operations, and other measures can have a decisive influence on the achievement of surprise in switching to combat operations with the unlimited use of nuclear weapons. (82)

The Soviet integrated approach to targeting NATO C^3I both prior to and during war is believed to be one of the two or three single most important aspects of Soviet military strategy toward Europe.

6 Special Soviet Problems

In the Western view, the Soviets are far from open in their discussion of problems or limitations. However, a major tenet of their methodological approach to military science is to surface and focus on important "contradictions," to estimate accurately the enemy and to take into full account any environmental considerations that might otherwise cause plans to be overdesigned, optimistic, or otherwise unrealistic. Consequently, there is considerable recognition, both explicit and implicit, of many of the difficulties they consider severe; indeed, much of the material presented in the preceding discussions was extracted from Soviet analyses of problems and ways of resolving them. Several of these problems are of special importance and worth a more detailed examination.

THE NATO NUCLEAR THREAT

The threat - particularly of nuclear weapons - posed by United States and NATO forces occupies a central place in the Soviet image of, and strategy for, war in Europe. Their concern has two important facets: NATO nuclear weapons and their impact on Soviet ground and air forces, and escalation from localized to intercontinental war.

In examining the threat posed by nuclear weapons to the Soviet Union, it is important to recognize that while nearly all of these weapons, especially those that would be encountered initially after an attack in Central Europe, are United States weapons, that are deployed under the operational commands of different nationalities. The United States retains ultimate control over the decision to use them, but the decision will be taken in close consultation with the allies. In assessing NATO strategy, therefore, the Soviets do not simply listen to what "Washington says." Rather, they consider also what is said in Europe, particularly in Bonn and at SACEUR Headquarters in Mons. Most importantly, they watch what NATO forces do in their exercises - exercises which have a political as well as a military aspect. Those exercises conform to the agreed NATO doctrine which includes a strong nuclear component. The Soviets have no good reason to doubt that NATO fully intends to use nuclear weapons to avert defeat (the main question is how) and NATO forces exercise for the eventuality. As much as many people might think the idea insane or unreasonable, that does not change the basic nature of NATO's doctrine and capabilities, and the manner in which the Soviets must assess the threat.

Nuclear weapons were first introduced into NATO defense forces and concepts to counter the Soviet strength in massive ground forces, and this is exactly what they do. The heart of Soviet strategy toward Europe is their ground forces. The critical attributes of their offensive, apart from the nuclear strike, are maneuver, rapid exploitation and subsequent occupation by tank, motorized infantry and more recently airborne troops. These operations depend on troops, supporting firepower, mobility and command/control, all of which are particularly vulnerable to the effects of nuclear weapons, and increasingly invulnerable to the effects of nonnuclear weapons.

As explained by a Soviet artillery officer, in a text on antitank warfare,

...Nuclear weapons have brought about considerable changes in the character of the armed struggle. With regard to antitank warfare, the essence of the revolutionary changes consists mainly in the fact that the troops are now in a position to destroy whole tank units with a single nuclear explosion and to put large tank units out of action in short periods by massed nuclear attacks. Moreover, the range of modern missiles makes it possible to perform such missions not only within the limits of the battle formations of the attacking enemy in the tactical depth, as was formerly the case, but practically in any depth.

Single nuclear attacks will be launched, depending on the weapon yield, against corresponding tank units. A superlow-(low)-yield nuclear missile can destroy a tank platoon (company) and one of medium yield – a tank company (battalion).

A group nuclear attack can also, depending on the yield of the missile or bombs, inflict heavy losses on the tanks of a tank battalion, armored or motorized infantry brigade and even division.

A massed nuclear attack of scores of nuclear weapons can inflict a decisive defeat on a tank group consisting of several armored or mechanized (motorized infantry) divisions and break up their offensive. The use of a large number of nuclear weapons of medium and large calibers in a massed attack may result in the rout of large tank groups and paralyze the actions of enemy army corps and field armies. This method of mass (group) destruction of tanks, or, to be exact, whole tank units and formation with their tanks, nuclear attack weapons and all other weapons, is decisive. (1)

The possible impact of the nuclear threat on Soviet operations is recognized.

> ...using the new means of destruction, the defending forces may successfully frustrate or weaken an enemy attack. (2)

> In connection with advances in military hardware, the content of the term "defense" also encompasses a number of new elements. Employment of nuclear weapons in the defensive operation and engagement increases the stability of defense and enables the defending force to mount heavy strikes against the opposing enemy force even before the attack begins. There is now greater potential for stopping an offensive in its tracks or substantially weakening the attack and destroying the attacking force in the course of defensive operations. (3)

Another concern associated with the nuclear threat is the damage that would occur to the Soviet Union itself should it come under attack. This is generally, although not always, related to world nuclear war, which the Soviets would like to prevent. The problem is how to prevent a war that begins in a localized area from escalating to intercontinental, or world war. As stated in all editions of Military Strategy:

> Simultaneously with preparing for a decisive battle with the aggressor during a world war, the armed forces of the socialist camp must also be prepared for small-scale local wars which might be unleashed by the imperialist. The experience of such wars which have repeatedly arisen during the postwar period shows that they are conducted by ways and means which differ from those used in world wars. Therefore, Soviet military strategy calls for the study of the means for conducting such wars in order to prevent them from developing into a world war and to bring quick victory over the enemy. (4)

While "small-scale local wars" is not a term generally applied to Europe, the basic principle is the same. The Soviets would like to decouple the United States from a war in defense of Europe, and devote considerable thought to the problem of restricting such a conflict. The Soviets recognize that there will always be a risk of escalation for there are limits to the extent that a European conflict can be decoupled from a world war. At the same time, while expounding the difficulty of limiting a war - rhetoric which in part appears designed to influence the West away from efforts to develop limited capabilities or to restrain Western expectations of being able to limit such a conflict - the Soviets nevertheless perceive the urgent need to contain such a war and to develop exactly such a capability for themselves.

INTELLIGENCE AND TARGET ACQUISITION

One of the most serious problems associated with the NATO nuclear threat pertains to tactical intelligence and target acquisition. Target acquisition is important because of the decisive nature of the nuclear threat facing the Soviets in Western Europe. All Soviet references to the importance of nuclear weapons in deciding the course of the battle and the war applies not only to the Soviet use of nuclear weapons but also to their employment by NATO against Warsaw Pact and Soviet forces. From the Soviet standpoint, therefore, the destruction of these NATO nuclear weapons is critical to success.

At the present time, the ground forces of the United States are armed with various ground means of nuclear attack. However, their main portion are tactical, the firing range of which is limited to several tens of kilometers. These means have been widely introduced among the troops. For example, the infantry (mechanized, armored) division numbers about 80 means for the delivery of nuclear weapons. With consideration of the reinforcement of the division with two or three battalions of 155-mm howitzers, their number increases to 116-134 units. It is completely obvious that the successful conduct of the offensive is unthinkable without the timely and dependable neutralization and destruction of these means.(5)

As a rough indication of the severity of the problem, NATO is generally believed to have some 7,000 nuclear weapons deployed on the continent. The Warsaw Pact is usually credited with 85 divisions in Eastern Europe and another 60 Soviet divisions in the Soviet Union west of the Urals. If it takes approximately 15 nuclear weapons to render a division ineffective, 2,175 nuclear weapons could "take care of" all Soviet and Warsaw Pact ground forces west of the Urals. While these types of calculations are not particularly meaningful, they do indicate to some degree the force that the NATO nuclear weapons could represent if they and their associated command/control and targeting were survivable, and the importance to the Soviets of destroying them. The problem, therefore, is one of adequate intelligence about those targets.

...the armed forces will be able to use their might purposefully and with the greatest effect only if they have adequate and reliable data concerning the composition, grouping, and nature of preparations of troops of a potential enemy, his most important military and economic targets, and the system used for their defense. This is not new. But in modern conditions it has acquired a special sense, since the successful employment, at the beginning of the war, primarily of strategic weapons, which advance victory over enemy in a decisive manner, depends upon intelligence data. The situation is similar to the role of reconnaissance in operations of the branches of the armed forces. Their course and outcome are determined to a great degree by the timely ascertainment of the location of enemy nuclear weapons and the disclosure of the concentration and basic groupings of the [enemy] troops and various important targets. (6)

The suggestion has been made that target acquisition for nuclear strikes need not be precise because a larger-yield weapon can be used to "make up" for faulty intelligence or errors in target location. Unfortunately, this is a gross oversimplification of the problem. Although the nuclear weapon represents enormous increases in firepower, it does not render target acquisition any the less important. Indeed, it is more significant than it has been in the past because the nuclear weapon is of such a size and cost that expenditure is not, relatively speaking, a trivial decision. One does not fire merely to suppress; one fires to kill or destroy a reasonably significant target and this necessitates highly accurate intelligence on the nature and location of objectives. This requirement is recognized in both the Soviet and United States literature. Nuclear fire requires somewhat less precision, but better target identification and analysis - which traditionally might have been viewed more as tactical intelligence than target acquisition. One of the important consequences of the introduction of nuclear weapons has been to turn tactical intelligence - signal, photographic, and agent - into "real-time forward observers" for the nuclear strike forces. For example:

The success of battle against enemy tactical nuclear means depends first of all on the timely discovery of them by intelligence. Intelligence has the mission of establishing the places of disposition of means of nuclear attack, discovering the system for controlling them, disclosing warehouses for nuclear ammunition and points for their assembly, and checking on their destruction. (7)

Because this is to be used for targeting, "Special trustworthiness and accuracy are required of intelligence data on means of nuclear attack." (8) Accurate intelligence gathering will be far from easy.

The enemy may have considerably fewer such weapons than guns and launchers capable of delivering these weapons to the target. Therefore, it is very important to receive reliable data in good time not only about the location of the means of nuclear attack but also of the presence of nuclear ammunition with them. Of course, this is a difficult task but its accomplishment is necessary and possible. (9)

Moreover, it will require knowledge of those special characteristics that distinguish nuclear from nonnuclear units.

In order to conduct the reconnaissance of tactical means of nuclear attack successfully, it is necessary to know their tactical and technical characteristics, reconnaissance signs, organization of the podrazdeleniya [battalions] and chasti [regiments] and the enemy's view on the procedure for the placement of these means in position areas and employment on combat.

Each type of means of nuclear attack has its own inherent reconnaissance signs. Common reconnaissance signs of tactical means of nuclear attack at the firing positions and close to them are considered to be: the presence, in the position area or close to it, of camouflaged guns (self-propelled or towed), launchers, and missiles; a large number of special-purpose vehicles, vehicles of various types, prime movers, and trailers; the preparation and disposition of firing positions at a distance of 4-12 km from the FEBA; the preparation of cover for the sections; the presence of approach routes to the firing positions; and a large number of radios and the special character of their operation. (10)

The target acquisition problem is further exacerbated (except for the case of a successful Soviet surprise attack on NATO) because the Soviets cannot assume that NATO nuclear forces will remain in peacetime locations once war appears imminent. NATO forces with nuclear capabilities -artillery, mobile land- and sea-based missiles, and aircraft - are highly mobile and are expected to be dispersed and moving or hidden in position to strike. As prudent military planners, the Soviets must plan on the basis of losing a major portion of NATO nuclear targets, perhaps as many as 75 percent on the eve of war if NATO goes on alert. The loss makes an initial nuclear strike difficult if not impossible in terms of accomplishing its assigned mission, the first priority of which is the destruction of NATO nuclear means. This problem is explained in The Offensive as follows:

> The simultaneous launching of nuclear strikes throughout the entire depth of the enemy disposition is possible only with the presence of the corresponding quantity of nuclear ammunition and means for its delivery to the target as well as complete and reliable data on the enemy objectives throughout the entire depth of his defense. But the attacker will not always have such capabilities and data. It is considered difficult to determine the location of all objectives reliably and accurately for the launching of a simultaneous nuclear strike against them even with the presence of modern means of reconnaissance.   And before destroying such objectives, final reconnaissance is required to refine their location. A portion of the objectives may be in motion or appear anew. Hence, the conclusion is drawn that one can hardly count on the fact that the attacker will succeed in destroying all important objectives with one simultaneous nuclear strike. In the course of the offensive it will often be necessary to launch nuclear strikes as the attacking troops advance and targets are disclosed for destruction by nuclear weapons. (11)

Target acquisition demands the most careful attention, since many of the nuclear systems are in constant motion.

Combating enemy tactical means of nuclear attack is a complex mission. This complexity consists of the number, high maneuverability, short stay time at one firing position, and the difficulty in reconnoitering them because they are guarded in an intensified manner, covered, and thoroughly camouflaged. According to the views existing in foreign armies, as a rule only one nuclear weapon can be fired from one firing position. Therefore, the stay time at one firing position is determined by the duration of the preparation for firing, the accomplishment of the fire mission, and closing down and is numbered in several minutes; after this, the means of nuclear attack depart to alternate positions or to other position areas. (12)

The sea-based and land-based missiles present the most difficult targets. Land-based aircraft may present a less severe problem because the Soviets understand there to be only a limited number of bases from which NATO's high-performance nuclear strike aircraft can operate. In short, there are limitations on the extent to which NATO nuclear strike air forces can disperse, and presumably, Warsaw Pact reconnaissance aviation would monitor continuously these potential dispersal bases.

The problem of target acquisition is of further importance because of its impact on the Soviet military assessment of the effectiveness of a mass, simultaneous nuclear strike. This in turn could influence perceptions of when and how to "go nuclear." Target acquisition is most difficult during a crisis if NATO has dispersed its forces and if fighting has not yet begun because of restrictions on reconnaissance activities - in particular, on mass air reconnaissance overflights - prior to the actual outbreak of hostilities. Once the war starts and reconnaissance units and overflights are possible, the problem will become less severe as targets are reacquired and carefully tracked. On the other hand, should NATO decide not to disperse to avoid provocation and destabilization, the Soviets would have an enormous incentive to launch immediately a mass nuclear strike - a strike that might well be maximally effective, require the least expenditure of resources and cause the least associated damage. A NATO decision, therefore, to remain nonprovocative in the midst of crisis greatly enhances the first strike capability of the Warsaw Pact.

RATES OF ADVANCE PLANNING

Planning and coordination are essential to any military operation, but are even more vital to the high-speed, combined arms offensive envisaged by the Soviets. This is reflected in the Soviet penchant for studying rates of advance and learning how to estimate the speed of troop movements under widely varying conditions. The rate of advance is probably the single most important parameter in describing the nature and duration of the war.

In an offensive battle or operation the basic indicator of tempos of troop operations are the tempos of attack, by which we mean the average daily advance of troops in the course of an attack, or in overcoming an enemy's defense - the average advance of troops in kilometers per hour of combat. (13)

The rate of advance is in direct correlation to troop movement spacing and scheduling; utilization of transportation nets; required reserves and logistic resupply; maintenance, which is particularly important for tracked vehicles such as tanks; coordination and exploitation of nuclear strikes; treatment of casualties; and, in general, the whole management of the war effort.

Soviet discussions of the exploitation following the nuclear strikes create an image of a highly orchestrated attack in which all forces have precise missions in accordance with an exact timetable.

Accomplishment of an assigned combat mission is regulated by a specific time. It is possible to defeat totally an enemy grouping and take the indicated line of region and still not accomplish the combat mission if this done late or inopportunely. The assigned mission must be accomplished at precisely the time indicated. Delay leads to interruption of interaction with adjacent units and to a breakdown in plans which have been developed. It allows the enemy to accomplish a maneuver of men and materiel, to make counter- attacks and deliver nuclear strikes, and to bolster his defense. Belated actions almost always are of a scattered and disorganized nature. Therefore, in the determination of the combat mission, the time of its accomplishment is calculated with the maximum possible precision, taking into account concrete conditions of the situation, and troops bend all efforts to ensure that the mission is accomplish- ed on time. (14)

What could be done over the course of days in World War II must now be compressed into minutes: "The broad maneuver and the rapid sequence of combat operations calls for a most exigent taking into account of the time factor, a calculation of every minute and second."(15)

This notion of precise timing, preplanning and adherence to schedules would appear very suspect if applied to a potential environ- ment of extreme destruction and gross uncertainty created by NATO nuclear weapons. There is, after all, no experience with a nuclear battlefield. The nature of NATO's defense posture, as well as the timing and manner in which NATO nuclear weapons will be employed are fraught with uncertainties. Early use by the Soviets could have severe repercussions on their planning - repercussions which are clearly recognized in their discussions of the types of environments in which their command and control system should be designed to operate. In this regard, the Soviets' emphasis on the speed, pace and timing of the attack in their literature is a study of contrasts and potential inconsistencies.

Although the Soviets would like to move as rapidly as possible, they recognize that it is important not to overdesign the offensive in an environment that will be "uncertain" at best. The following passages are illustrative:

> Thus, the combat mission is the initial basis from which all subsequent work is done, both in organizing and in conducting the offensive. Performance of the combat mission serves as the basic criterion in evaluating the operations of troops. Therefore, a proper determination of the content and depth of combat missions is of the greatest importance. (16)

> A miscalculation in concentration of efforts or unskilled accomplishment of it under conditions of employment of nuclear weapons conceal a considerably more dangerous embryo of defeat, since a defending enemy possesses high mobility and great fire power. (17)

> Thus, the contemporary meeting engagement is characterized by: an intense fight to capture and return the initiative; deployment of troops in combat formation chiefly from columns, simultaneously with the initiation of combat; insufficient clarity of the situation, sharp and rapid changes and high speed of combat; a rapid change of the combat formation of troops; the development of combat on a wide front; freedom of maneuver and the presence of open flanks for both sides.

> The use of nuclear weapons and the high mobility of troops will inevitably lead to rapid and radical changes in the situation.

> In contemporary conditions the situation changes sharply, and therefore information is outdated very quickly; it loses its value and can even lead the commander to error. (18)

The obstacles to precise planning in this environment are quite formidable.

> While conducting the offensive at high rates, troops will not only have to complete the defeat of a defending enemy, but also pursue him, wage a meeting engagement, repulse counterattacks, force water obstacles, etc. In such a situation it is very difficult to provide ahead of time for concrete missions to defeat particular groupings of a defending enemy situated at a great depth. (19)

Troops may also be forced to operate in an environment of radioactive contamination.

> The effect of radiation on troops depends on the intensity and duration of the radioactive influence, and these factors must be taken into account in determining the means of carrying out missions in this situation.

The intensity of the effect is determined by the degree of radioactive contamination of the terrain and by radiation levels, but its duration is a function of the length of time troops are in the contaminated regions. The dimensions of the contaminated territory also have a direct effect on the execution of combat missions by troops and on the whole course of their actions. The area of radioactive contamination of terrain and the levels of radiation compose the fundamentals of a radioactive situation, and therefore they must be taken into account first of all in determining the means of troop operations and solutions to the questions of their control. Both the area of contaminated territory and the levels of radiation in it are a function of quantity and power of the nuclear munitions used by both sides, the type of altitude of the bursts, the time elapsed from the moment of each burst, the speed and direction of the wind, the relief of the terrain and nature of the topsoil, and atmospheric phenomena. For instance, it is known that the area of contaminated territory with dangerous radiation levels two or three hours after a surface burst of one very powerful nuclear warhead comprises tens of thousands of square kilometers. The contaminated zones will be especially widespread in the case of grouped nuclear strikes. In the case of repeated nuclear strikes the dimensions of the contaminated zone may also increase significantly. (20)

The possibility of immense radiation may have led to the use of special units at Army- and Front-level command posts simply to monitor the radiation situation.(21) The problem includes not only the effects of radiation, but of fire, flood and rubble as well.

With high rates of forward movement and operations along a broad front and at great depths, the troops must obviously overcome more frequently than before, obstacles, zones of destruction and inundation, regions gripped by fires, and, especially, zones of radioactive contamination created by the defenders. (22)

This has led to numerous Soviet calculations of rates of advance in the presence of rubble and other obstacles, (23) and warnings regarding the use of their own weapons, particularly in terms of surface burst.

It is not precluded that surface nuclear bursts can be planned against deep objectives, but it must be very well planned as to what kind and where (along the path of tank forces), inasmuch as this may create zones of radioactive contamination, destruction, inundation and fires. (24)

NATO plans involve two different approaches to employing nuclear weapons against Soviet troop operations. The first and most effective approach is to attack troop concentrations and the transportation nets (roads, bridges, railroads and so forth) in front of the advancing troops.

The second approach, to attack the transportation nets behind the troop units to cut off their logistic resupply, has been proven generally ineffective because moving the troops themselves requires at least ten times the effort and transportation capacity that is required merely to resupply them. Moreover, the impact of the first approach on time schedules is severe, while the latter ensures generally much more time to reschedule along alternate means and complete deliveries before significant impact at the front is felt. In fact, when the war goes nuclear, the Soviets might well plan to discontinue all shipments into the front until NATO strikes have been completed, and then replan and reschedule all shipments around the NATO nuclear strike areas. This flexibility may not be enjoyed near the FEBA, where timely reinforcement by second-echelon forces may be critical to sustain the offensive and develop breakthroughs in an effective manner. For this, troop maneuver is essential, and the potential impact of NATO strikes on troops and transportation nets in advance of their movement is recognized by the Soviets. One interesting World War II example focused upon in their literature is that in which the Allies interdicted in front of an important German reserve army and effectively blocked its movement and subsequent use to halt the advance from Normandy. As described in Voyennaya mysl':

> The problem of combating strategic reserves is not new. This can be seen in the experience of World War II. For example, one of the most important problems of the U.S. and British air forces in preparing for the Normandy operation in 1944 was the disorganization of communication in the rear area of German fascist troops with the objective of disrupting the normal supply of material and reserves to German groupings located on the Northern Coast of France. The plan for Operation Overlord included strikes against railroad systems of France and Belgium within a radius of approximately 300 kilometers of the landing area and the destruction of railroad and motor vehicle bridges over the Seine and Loire rivers. This would disrupt the normal transfer of reserves to the German fascist troops in Normandy. As a result of the air raids by the Allied forces 24 bridges were destroyed on the Seine alone. During the landing and the following period of battle on the beachhead Allied aviation isolated the main areas of combat action from German reserves in the inner regions of France, from the East, and from the coast of the Straits of Dover. (25)

A primary concern of the Soviets is the impact of NATO nuclear weapons on their force movements. While this concern applies to the movement of all echelons, it has focused in recent years particularly on the movement of the second echelon and reserves. An additional problem in this regard is the threat posed by the possible use of atomic land mines, i.e., atomic demolition munitions (ADMs), especially to advancing troops.

In the final analysis, Soviet planning encounters two strongly opposing forces - one which stresses "go as fast as possible or you will be destroyed by the opposition's nuclear weapons," and the other which warns "do not plan above your capabilities or you are equally well doomed to confusion and defeat." On the other hand, Soviet use of nuclear weapons makes high rates of advance possible, while on the other hand, their use by NATO could slow down rates of advance and create .choke points leading to traffic jams, which could become lucrative targets for further NATO strikes. There is extensive analysis in the Soviet literature on the damage caused in particular by NATO nuclear weapons and its impact on troop operations.

CENTRALIZED CONTROL AND AUTOMATION

The Soviets have been forced to look to automation for a solution to the dual problems of compiling the vast amount of information and the paucity of time in which to analyze it.

> Modern information technology enables us to transmit, receive, re-request, check, evaluate and display in graphic form a mass of data within a sufficiently short processing time. Even more complex logic processing of data is being done: comparison, evaluation and generalization. All this makes it possible to liberate people from accounting and other difficult but mechanical work, and to turn the intellectual potential of the commander to the solution of funda-mental military management problems. (26)

That solution, however, is not without its problems, chief of which is the combining of the complete experience and intellect of man with the computer. This dilemma is a common one and not unlike that encountered in the West. As explained in Concept, Algorithm, Decision: The "automation" position is, "Here you have the cybernetic industry and its capabilities, so use it. If the capabilities are inadequate tell us what you need and we will do it." The management response is, "We are ready and want very much to use cybernetics and you are welcome to expand its capabilities. We place great value on the computer. But tell us how it will help us to solve management problems and prove that it has the advantages which you say it has. Otherwise, it will be hard for us to understand how to use it."(27) This problem and those of software appear to be causing the Soviets some difficulties.(28) Automating the command decision process is evidently not a simple task and its benefits may not yet be realized.

At issue here is large-scale coordinated and centralized planning, high-speed rates of advance and command at unit and subunit levels. All these appear to be interrelated and of considerable concern in the Soviet military press – a concern that may be related to that with the structure and organization of command and control at the tactical and operational-tactical levels.(29) Although this issue is not well explained in the open literature, it too may reside in dissatisfaction with the overall organization in planning and co-ordinating a major high-speed offensive. Factors included here are the time required for all plans to be drawn up, approved and disseminated, following the transmission of the strategic concept and missions from the STAVKA of the Supreme Command to the commands and staffs; the accuracy and effectiveness of coordination between forces and branches; and the flexibility in subsequently changing plans to conform to new situations, as for example might be encountered in transitioning from conventional to nuclear operations.

Part of this problem, with which the Soviets have grappled over the years, stems from the conflict between the traditional centralized control of the Soviet military system, which is evidently even more important in a nuclear environment, and the need for independence at the lower command levels, also of apparent significance in a nuclear war. On the one hand, activities must be controlled from the top to accord with a single plan and concept of operations and to provide maximum flexibility in the hands of the strategic leadership. On the other hand, some degree of initiative is required at the lower operational levels to cope with unforeseen situations that demand fast reaction.

In this regard, the Soviets are also aware that extensive automation is required to cope with the sheer volume of information and to perform calculations in order to determine the best military option. It is important to recall the Soviet control from the top was accomplished in World War II in a relatively slow-moving environment. Where the course of combat is accelerated by orders of magnitude, such attention to detail at the very top may no longer be possible, even with the aid of automation, because of the stunning rapidity with which situations change and the nonavailability of time in which to understand the changes, assess their implications, and weigh the alternatives.

NUCLEAR WEAPON STOCKPILE

One final problem worth noting, and mentioned earlier, may no longer be a problem - the shortage of tactical nuclear weapons. Throughout the Soviet literature of the early and mid-1960s, there was projected a sense of scarcity of tactical nuclear weapons. One of the best such examples relating to the 1960s is contained in Khrushchev's memoirs:

> There were incidents when Marshal Grechko insisted that we develop a tactical missile with a small nuclear warhead that could be used by our infantry against an advancing army. I agreed with Grechko that it would be good to arm our troops with tactical nuclear weapons at the platoon and regiment level or even at the division level, but I had to explain to him that the smaller the explosive charge of a warhead, the more raw (fissionable) material you need - and we

simply didn't have enough raw material to go around. Therefore, we
had to concentrate first and foremost on intercontinental - that is,
strategic rather than tactical missiles. (30)

This impression of scarcity is not reflected in the unclassified literature
of the 1970s. Further, a <u>Voyennaya mysl'</u> article from the late 1960s
refers to a period of limited supply as being in the "recent past."

It appears quite possible that there have been two major and <u>equal</u>
expansions in Soviet theater capability during the late 1960s and 1970s.
First, the so-called conventional buildup that has received the major
publicity; and, second, a tactical nuclear buildup that has, on the
contrary, been largely neglected. This study concludes that the growth
in tactical nuclear capabilities, operational concepts and Soviet interest
in, and exercise of, alternative forms of tactical nuclear warfare is at
least as impressive and important to recognize as the conventional
buildup in analyzing Soviet military strategy in Europe. It is considered
extremely doubtful that the Soviets still suffer from a shortage of
tactical nuclear weapons; indeed, it is more likely that they possess a
stockpile considerably in excess of and qualitatively superior to that of
NATO. Moreover, within recent years, the appearance of the Backfire
Bomber and the SS-20 IRBM gives the Soviets an arsenal of theater
nuclear delivery systems of greater range than most of the delivery
systems at the disposal of NATO.

7 Contemporary Issues of Soviet Military Strategy toward Europe

The preceding chapters have presented, in Soviet terms where possible, discussions of the more important concepts that underlie Soviet military strategy toward Europe. This chapter will proceed from that basis to consider the broader political-military issues of Soviet military strategy that are of current interest. The discussion of these issues has been organized in individual sections as follows:

- Soviet objectives,

- The role of nuclear weapons,

- Conventional war and transition to nuclear operations,

- Chemical warfare,

- Escalation to intercontinental war,

- Superiority and war initiation and

- The scenario.

While there is much discussion in the Soviet unclassified military literature of basic elements of strategy and principles of war, there tends to be considerably less of practical importance in those areas that bear heavily on the broader political-military issues. As a consequence, much of the analysis of these issues is of necessity inferential or deductive. The major problems in such an analysis are: first, mirror-imaging Western values or benefits, i.e., attributing to the Soviets what the West "knows" is right; and second, the tendency to find what one is looking for, particularly when it supports an acceptable policy or "nice" conclusion. A third and related difficulty is that, to a certain extent, these issues reflect Western perhaps more than Soviet concerns. Many of these may be "nonissues" to the Soviets or secondary in that they are automatically resolved when a decision is reached on what in their view is a more important issue.   Finally, as will be exphasized in the concluding section, all of these issues are heavily scenario dependent. In the absence of specific details on what actually is happening and why, one can only examine the issues in general terms.

SOVIET OBJECTIVES

Soviet objectives bear directly on all their plans and actions.   This discussion, therefore, will review three topics: 1) the primacy of fundamental political objectives; 2) armed conflict and strategic goals; and 3) Soviet interest in destroying Europe.

Political Objectives

It is clear in the Soviet literature that military strategy is subservient to political objectives and strategy. For example:

> Politics determines the priority and strength of the blows inflicted on the enemy, the measures taken to strengthen allied relations within the coalition and the general strategic plan of the war, which is directed at the quickest possible rout of the enemy or at a drawnout struggle and the gradual exhaustion of the enemy's forces. At the same time politics, by taking into account the strategic possibilities at its disposal, must determine the speed and the intensity of the military actions, and also the forces and means it is necessary to mobilize in order to attain the aims intended, etc. In doing so, politics takes into account not only the aims of the war but also those of the post-war settlement and subordinates the conduct of the war to the attainment of these aims. (1)

As stated by Major General V.I. Zemskov, editor-in-chief of <u>Voyennaya mysl'</u>, the major decisions are made by the political leadership.

> ...the decision to employ such devastating implements as nuclear weapons, has become the exclusive prerogative of the political leadership. It is primarily the political, not the military leaders who determine the necessity of employing mass destruction weapons, who specify the principal targets, and when they are to be hit. (2)

There is no debate on this point: the political (Party) objectives come first and determine the context for military strategy.   This is clearly stated throughout Soviet political, Party, and military literature and explains the importance, in assessing issues of strategy, of keeping always in the forefront the basic political objectives that will condition the consideration of alternative military strategies.

There are three main underlying Soviet objectives in waging war:

first, to preserve the Soviet Union proper; second, and of lower priority, to preserve gains made in the building of worldwide socialism, especially in Eastern Europe; and, third, to extend political, military and ideological hegemony in building worldwide communism under Soviet leadership.   This third objective continues to be the long-term goal of the revolution, but it remains subordinate to the interest of the socialist homeland - the Soviet Union.   The Soviet leaders have historically manifested little tendency to press militantly toward the goal of world revolution whenever this might place in jeopardy the primary goal of national security.

Several important consequences emerge when these political objectives are applied in the context of Western Europe.   First, in building worldwide communism and extending the revolution, Europe is the highest priority "target" because of its location and resources. Achieving hegemony over all Europe is therefore a major objective.   For this purpose, it is necessary to decouple the United States and Europe - to divide and conquer.   Second, the Soviets recognize that they can gain considerable benefits from Europe in peacetime through trade and economic assistance - benefits that may warrant maintaining peace rather than risking war.   By far the most important consideration in this regard is the possibility of worldwide nuclear war.   As quoted in the third edition of Marxism-Leninism on War and Army:

A new world war, which will take on an unprecedented destructive nature and which will lead to the destruction of hundreds of millions of people, not only would not accelerate, but would delay the transition of humanity to socialism; without war, man will make the transition to socialism more rapidly and easily. (3)

To the extent that direct conflict is regarded as excessively dangerous, the Soviets will proceed by fostering the growth of internal Communist parties, by making it clear to the Europeans what they will lose in the event of war and by obtaining through "peaceful coexistence" all possible means from Europe and the United States for building the Soviet scientific and industrial base.

At the same time, they are striving for total superiority so as to facilitate their task and minimize the risk involved by ensuring that the United States will not start the war.   This is one reason why strategic nuclear superiority is of primary importance to the Soviets.   Such a posture is for the purpose of deterrence, but not in the sense used in the West which is coupled with notions of retaliation, destruction and the end of the political process.   The Soviets do not share the West's pessimism about the future of mankind in the event of a nuclear war; (4) instead they see armed conflict, including nuclear conflict, as an important and usable tool of politics.   While the consequences of all-out nuclear war are well recognized, this does not mean it is to be avoided at all costs or has ceased to be a tool (as opposed to an end) of politics. Because of its potentially dire consequences, it is even more important for the political leadership to be fully prepared for such a contingency.

Such preparation has become the first priority of Soviet military science. Their most immediate long-term objective has been therefore to achieve the capability (superiority) to win all forms of armed conflict, beginning with the most important, nuclear war.

Armed Conflict Goals

The Soviets would prefer to build communism through infiltration and revolution rather than through direct conflict. This is particularly true where the antagonist is respected, e.g., Germany and the United States, and especially where the risk of all-out nuclear war is significant. However, when undertaken, armed conflict is to be fought to a victorious end, maintaining in the meantime proper respect for military principles and sound military strategy.

According to the Soviet literature, victory is attained only through the destruction of the enemy's forces and the domination and control - hegemony - of Europe by means of covert or coercive mechanisms, thus ensuring that the enemy can never again challenge the Soviet Union. This would be accomplished as swiftly and decisively as possible. All forces and means would be employed without hesitation if in the Soviet assessment this would bring about victory more quickly and efficiently.

In a war in Europe, several immediate strategic missions would emerge. Explicit examples of such missions are frustrating a NATO nuclear attack, delivering a rapid preemptive strike, forcing countries to withdraw from the aggressor NATO coalition, disorganizing the enemy's deep rear, and destroying strategic groups of forces on the continental and oceanic theaters. (5) In developing these missions, the Soviets would take into consideration not merely the war in Europe, but also a potential world war. Missions would be established and tasks assigned to the major force groupings bearing in mind the longer term goal of seizing and occupying or otherwise controlling Europe. These objectives obviously affect the manner in which targets are selected and forces assigned for their destruction or seizure.

Soviet Interest in Destroying Europe

The Soviets certainly have the capability to destroy Europe - a capability which serves as a constant reminder to the Europeans of the devastating risks of nuclear war. Yet the active realization of that capability - especially in the initial phase - appears to be contrary to their political objectives. The Soviet objective

> ...is not to turn the large economic and industrial regions into a heap of ruins (although great destruction apparently is unavoidable), but to deliver strikes which will destroy strategic combat means, paralyze enemy military production, making it incapable of satisfying the priority needs of the front and rear areas and sharply reduce the enemy capability to conduct strikes. (6)

The Soviets' preferred operational strategy appears to be to seize and occupy Europe without destroying the prize for which the war is being fought. The types of resources that the Soviets wish to preserve for their own use are transportation, industrial and economic assets, geography and manpower - particularly scientific and technical personnel. These valuable assets are to be preserved for the expansion of communism, and for the benefit of the Soviet armed forces and the economy of the Soviet homeland.

THE ROLE OF NUCLEAR WEAPONS

It is believed that the Western perception of the role of nuclear weapons in Soviet strategy, while seldom examined in detail, is one of the principal determinants of NATO's approach to its own strategy. It is important, therefore, to examine the Soviet view of the role of nuclear weapons as carefully and realistically as possible. Key issues in this regard appear to be the role of nuclear weapons in deterrence or war fighting; the utility of limited or selective use; and Soviet use of weapons based in their homeland.

Deterrence or War Fighting

Since the mid 1950s, the Soviets have held that a major war with their natural enemies, the Western capitalist states, most likely would start as, or quickly become, a nuclear war. Hence, although they prepare for alternative contingencies, the chief task of Soviet military strategy since that time has been to build, equip and train the forces to win a nuclear war. While NATO strategy has changed over the past 20 years, it also remains a strategy that calls for the use of nuclear weapons. However, while war fighting has governed the development of nuclear forces in the Soviet Union, deterrence appears to have been the major impetus for their development in the West.

This distinction in the West between war fighting and deterrence can be crucial. Because many Western leaders believe nuclear war fighting to be impossible, Western forces are designed to deter. That conclusion tends to be attributed to the Soviets, as well. However, if we are to judge according to Soviet literature and force development, attributing these beliefs to the Soviets is most dangerous if not patently false. The Soviets may well desire to prevent war and may well build their forces with what can be interpreted as deterrence in mind. Yet theirs is clearly a different kind of deterrence - one that is derived from the possession of a war-fighting capability.

This is by no means a trivial distinction - for it results in tangible differences in capabilities. In the West, deterrence provides for primary emphasis on the offensive nuclear delivery systems, on a retaliation blow, and on the ability to inflict unacceptable damage. According to the Soviet view of deterrence as a war-fighting concept, the emphasis goes far beyond the delivery systems to include all forces and means, command/control, reserves, countermeasures and recovery, as well as a preemptive strike, a disarming counterforce strike, and subsequent war through to and including victory. Such a concept of deterrence is wholly alien to the West. Economically, of course, the peacetime cost of the war-fighting option greatly exceeds that of deterrence. To the extent one's objective is a war-fighting capability, command/control is perhaps its most essential component. For that reason, significant changes and serious improvements in command/control have been underway in the Soviet Union continuously since at least 1960, while NATO C^3I has suffered a decade of neglect and is now "by far NATO's most grievous deficiency." (7)

The differences between the Soviet and the NATO approach to force development are also so significant that the types of numbers comparisons most often encountered in the Western literature have limited validity. The service roles and missions, as well as the objectives and doctrines, are diametrically opposed, while weapons deployments and related strategies are in different phases of development and moving in opposite directions. NATO strategy, still oriented toward war fighting in the late 1950s, has been deterrence oriented since 1960, while Soviet strategy, which aimed at deterrence in the late 1950s and early 1960s, has been moving steadily toward war fighting. The principal NATO strike force is forward-based tactical air in Western Europe; the Soviet counterpart is a ballistic missile force based in the Soviet Union. NATO weapons greatly outnumbered those of the Soviets in the 1950s and 1960s, a fact which probably accounts for the basic Soviet deterrence orientation in that time frame. In recent years, however, NATO deployments are believed to have decreased, with considerable pressure for further reductions, while Soviet deployments have been steadily increasing. This increase has yet to be widely taken into account in Western literature. Plans and strategies also stand in marked contrast: NATO's are structured for defense while those of the Warsaw Pact, for offense and invasion. NATO forces and command/control are designed to survive in a conventional war, while Soviet forces and command/control are designed to survive and win a nuclear war. NATO strategy emphasizes defense and the second strike, while Soviet strategy stresses offense and the first strike.

Limited Nuclear War

In considering the Soviet strategy for employing nuclear weapons against NATO forces, an important issue is whether the Soviets will fight a limited nuclear war, or launch a mass, indiscriminate attack. If the latter approach is used, how can the notion of "mass" be defined and can such a strike be a politically usable tool for the Soviets?

It is useful to break down this problem into two components: the Western view of limited nuclear war, and Soviet views on limiting the consequences of a nuclear war in Europe.

As defined in the West, limited nuclear war encompasses those varieties known as constrained battlefield, limited interdiction, or regional options. The objectives underlying these employment concepts are to limit escalation, terminate the war, stop the advance, and so forth, but usually do not include victory.

The Soviet literature indicates that politics would guide the strategy of the war and the intensity with which it would be pursued. However, the Soviets are quick to point out the need to observe traditional principles of military strategy in the process:

> Conditions for the achievement of the set aims can be created only combined with an excellent knowledge and careful consideration of specific military conditions, and of the laws governing the conduct of the armed struggle. (8)

The key considerations of military science are the aims of the war, the postwar settlement, and the laws that govern the military strategy for the conduct of the conflict. In accordance with these concerns and the notions of limited nuclear war put forth in the Western press, the Soviets continue to examine carefully all possibilities. As stated by Army General V. Kulikov, Chief of the General Staff and Soviet First Deputy Minister of Defense, in Kommunist in February 1973:

> Research is being carried out to ascertain more profoundly the probable nature of a future war. Military science devotes great attention to the quest for means for reliably repulsing a surprise attack by an aggressor and to the further elaboration of the most effective methods of organizing and implementing decisive military actions on the most varying scales. The range of questions relating to this problem embraces the preparation and performance of operations and combat actions by all services of the Armed Forces in nuclear war. Here the efforts of military theoreticians are directed toward studying the planning and conduct of operations in various theaters of military actions, restoring the troops' combat capability after enemy nuclear strikes and other questions. [Emphasis added.] (9)

Evidently, Soviet military science is being applied to the examination of alternative forms of theater nuclear war. However, at this stage it is still research. In discussing the characteristic features of the present stage in the development of military science, General Kulikov also states that: "Military strategy has determined the most expedient ways of repulsing aggression and inflicting a crushing retaliatory strike and methods of using nuclear and conventional weapons in the course of a strategic offensive by major groupings." (10)   He reiterates the importance of using the basic principles of operational art that have been "...formulated for the use of nuclear weapons in operations and combat actions by formations of the different services of the Armed Forces - principles concerning, in particular, the organization and delivery of massed nuclear strikes."(11) Such statements balance the research by maintaining the presence of military strategy and the laws and principles of armed conflict.

While there is debate over alternative forms of warfare, little evidence has been found in the Soviet literature to suggest any interest in limiting objectives or in restraining employments <u>within</u> (rather than <u>to</u>) the theater of operations once the war goes nuclear - to conduct a little nuclear war within a larger conventional war. To the Soviets war is war; it is combined nuclear and conventional war and not either disjunctively a conventional or a nuclear war or something in-between.

Furthermore, the overwhelming majority of Soviet statements indicates a strong disposition against the possibility of a limited nuclear employment within a larger theater of operations. This is revealed first, in the stress placed on seizing the initiative and mounting a strong offensive; second, and closely related, in the need, as a fundamental principle of war, to attack the enemy and completely destroy him throughout the entire depth of his defense; and third, in the importance attached to destroying all targets as soon as they are acquired.

A delay in the destruction of means of nuclear attack will permit the enemy to launch the nuclear strikes first and may lead to heavy losses and even to the defeat of the offensive. The "accumulation" of such targets as nuclear weapons and waiting with the intention of destroying them subsequently is now absolutely inadmissible. (12)

Perhaps most important is the universal belief in the potential decisiveness of the first strike, and the inherent difficulty in assuming that "one of the opposing groupings having nuclear-missile weapons at its disposal will be reconciled with defeat in a limited nuclear war without using all means of combat." (13)

Further, the Soviets are skeptical that a nuclear war can be kept limited to less than the entire theater of operations. They recognize that the situation will be very confused in the fog of war, that the enemy's intentions will be unclear, and that the problem of distinguishing between a limited employment and a limited strike as an initial phase of a larger attack will be virtually impossible. However, the absence of information on the situation should not prevent positive action.

The situation is well known where incomplete information about the situation does not release the commander of his obligation for making a timely decision. The worst of all is not to decide on anything or to decide late. The one to be rebuked is not he who under difficult conditions of a situation has made a decision, although not necessarily the best one, but he who, fearing responsibility, did not make any decision at all and thus placed the troops in an extremely difficult position and did not ensure fulfillment of the assigned mission. .. This fundamental thesis most corresponds to the nature of operations in a nuclear war, in which bold decisions full of initiative will find widest application. (14)

Preplanning required to cope with severed communications would tend to be worst-case planning.

This is further exacerbated by their need to anticipate and initiate actions before NATO goes nuclear.

> One of the decisive conditions for success in an operation is the anticipating of the enemy in making nuclear strikes. (15)

> In the military, one cannot be guided by the principle of "better late than never." Prediction in military affairs, particularly when one takes into consideration a potential nuclear missile war, should correspond in full to the principle of "the sooner the better." (16)

These strictures are believed to correspond to a very strong theme throughout Soviet strategy opposing any significant notion of limited nuclear employment within the theater.

Further, any very small scale use, such as that often suggested in the Western literature, is referred to as "insignificant." Any introduction of new capabilities into a conflict must be of sufficient quantity so as to bring about real change, unless one can clearly identify a limited employment capable of producing significant results.

One specific rationale for a limited use of nuclear weapons has been found in the Soviet literature. It applies only to a theater operation and is a limited defensive response designed to confuse or mislead the enemy and buy time while preparing the combined arms armies - particularly the ground forces - for a subsequent massive nuclear strike. The example often used to illustrate the rationale for this type of limited response is taken from the Battle of Kursk:

> In other words, a shift to the defense foresees only a temporary rejection of the initiative, and its chief goal is a subsequent seizure of the initiative with a renewal of the attack. We know, for example, that in the Battle of Kursk the Soviet High Command knowingly rejected anticipating the enemy in shifting to the attack so that, having given the enemy this opportunity, it could grind his strategic groupings in the course of defensive operations and then deliver a crushing blow against them. Such a decision is even more remarkable in that our troops were fully capable of shifting to the attack first, and the premeditated defense was not a sign of their weakness. Seizure and firm maintenance of the operational-strategic initiative were planned subsequently and really were achieved in the course of the armed conflict which developed in the Kursk bulge. (17)

Such use also appears to be the Soviet counter to a NATO conventional attack or conflict wherein NATO first initiates a limited use of nuclear weapons. The passage quoted suggests that the Soviets might respond in a limited fashion to solidify their gains or temporarily deter NATO and buy time while they reposture (i.e., transition from conventional defense to nuclear offense) for a decisive nuclear strike and associated exploitation.   Thus, limited employment of nuclear weapons in a restricted area appears to be considered as one means of transition from one form of combat to another in the event they are surprised by a NATO first use of nuclear weapons or choose to let NATO go first in what they assess to be a very limited use of nuclear weapons (e.g., fewer than ten).

The weight of political evidence also appears to stand against limited nuclear engagements.   The Soviet war aims with regard to Europe are clearly to "free" Europe and make it safe for the future growth of socialism.   No limitations on the political goals have been identified; war will be both militarily and politically decisive.

Selective Nuclear Employments

The general impression in the West of how the Soviets apply force emphasizes above all their use of "mass."   This impression can be misleading, however, because "mass" is rarely defined, and there is an implicit Western tendency to equate "mass" with "overkill."   "Massive" to the Soviets does not mean everything; it merely signifies that which is required to do the job.   In fact, the Soviets may be inclined increasingly toward an attack that is not only massive, but also selective and damage limiting.   The Soviet objectives relative to Europe are to seize and occupy, to turn the "military-political, military-economic, military-geographic, and directly operational strategic elements" of the theater to their own use.

While the Soviet strategic target list in <u>any</u> theater includes a wide variety of targets, there is reason to believe that the Soviets may limit their initial nuclear attack against Western Europe only to those targets of greatest importance - vital command and control points, nuclear forces that pose an immediate threat, major military-economic targets such as ammunition supply dumps, tank and truck parks, and major troop concentrations whose destruction is critical to the initial period of the war.

> In selecting any specific region as the target and determining the sequence of nuclear strikes against it, first and foremost, it is necessary to determine the effect the strikes will have at a given time, the influence of the target on the progress of armed combat and on the functioning of the entire life of the country.

> At present political conditions will be considered when selecting regions for delivering nuclear strikes on a country-wide scale and when determining the number of objectives, the priority of inflicting strikes, and the methods of destruction of industrial, administrative-political and other centers. (18)

Specific reference is made to the attitude of the population of targeted cities and economic centers.

Prior to reaching the decision to employ nuclear weapons (in that case when they have already been employed during the course of combat action) it is necessary to take into consideration the importance of the city as a military, administrative, political, and economic center and the attitude of the populace of the city toward our army. (19)

More recently the following additional consideration has been set forth:

The decision to use a nuclear weapon involves the resolution of contradictions that never occurred in wars of the past. The moral aspects, including the guarantee of maximum safety to friendly advancing forces, and vital time factor (precipitant use of tactical nuclear weapons can have just as serious consequences as a delay), and many other factors pose complex problems. (20)

The concept of avoiding the targeting of cities is also clearly suggested in Voyennaya mysl': "Political motives can force the abandonment of strikes against extremely important economic and military targets or their implementation with smaller forces and means of a selective basis." (21) [Emphasis added.]

The Soviets may have considerably greater flexibility and control in their nuclear strike capability than is commonly supposed. Flexibility would include a basic attack plan broken down by country, by strategic regions within the larger countries, by target classes according to the time impact of the destruction of each target, and by political implications of the strike. There is major interest in identifying choke points, again to minimize the number of weapons required to achieve a given effect. Further, it is believed that alternative nonnuclear means for attacking important targets have been devised for those against which nuclear strikes may be inappropriate. Chemical weapons may be a particularly effective substitute for nuclear weapons in this regard. (22)

It is hypothesized that the Soviets possess their own means of limiting destruction in a theater war, but that these limitations do not correspond with a limiting of their objectives within the theater or with Western notions of limited nuclear war. Soviet interests in limiting nuclear war are believed to be based upon the desire for a military and political victory which includes the seizure and occupation or control of a largely intact postwar Europe.

Use of Soviet-Based Systems

Since the late 1950s, the center of gravity of the Soviet nuclear threat to Europe has been based in the Soviet Union. However, the recent growth in front nuclear capabilities - in surface-to-surface missile artillery and tactical aviation - has given rise to the theory that the Soviets may be preparing to fight the war from East European territory, without having to rely on Soviet-based aviation and medium- and long-range missiles. The tacit impetus is a desire to limit the war and reduce the risk of escalation by avoiding the use of systems based in the Soviet Union.

While this possibility should not be discounted, no support for it has been found in Soviet military literature; there is, however, considerable support for the proposition that Soviet-based forces remain the basis of their nuclear capability for war in Europe. A more rational explanation for the increase in the missiles and the tactical aviation may be the Soviet shift from a defensive to a genuine offensive capability. These systems are clearly vital to an effective offense - particularly the ground attack tactical aircraft which have the ability to locate and destroy mobile targets, especially NATO nuclear means, to achieve quickly air superiority, and to support a high-speed offensive.

CONVENTIONAL WAR AND TRANSITION
TO NUCLEAR OPERATIONS

In the mid-1960s, the Soviets began an expansion and modernization of their ground and air forces. The subsequent increase in equipment - tanks, surface-to-air missile defenses, frontal aviation, antitank capabilities, artillery, and so forth - have been viewed in the West as a massive conventional buildup of far greater proportions than that required simply for defense or for maintaining control over the satellites. To prevent any tendency to lower the nuclear threshold in return, the main United States reaction has been to emphasize that NATO's vastly greater resources and people could provide a better conventional defense than the Soviet offense, and that NATO, particularly its European members, should not be deterred from building up a conventional defense capability.

In interpreting the Soviet conventional buildup and the related analyses, it is important to understand this background and recognize that over this same period of time, the principal U.S. policy objective in NATO strategy has been to raise the nuclear threshold - to shift the NATO defense planning from nuclear to conventional defense. The following propositions ought to be highly suspect: 1) the Soviet buildup is intended for conventional warfare; 2) the Soviet buildup in nuclear capability is only to deter NATO from using nuclear weapons; and 3) NATO will enjoy the option of first use of nuclear weapons if conventional defense falters. The following discussion is designed to broaden this interpretation, hopefully without going too far in the other direction.

The Soviet View of Conventional War

In examining the discussions of conventional war in the Soviet literature and their conventional force development, it is essential to draw several distinctions between possible types of war: between conventional aspects of a nuclear war and a truly nonnuclear war; between a conventional war and an initial conventional phase; and between a World War II type of conventional war and a conventional war conducted under the threat of nuclear use.

In the first case (as explained earlier) nuclear weapons do not render conventional forces obsolete. The basic message was clearly stated in 1962:

> In the future war, the initial period, which can exert decisive influence not only on the course, but also on the ultimate result of the battle, will be of the greatest significance. Here our military doctrine considers that regardless of how great is the role of the nuclear missile, the requirement for other forces remain, and mass armies will continue to exist. In a modern war, victory can be achieved only by the combined efforts of all branches of the armed forces and all types of troops. (23)

The vast majority of Soviet "conventional" force improvements such as armored vehicles, tanks, air defenses, and command/control have been designed with nuclear war fighting in mind.

Most Soviet statements about conventional capability do not refer to large-scale conventional war, but rather to specific missions at the unit and subunit level in a nuclear war. (24) Implicit in this is the recognition that in certain situations, the use of nuclear weapons may be inadvisable and, therefore, subunits and units must be able to fight without them. Moreover, nuclear weapons may be unusable for several reasons including the desire to capture critical geographic areas or important facilities intact; (25) the possibility that severe disruptions in command/control may prevent units and subunits from calling for nuclear fire; and because nuclear weapons may be severely attrited by NATO and hence not available to support all ground forces. Thus, "conventional" forces and equipment are as essential to the Soviet nuclear war-fighting posture as they are to a nonnuclear capability.

In addition, the Soviets require conventional capabilities to further policies in nonnuclear crisis situations, both in Europe and in other areas of the world such as the Middle East. In fact, the importance of conventional capabilities for waging local wars, which are the wars of greatest significance to the Soviets in advancing the spread of socialism or preventing its rollback, was demonstrated most visibly and with the greatest impact by the Middle East wars of 1967 and 1973 and the invasions of Hungary in 1956 and Czechoslovakia in 1968. Nuclear weapons would probably be used in these types of counterrevolutionary or national liberation wars only if another nuclear power were involved, since in these instances Soviet conventional strength is usually more than adequate.

The broad rationale for "conventional" capabilities is very well summarized in the second (1969) edition of Methodological Problems of Military Theory and Practice, as follows:

All these (conventional) means preserve their value because of a number of reasons. In the first place wars without the utilization of nuclear weapons are possible. In the second place, if nuclear weapons will be used, then with their help it is not possible to solve all problems of armed combat; one cannot, for example, occupy the enemy's territory. Thirdly, on some objectives the utilization of nuclear weapons can be simply inadvisable. One must take into account that the utilization of a nuclear weapon under certain circumstances can interfere with the actions of our own troops. Finally, many conventional forms of weapons can be used very effectively for the annihilation of nuclear means of the enemy. (26)

Further, to ensure that the Soviet military do not misinterpret the development of conventional capabilities and discussions of conventional conflict that emerged in the mid-1960s, guidance was presented in a December 1968 article in Communist of the Armed Forces by the well-known Soviet military theoretician, Colonel V.M. Bondarenko, Candidate of Philosophical Sciences.

The second circumstance (errors in understanding the "revolution in military affairs") is a more serious one. It is involved with the fact that in our times conditions may arise when in individual instances combat operations may be carried out using conventional weapons. Under these conditions, the role of conventional means and the traditional services of armed forces are greatly increased. It becomes necessary to train troops for various kinds of warfare. This circumstance is sometimes interpreted as a negation of the contemporary revolution in military affairs as its conclusion.

One cannot agree with this opinion. The point is that the new possibilities of waging armed struggle have arisen not in spite of, but because of the nuclear missile weapons. They do not diminish their combat effectiveness, and the main thing, they do not preclude the possible use of such weapons. All this forces the conclusion that the present situation is one of the moments in the revolution in military affairs. It flows out of this revolution, continuing it, instead of contradicting it.

On the basis of this, we are able to define the contemporary revolution in military affairs as a radical upheaval in its development, which is characterized by new capabilities of attaining political goals in war, resulting from the availability of nuclear missile weapons to the troops. (27)

Parallel to the nuclear revolution, improvements in conventional arms were also made - in rifles, air defense, antitank means, armored vehicles and so forth. As noted earlier, these improvements are not, however, intended simply for conventional warfare. At the same time, the Soviets have put considerable effort into providing for a nonnuclear or conventional combat option in a NATO context. We can infer this from the fact that a major portion of Soviet military science is directed toward understanding the nature of future nonnuclear war and that of the enemy's forces, capabilities and strategies.   In 1961, the United States adopted the flexible response policy - a policy which involved an initial conventional phase, with a subsequent shift to nuclear use when it becomes apparent that vital areas or forces are in jeopardy.   The expansion in Soviet military thinking in the mid- to late 1960s to provide for a war that would begin conventionally, and later involve the use of nuclear weapons was an accommodation to that United States shift in policy (and that of NATO in 1967).

The timing of that change in NATO strategy is suggested in a 1966 Voyennaya mysl' article on "The 'Nuclear Threshold' in NATO Strategy" in reference to the December 1962 Nassau conference between Kennedy and Macmillan. (28) The article references a London Times article from the summer of 1963 in which Kennedy was cited as stating that a shift in NATO strategy from nuclear to conventional emphasis would take place, although there was a recognition in the Kennedy Administration that no amount of buildup in conventional capabilities would enable NATO to back off too far from a nuclear strategy.   The Soviet recognition and interest was clearly expressed in Voyennaya mysl' in 1964.

> Under certain conditions of a war the strategic air force may be a most dependable and effective means of augmentation of strategic efforts. This may be especially true when the enemy has started the war without resorting to nuclear weapons.   In such a case the augmentation of efforts will mainly take the same form as in past wars, by the use of conventional weapons. (29)

It was stated, further, in 1967 that,

> ...in recent years, foreign military theoreticians have expressed their thoughts more and more often on the possibility of the unleashing of war in Europe without the use of nuclear weapons. For example, the military-political leadership of the United States and the North Atlantic Alliance proposes that the conception of "forward defense" and the strategy of "flexible response" on the whole must be based on the use not only of nuclear but also of conventional weapons. Hence the quite firm stand on the variant whereby a world war can be unleashed and waged for some time only with conventional means of conflict, and nuclear weapons will be used sometime in the course of military operations. (30)

The editor of Voyennaya mysl' made his point in 1969:

> The NATO strategists are also able to conduct a so-called war by stages, in which the means of armed conflict are to be put into operation in sequence. In the first stage, the use of "sufficient non-nuclear forces" is specified, in the second stage, tactical nuclear

weapons, and in the third stage, strategic missile means. If such a
war occurs, a constant increase in strategic pressure and a multiple
change in the nature, scales, methods, and forms of military
operations will be characteristic of it.   Its culminating point
coincides with the moment of transfer to the mass use of strategic
nuclear weapons.   In light of this, war by stages constitutes a
variation of general nuclear war. (31)

This is then, really, a variant of nuclear war. This is important because
in the Soviet literature, nonnuclear conflict is a phase, not a whole war.
    The Soviet study of this conventional phase has focused largely on
the lessons of the Great Patriotic War. It is, however, recognized that
there are limits to that approach because of crucial disparities between
the conventional war fought in the 1940s and a future phase of such a
war fought under threat of nuclear use. The opposing sides' views of the
conventional phase must be reiterated as a further distinction: the
Soviets place priority emphasis on the nuclear transition, treating the
conventional aspects of the war merely as a phase; the West, on the
other hand, stresses the conventional defense in a largely conventional
war, treating the nuclear means as a deterrent or as a threat to be
unleashed only as a last resort when conventional containment fails.
The Soviet approach to the conventional phase is conditioned by the
recognition that the war can go nuclear at any instant.
    Thus, Soviet descriptions of the conventional phase are astonishingly
similar to those of the nuclear war, with only the nuclear rhetoric
excised. As indicated earlier, reserves are handled similarly, the front is
porous in both cases, major force engagements are avoided, the primary
targets are always the nuclear means and command/control, and
surprise is equally critical and employed to achieve the requisite
correlation of forces without major mobilization.   In brief, the
conventional phase is designed with transition to nuclear war foremost
in mind and as a result, ends up looking very much like a nuclear attack
-- apart from the absence of nuclear weapons and the increased use of
artillery and especially tactical air to compensate for the lack of
nuclear firepower.

The Nature of the "Conventional" Expansion

While there was a brief period of time in the late 1950s and early 1960s
when it appeared that the Soviets emphasized nuclear weapons to the
detriment of conventional forces, the mid-1960s terminated this phase
with the clear conclusion that multimillion armies would be as
important in future wars as they had been in the past.
    One flaw in our perception of the threat to Europe is that the
Soviets appear to have cut back their armies in the late 1950s, with the
result that their subsequent expansion in the late 1960s and 1970s seems
magnified. One explanation for that cutback is that the Soviets were
facing a manpower shortage in the late 1950s and early 1960s as a result

of the decline in birth rate during World War II. As pointed out by Dr. William F. Scott, the number of 18-year-old Soviet males eligible for the draft fell from over two million to under one million in the period from 1957-1963. (32) Hence, a large army in this time period may have been considered impossible, especially considering the emphasis Khrushchev had placed on building up the Soviet economic and technical base, a task which also required great numbers of people.

It is also possible that the cutback in force levels was the result of a temporary emphasis on a policy of nuclear deterrence. The Soviets' first military priority at that time was clearly in the strategic missile field - IRBMs, MRBMs, ICBMs, SLBMs, and so forth. To this end was probably devoted virtually all research, development, test and acquisition funds and technical people in the early to mid-1960s. Evidence of this is available in a 1965 Voyennaya mysl' article on military economics in which it is explained that "the production of nuclear-missile weapons requires greater budgetary appropriations for the solution of complex laboratory design problems," (33) and conventional weapons development receives a "considerably lesser amount of materials and fuel as a whole." At the subsequent Twenty-third Party Congress, the accomplishments of the Strategic Missile Force and atomic missile submarines were referred to as "titanic work," implying that vast resources were vital to their development.(34)

Thus, a cutback may also have been a necessity - a temporary expedient - which Khrushchev sought to cover with his nuclear war scare pronouncements. At the same time, the cutback had some important advantages. For example, it enabled Khrushchev to carry out substantial "weeding" of the military - thus eliminating "unproductive officers" including personnel who were unable mentally to make the transition from World War II-type thinking to that required for the revolution in military affairs. The cutback also provided a deception means by which Khrushchev could show the West that Russia had changed and was intent on peaceful coexistence, and that it would behoove the West to embrace these changes and remove trade restrictions with the Soviet Union and Eastern European nations.

In 1961, the Soviets clearly recognized the need for mass, well-equipped land and air forces. And, in the mid-1960s, when sufficient draftees were once more available, the Soviets began to expand and modernize completely all forces. Since then, approximately 150,000 men have been added to the Soviet forces in Eastern Europe, including 70,000 men and five divisions deployed in Czechoslovakia since 1968. (35) During their modernization drive, the Soviets have introduced in quantity new high-quality fighting equipment including: two modern tanks (The T-62 and T-72); armored self-propelled artillery (122mm and 152mm); antitank guided missiles; armored personnel carriers (APCs), including airborne combat vehicles (BMDs); amphibious combat vehicles (BMPs) that combine the features of light tanks; APCs and guided missile carriers; armored reconnaissance vehicles (BRDMs); attack helicopters, including the heavily armed MI-14 HIND and MI-8 HIP, and massive quantities of mobile air-defense capabilities, both guns (S-60/57 and ZSU-23/4) and missiles (SA-4, SA-6, SA-7, SA-8 and SA-10). (36)

The Soviet Frontal Aviation now includes 16 air armies, of which four are located in Eastern Europe. These forces have also undergone extensive modernization with late-model MIG-21s (FISHBED), MIG 23s and 27s (FLOGGER-B and D), SU-17s (FITTER), and SU-19s (FENCER). Nearly 80 percent of the fighter/attack elements in Frontal Aviation are now made up of these four aircraft, providing the Soviet forces with a significant new capability to conduct deep-air and interdiction missions employing nuclear or conventional munitions, and to attack high-value targets such as command centers, nuclear storage sites and systems, stockpiles of ammunition and equipment, and lines of communication including naval ports and airbases critical to logistic supply. (37)

While the overall size of the general purpose forces portion of the navy has remained constant, the ships have been steadily replaced with modern versions including one KIEV-class light ASW carrier (with two more under construction), two MOSKA-/class ASW helicopter ships, and 230 other surface combatants. The Soviets have also acquired a long-range ocean-going amphibious assault capability that includes numerous ships and approximately 12,000 naval infantry. (38)

These and many more improvements do not represent mere modernization, a "significant uprgrade," or, as portrayed in the West, those of a conventional or general purpose force nature. Rather, they signify the development of a true offensive, combined arms, and nuclear war-fighting capability. This is most visibly represented by the additions to nondivisional combat capability (at Army and Front levels), improvements in logistics support capabilities that now enable them to sustain a high-speed attack, and command/control improvements. The interest in nuclear war fighting has continued - even intensified - up through the present time. As explained in the prestigious Soviet Military Historical Journal in 1978:

> ...on preparation for and conduct of a battle by combined arms formations...the principal attention is now being devoted to theoretical development and practical testing, in the course of tactical exercises, of new procedures and methods of combat use of men and equipment in conditions involving the use of nuclear weapons. (39)

The article stresses new methods of accomplishing breakthroughs, increased depth of fire and combat missions, operations by formations separated from the main forces, use of forward detachments and airborne troops, and so forth, all in a nuclear context. More specifically:

> Use of nuclear weapons and change in the nature of enemy defenses have made it possible to perform a breakthrough at lower tactical densities of men and equipment than is the case for combat activities involving conventional weapons alone.

...It has become possible to make the main strike against the strongest grouping in the enemy defenses and attain the goal of the battle within a short time.

...Increasingly greater use of nuclear weapons and active battle against enemy nuclear weapons are becoming typical traits of combined arms formation defense.(40)

On the basis of the material examined, it is believed that the expansion in Soviet "conventional" capabilities which has caused increasing concern in the West in recent years does not represent a shift in emphasis regarding the nature of the conflict - nuclear to conventional - but rather is a shift to or realization of a true war-fighting, dual-purpose, offensive, preemptive capability. With this perspective in mind, the Soviet book The Offensive takes on a very different character, and the main emphasis on "combat readiness" introduced by Marshal Grechko in the 1970s becomes more understandable. Moreover, this realization may serve to clarify issues that the massive Soviet military improvements have raised even in official documents and that led the United States Secretary of Defense in 1978 to conclude that "...the Soviets may be less well intentioned than we would wish them to be." (41) Insofar as a major war in Europe is concerned, the Soviet threat is at present as much nuclear as it was in the mid-1960s, except that it now possesses significantly greater credibility.

Advantages of a Conventional Phase

Another aspect of the Soviet interest in a conventional phase - as opposed to conventional war - involves the undoubted advantages which can accrue from it. These advantages - stated most forcefully in the Soviet literature from the late 1960s through the 1970s - all relate to the problems inherent in an initial nuclear strike; that is, in transitioning from a "peacetime" posture to that of a high-speed nuclear offensive. In general terms, a conventional phase enables the Soviets to execute more effectively the transition, initiate an attack, launch a surprise nuclear strike and exploit it.

Numerous specific benefits that may be derived from a conventional phase are discussed in the Soviet literature. While it is assumed that the majority of these would accrue to the Soviets, there is a recognition that some would also apply to NATO. First, a conventional phase enables the Soviets to increase their readiness by providing time and "cover" to bring nuclear weapons forward from the rear areas.

Such a beginning of war can create favorable conditions for the movement of all nuclear forces to the regions of combat operations, bringing them to the highest level of combat readiness, and subsequently inflicting the first nuclear strike with the employment in it of a maximum number of missile-launch sites, submarines and aircraft at the most favorable moment. (42)

Second, a conventional phase gives the Soviets time to conduct massive reconnaissance flights to reacquire the targets which were lost as NATO dispersed prior to the war, and consequently execute a much more effective initial strike.   Moreover, under "cover" of the conventional conflict, the strike can be accomplished with greater surprise.

> ...the movement of nuclear forces into regions of combat operations will be conducted in conditions of constant and active counter-measures of the defending side.

> It is necessary to insure not only secrecy in bringing nuclear means to the regions of combat operations, but also constant protection of them from enemy strikes and secrecy in maximum speed in the preparation of the first strike.

> The skillfully organized struggle against reconnaissance, the sup-pression of his radio-technical means, especially early detection systems, false and deceptive operations, and other measures can have a decisive influence on achievement of surprise in switching to combat operations with the unlimited use of nuclear weapons. (43)

This principle is restated in the Military Historical Journal in 1978: "Highly important principles have been developed in the course of Soviet strategy's development: constant readiness. . .; decisive mass-ing. . .; covert preparations for and conduct of surprise strikes during repulsion of aggression;. . .(44)

Third, a conventional phase allows the Soviets time and cover to increase the survivability of their forces - in particular, by moving naval forces out of ports and into the broad ocean area where they would be much less vulnerable and by dispersing air forces.

It is recognized that while the Soviet forces are close to West Germany, they are not as well positioned to exploit a nuclear strike as they would be if they were already in West Germany, had actual knowledge of the defense posture, and were in possession of many critical features of the terrain.   A conventional phase, therefore, provides the opportunity to move first-echelon forces well into West Germany through the NATO screening defense and test the nature of the main forward defenses. Only then are they in a position to identify the targets for operational-tactical nuclear strikes to facilitate the breakthrough and to rapidly exploit the nuclear strike.(45)

A less immediately realizable advantage of a conventional phase discussed in the Soviet literature is the additional time it provides for mobilizing the economy and placing it on a strict military footing. (46) This could help to prepare for the possibility of an escalation to world nuclear war.

It has been shown the Soviets place considerable emphasis on airborne operations. Assault units are to be inserted into NATO's rear areas for numerous purposes including sabotage, seizure of critical features of the terrain, destruction of command/control/communica-tions facilities, capture of airbases and critical political-administrative control points (i.e., governments), and reconnaissance of NATO nuclear capabilities. It take time to insert these units, put them into operation, enable reconnaissance teams to report back, and prepare for the exploitation. A conventional phase provides the Soviets with the time required to reap the benefits of these operations before the war goes nuclear.

Perhaps most important is the opportunity provided by the conventional phase to improve further the correlation of forces in the Soviets' favor by attrition of NATO nuclear forces and command control (47) and disrupting NATO's rear, while simultaneously increasing the survivability and combat readiness of their own forces. The success of these attacks - especially on NATO's nuclear means (48) - is viewed as a critical determinant of the likely winner following the transition to nuclear war.

Transition to Nuclear Operations

Because the initial nuclear strike is regarded as a decisive determinant of the course of the war, considerable thought and analysis will be reflected in the decision to transition to nuclear operations. One of the most important assessments in this regard pertains to the impact of the initial strike on the nuclear correlation of forces. (49)

> ...the correlation of forces in a nuclear war remains one of the most important criteria by which it is possible to judge the success of combat operations, and also to select the most expedient variants of the operations. (50)

> ...the best variant of a nuclear strike is the one which ensures the greatest correlation of forces in our favor after the strike is delivered. (51)

Soviet calculations of the correlation of forces must take into account various factors: the readiness of enemy forces, the number of enemy forces acquired and targeted, the readiness of Soviet forces, and the survivability of Soviet forces, or as they put it, the probability of "nondestruct" at launch. Following a consideration of these variables, the advantages of a conventional phase and the difficulties in launching a strike at the beginning if NATO has moved to a full alert posture are apparent.

Another basic military consideration associated with a Soviet decision to initiate nuclear operations is the determination to preempt any large-scale NATO use. The detection of any such NATO preparation, therefore, is a top-priority task of Soviet military intelligence. The case of a limited NATO use is far less certain because of other Soviet considerations - in particular, the readiness of their own forces to carry out and exploit a simultaneous strike. If this readiness is insufficient, the Soviets might ignore a small-scale NATO use, or respond in kind while striving to mislead NATO regarding Soviet intentions to launch and exploit a mass simultaneous nuclear strike. This, however, would not be a desired condition; the Soviets would far rather preempt any NATO actions through a surprise attack.

The critical question remains: When and how the transition to nuclear means will occur?   The length of the conventional phase as discussed in the Soviet literature is described variously as very short, a few days, "as much as 4-5 days,"(52) and "for some time." (53) These discussions are difficult to interpret because to a certain extent they appear in analyses of Western exercises and thought and may not necessarily reflect Soviet strategy. For example, in the 1970s the West has observed a tendency to prolong a conventional phase in Soviet exercises.   To what extent does this merely "correspond" to Soviet perceptions of NATO strategy? The following 1969 statement regarding NATO exercises by the editor of Voyennaya mysl' suggests a possible answer:

> First on the duration of the non-nuclear operations. This is an extremely important question the answer to which is of great importance, because it predetermines the resolution of many other missions involving the conduct of military operations. The duration of this stage depends on many factors, and in particular on the capability of both sides to continue the struggle without the use of nuclear weapons. Usually at NATO training exercises, the duration of the non-nuclear stage depended on the capability of the troops to hold the advance defensive line. Recently the tendency to increase its duration has begun to appear, and it is possible to conduct large-scale operations in the course of this stage. (54)

Implicit in the quote is the recognition that either side's decision to go nuclear will be strongly influenced by its ability to continue the struggle without the use of nuclear weapons. It follows that the Soviets should be expected to transition when a Soviet conventional breakthrough appears imminent. According to NATO strategy and exercises, NATO would go nuclear either in response to a Soviet first use or to avert such a breakthrough and subsequent capture of significant territory or forces. For example, as stated by the United States Secretary of Defense in 1977:

> In structuring U.S. nuclear forces, attacks in Central Europe or in Korea are considered the most likely to call for backup. A decision to use tactical nuclear weapons would depend upon (1) an enemy conventional breakthrough which could not be countered, or (2) his first use of nuclear weapons. (55)

The critical time for this breakthrough would be early, perhaps even toward the end of the first day of combat. This would also be a natural point for the Soviets to decide to go nuclear from the standpoint of their own force survivability, because it is at that precise juncture that the decision to commit the second-echelon armies would need to be made. Those are the forces that complete the victory, destroy the opponent's forces and consolidate the gains. The first-echelon forces make the breakthrough and proceed immediately into NATO's rear to seize their first strategic objectives, leaving the problem of developing the breakthrough and destroying the forward NATO forces to the second-echelon forces. During the initial conventional phase, these second-echelon forces would be very carefully concealed and maneuvered so as to prevent NATO from striking them with nuclear weapons. (56) When they become committed and move forward, they become highly vulnerable to NATO nuclear attacks. Hence, a logical point of transition is just before the NATO decision to go nuclear is communicated and when the Soviet initial strike would be most exploitable, i.e., following the breakthrough. By this time, strong points of NATO resistance (targets) would also have been identified and could be attacked to assist the breakthrough in sectors of the front where the Soviet advance had been halted.

There is a tendency in the West to believe that NATO will be able to opt for first use of nuclear weapons, and that if the Soviets should prove successful conventionally, they would continue in that mode and not risk nuclear war. Neither belief seems to be supported in the Soviets' military literature; neither takes into account the great importance they attach to surprise.

> The successful beginning and development of combat operations by conventional means of destruction by one of the sides and the quickly growing danger of use of nuclear weapons by the other side might force the one side to abandon operations only by conventional means considerably before it succeeds in resolving the outlined minimum of missions despite the favorable premises for this. Finally, the duration of operations with the use of just conventional means can be sharply decreased for the purpose of achieving greater surprise of a nuclear strike and faster destruction of the enemy. (57)

The Soviets' approach to transitioning is conditioned by four major factors. The first factor is that the war will most likely go nuclear. The second is that it is necessary to strike first and be ready to initiate nuclear operations "at the drop of a hat." All nuclear forces are to be continuously ready with targets designated, and army and navy forces have missions assigned with possible rapid transition in mind. The third is that the time to transition is that which is determined to be the "most favorable time." (58) There is no suggestion of waiting as long as possible, prolonging the conventional phase, or waiting until NATO is determined to initiate nuclear operations; of all the variables, the Soviet assessment of the relative results of the nuclear battle would appear to be the most dominant aspect of the military input (both for and against) to that strategic decision. The fourth aspect of their approach is the maximum effort to mislead and otherwise deceive NATO so as to achieve maximum surprise. The crucial question is: When is "the most favorable time"?

THE CHEMICAL WARFARE OPTION*

Between the "conventional" and "nuclear" options is another dimension of Soviet capability and strategy that is often neglected in Western studies of the Soviet and Warsaw Pact threat to NATO. This is the chemical warfare (CW) option, (59) an area in which the Soviets recently have grown increasingly interested - perhaps because of the unique advantages it provides as a result of the asymmetry in United States/Soviet chemical warfare capabilities. This asymmetry has become so serious that by 1979, it had become one of the most lopsided among all the United States/Soviet capability comparisons. The Soviets have an overwhelming superiority in all aspects of CW capabilities - munitions stockpiles, testing facilities, training activities, equipment, personnel and force structure. Furthermore, the Western attitude about this facet of preparedness is characterized by widespread apathy and repugnance, while the Soviet attitude, as in other endeavors, is one of serious concern, focused on the need to develop a war-fighting capability and readiness for chemical warfare. This asymmetry in effect invites Soviet use of chemical warfare agents in a theater conflict and makes its assessment in Soviet strategy all the more important - rivaling that of Soviet command and control.

Chemical weapons are unique among modern weapons in that they impact only on living targets - that is, they kill people without destroying physical facilities or equipment. There are several types of chemical warfare agents, with widely differing properties. Some are colorless, some odorless; others can be seen, as, for example, in an approaching cloud, and some can be detected by their characteristic smell. Some are quickly dissipated and lose their effectiveness in a few minutes; others persist - or can be made to persist - for several hours; and the more persistent agents, either by nature or by the addition of thickeners, can last for several days or more, depending on the atmospheric conditions.

Chemical weapons are basically area munitions; they affect anyone who is not properly protected both at the time of agent delivery to the area or, as in the case of the more persistent agents, anyone who subsequently enters the area without proper protection. The extent of lethal areas depends on the type and number of munitions employed - with several munitions normally used to "blanket" the area of interest - and on a number of outside factors, such as weather, terrain, local vegetation, etc. Areas that can be efficiently attacked with a single salvo of a few rounds of the larger weapons, i.e., bombs and missiles, may be roughly the size of a major logistics area depot or airbase, and areas which might be attacked with a few battalion volleys of artillery might be the size of an antitank defense position.

Effectiveness of CW munitions is also quite sensitive to the

---

*Based on research conducted jointly with Ms. Amoretta M. Hoeber.

readiness of the unit under attack. Such readiness involves the use of individual and group protective equipment, decontamination capabilities, and, of exceptional importance, training in the use of available equipment. Chemical warfare is unique in that considerable protection and readiness to cope with the resulting environment, while technically and physically demanding, can be achieved at relatively low cost. The measures that need to be undertaken, however, are often cumbersome and inconvenient; no one likes the idea of having to remain inside special clothing and to wear gas masks while fighting a war - unless perhaps they understand the threat and want to survive.

The Soviet Union has invested heavily in all aspects of offensive munitions, protective equipment, specialized personnel, and widespread training and indoctrination. They have a wide variety of agents deliverable by all major launchers - artillery, multiple rocket launchers (MRL), tactical (FROG) and operational-tactical missiles (SCUD), air-delivered bombs, and spray tanks.

Chemical warfare preparedness is designed into most modern Soviet-combat vehicles including the newer tanks, armored personnel carriers, combat vehicles (BMPs, BRDMs), and support vehicles such as missile transporters, command vehicles, air defense (SAM) vehicles and even trucks. There is available considerable individual protective equipment and specialized equipment for decontamination. Soviet soldiers all possess personal masks, reusable protective clothing, chemical detectors and "effective" atropine-based compound syringe antidotes. Such capabilities cannot be assumed to be merely defensive; they are designed and deployed for use as part of the Soviet offensive capability, i.e., to enable Soviet troops to exploit the results of the employment of their own chemical weapons. Chemical defense units are organic to every Soviet command from front to regiment. Smaller units, even those of company size, are assigned special chemical troops. There are scores of Soviet generals prepared for chemical warfare and some 70,000-100,000 full-time chemical warfare officers and men. Training in the use of equipment for the purpose of fighting during chemical attack is standard and is emphasized in all individual and unit training which, as a further indication of their seriousness, includes operating in live nerve-agent environments.

As expressed by top level United States Army officials: "The Soviets are so immersed in chemical weaponry, tactics, doctrine, equipment and personnel, and so much of their training centers around the use of lethal agents, that it would be odd, from a military standpoint, if they did not employ them." (60)

Soviet use of chemicals must be considered likely - not only in a nuclear war, but also in a conventional war, a possibility that until recently has been discounted or ignored. Against all the major Soviet targets in Europe - NATO antitank defense, NATO nuclear capability, including command and control, NATO reserves, and NATO tactical air - chemical weapons offer important advantages that complement rather than duplicate the effectiveness of both conventional and nuclear weapons. Barring a good protective posture, fast-acting, nonpersistent agents, such as hydrogen cyanide delivered by multiple rocket launchers, coupled with normal artillery preparation and smoke delivery can effectively neutralize NATO antitank defenses within a few minutes without inhibiting Warsaw Pact armor operations.   Should nuclear weapons not be used, chemical weapons with persistent agents would likely be very important in disabling NATO nuclear capabilities, such as airbases and nuclear supply depots. A few repeated strikes with persistent agents could put unprotected NATO bases out of action for extended periods of time.   Many command/control targets - radars, ground control stations, navigation transmitters, and so forth - are neither large enough to warrant a nuclear strike nor vulnerable enough to ensure destruction with one sortie of conventional munitions. For the destruction of such targets, generally unprotected against chemical agents, chemical weapons may be the most efficient means in a nuclear or conventional context.   Finally, the movement of NATO reserves, already a severe problem given their deployment, could be seriously impeded by the application of the more persistent chemical weapons to block important transportation routes.

The considerable effectiveness of CW weapons in disabling particular forces and contaminating particular areas would not depend merely upon lethal doses of chemicals being delivered over the entire target.   Sublethal-dose areas that can impose physically disabling effects will extend well beyond the lethal-dose areas. These sublethal effects, for example the optical pain and miosis (61) caused by very small doses of nerve agent, will prevent or seriously degrade the performance of missions such as aiming, sighting, instrument reading and flying.   In this manner, the effectiveness of these weapons is increased well beyond the usual estimates that are based only on effects in the lethal areas.

In general, chemical weapons offer very significant advantages to the Soviets in any kind of war, nuclear or conventional.   Considering those advantages - many of which are a result of the "marginal" United States/NATO preparedness either to cope with CW employment or to subject the Soviets to the same environment throughout the depth of their offensive deployment - it is difficult to believe that the Soviets would not capitalize on their capabilities in any major conflict in Europe. The benefits to be derived - disabling NATO tank defenses, paralyzing NATO nuclear capabilities, rendering inaccessible logistics areas and equipment depots, and hence greatly shortening the war - are far greater than any additional incremental risk associated with their employment over that of the basic war itself.   It is assessed that chemical warfare agents would be employed by the Warsaw Pact forces very early in a war with NATO and that their use is an important element of Soviet strategy for war in Europe.

ESCALATION TO INTERCONTINENTAL WAR

Any consideration of the prospects for limiting a nuclear war to a critical theater such as Europe must attempt to answer a most critical question: Will the war escalate to all-out world nuclear war? Put in another way, can nuclear weapons be used by the United States or NATO to counter Soviet aggression in Europe, or, would their use inevitably lead to a general nuclear war?

This is a difficult question to address, first, because of the missions initially associated with theater nuclear deployments; second, because of Alliance considerations; and third, because of the relative paucity of Soviet literature about the issue and the ever-present problem of mirror imaging our own logic in interpreting what little there is that is relevant. No one can "prove" in advance the abstract proposition either that nuclear war in Europe can be limited or that it cannot. But sound strategic analysis always involves judgments concerning what appears probable in specific situations and under concrete circumstances that change over the course of time. The following discussion will serve to highlight the reasons why the Soviet leaders might well view the European situation in a very different light from the way they conceived it 20 or even 10 years ago.

Evolutionary Problems of Decoupling

The first of the problems cited above may well have originated in the early 1950s when the United States decided that it could ill-afford to prepare to wage a number of localized wars whenever and wherever the Soviet Union chose to start them, that any war other than a local skirmish would trigger a general nuclear war with the Soviet Union, and that consequently the United States would, in effect, prepare only for war with the Soviet Union. Although there is some question as to whether this was declaratory bluff or action policy, the development and deployment of United States nuclear capabilities in the 1950s appear to have been regarded as confirmation of this "massive retaliation" policy. As observed by Dr. Henry Kissinger in 1960: "Current military policy still holds the view that any aggression involving the Soviet Union or Communist China is general war, by definition, which will bring our retaliatory force into play at the outset." (62) At the time, this view was probably held by the Soviet Union as well.

In the mid-1950s, many of the United States strategic forces were deployed mainly in the one theater whence they could pose the most salient threat to the Soviet Union. Thus, the European theater became the center stage in the strategic nuclear play. This was perceived clearly by the Soviets, who understood that the United States transatlantic deployments were positioned to strike the Soviet Union.

It was not until the external strategic ICBMs clearly became the dominant force in the late 1960s that the setting grew favorable for the possibility of regional or theater nuclear war as distinct and separate from strategic global war.   Accordingly, West European strategic analysts who had thought that the NATO area was fairly secure in the era of United States strategic nuclear superiority, despite Warsaw Pact regional conventional capabilities, became increasingly apprehensive over the theater balance as the superpowers moved first toward "strategic parity" and then toward potential Soviet superiority.

Alliance Considerations

The second problem is associated with the fact that no one favors the prospect of having a nuclear war fought on his territory. As the danger of nuclear weapons use increases, the host country would immediately seek to broaden the geographic scope of the battleground.   This certainly presents a problem to both the United States and the Soviet Union, although much more so to the former, because of the political asymmetries between democratic and communist systems.   On both sides, however, it is difficult to discuss a limited nuclear war in Europe because the Europeans do not wish to see Europe become a battleground while the homelands of the major combatants remain sanctuaries.

When the United States sought to limit the scope of the nuclear battlefield in the late 1950s and early 1960s, the Soviets loudly proclaimed that the United States would not be immune. There appear to have been two principal Soviet motivations for that statement: first, to discourage United States or NATO efforts to strengthen NATO's hand within the theater; and second, to indicate that the United States was attempting to turn Europe into a nuclear battlefield while protecting its own territory.   The Soviets were trying to isolate the United States from Europe, and thus fracture NATO.   Fostering this suspicion in Europe has been one of the main objectives of Soviet political warfare since nuclear weapons were first introduced into that area in the mid-1950s.

This problem has further confused the issue of escalation, although many people, in reading through the fog of political rhetoric, appear to have reached the conclusion that neither the United States nor the Soviet Union is interested in escalating a European conflict into a general nuclear war.   The fundamental problem is not one of deployments, but rather, of weapons and targets. As President Kennedy stated during the Cuban Missile Crisis, the United States would look upon any missile fired from Cuba as though it were fired from the Soviet Union.   The idea that Soviet nuclear weapons, independent of where they are based, could be employed against NATO without any NATO (American, British or French) nuclear retaliation against the Soviet Union itself is basically repugnant to Europeans. In the eyes of West Europeans, such a concept lacks the elementary requirement of successful deterrence, for it gives the Soviets on a silver platter, as it were, the option of using nuclear weapons with impunity - with no need to fear retaliation.

To a large extent, this is an emotional problem and hence unlikely to be resolved. Moreover, it also serves as a red herring, drawing attention away from the more important aspects of the coupling problem. As indicated earlier, the issue serves mainly to isolate the United States and fragment the NATO alliance so as to diminish the prospects for combined action in time of war. Further, it shifts the attention away from two extremely critical questions. First, from the European perspective, is the distinction between theater and intercontinental war all that important? The Soviet objectives in both cases may be very similar - to seize and occupy a Europe that is as intact as possible. Second, from the United States perspective, is a theater war a dysfunctional way to start a global war because of the possible loss of surprise; that is, it can be used by the Soviets to "cover" preparations for a surprise strategic nuclear strike? Soviet military doctrine in the mid-1960s adopted the proposition that a global nuclear war could start in two ways - with a surprise attack or through escalation of a local war. Further, it has been noted that the Soviets emphasize the opportunities the conventional phase presents to cover preparations for nuclear war and therefore the more effectively to execute a surprise attack -both in the theater nuclear and in the intercontinental nuclear contexts. Perhaps the main dangers for NATO in strategy formulation, force development and planning, are the sharp but shortsighted and artificial distinctions drawn between theater and world war, between conventional and nuclear war, and even between tactical or theater nuclear and strategic nuclear war.

Stated Soviet Interests

While the Soviets reiterate in their literature the likelihood of escalation from theater nuclear to global war, they also recognize certain important differences between those two types of war. Evidence of this has been found in the public Soviet response to the Schlesinger selective targeting strategy, as well as in the approach to tactics - an approach which emphasizes defensive operations in the theater but not in strategic operations.

> This does not mean that defense as a forced, temporary type of troop combat operation will not have a place in a future war. Our troops should study and master defense in order to master all forms of military operations. But here we are speaking of operational and tactical defense. Strategic defense and defensive strategy should be decisively rejected as being extremely dangerous to the country. (63)

Further evidence is derived from the principal goal of the Soviet Union which appears to be the avoidance of strategic, or general, nuclear war.

> The question of consequences of war is being restated in our time due to the possibility of employment of nuclear weapons. "Under

present-day conditions," stated Brezhnev, "a nuclear world war would result in hundreds of millions of deaths, in the destruction of entire countries, in contamination of the earth's surface and atmosphere. Communists must draw from this the most serious political conclusions. The struggle to prevent the threat of a new world war has now become one of the most important conditions for successfully fulfilling the tasks of building socialism and Communism, and development of the entire world revolutionary process." (64)

One of the clearest statements of Soviet interest in limiting war is contained in a critique of a Soviet book on war and peace in the mid-1960s, when the question of limited nuclear war was being carefully scrutinized. (65)   The author of the review is Lieutenant Colonel Rybkin, who is associated with the Lenin Political-Military Academy and thus speaks from the Party dimension of the military. Colonel Rybkin is often cited in Voyennaya mysl' and elsewhere for his noteworthy contributions to military literature. The book under review suggests that local wars initiated by the capitalists have as their goal the undermining of the world system of socialism, and further, that such wars can turn rapidly into worldwide nuclear war. These common propaganda themes come under illuminating criticism in Rybkin's review.

In the first place not every local war has the aim of directly undermining the world system of socialism. The imperialists conduct the majority of such wars against the national liberation movement. This, of course, indirectly damages the socialist camp insofar as it is a blow against the united front of progressive forces.

In the second place, historical experience has shown that only two local wars have turned into world wars.... The author says further that "it is entirely possible" that the aggressor will use nuclear weapons in a local war. This is a correct statement, but again it is doubtful that this would "immediately" turn the war into a world war. Everything depends upon the specific conditions. In any case, it is in the interests of the Soviet Union and all progressive mankind to put an end to the local war or to limit it and defeat the aggressor with limited forces. Solving this problem is one of the important tasks in developing military theory in its present stage. (66)

This concern about small-scale wars is also present in Sokolovskiy's Military Strategy.

Simultaneously with preparing for a decisive battle with the aggressor during a world war, the armed forces of the socialist camp must also be prepared for small-scale local wars which might be unleashed by the imperialists. The experience of such wars which have repeatedly arisen during the postwar period shows that they are conducted by ways and means which differ from those used in world wars. Therefore, Soviet military strategy calls for the study of the means for conducting such wars in order to prevent them from developing into a world war and to bring quick victory over the enemy. (67)

In comparing the available Soviet literature of the 1970s with that of the early and mid-1960s, one of the most noticeable differences appears to be a certain separation of strategic from theater war. Recent discussions on the conduct of theater operations (e.g., in The Offensive and The Basic Principles of Operational Art and Tactics) seems to be much more detached from strategic war than similar writings have been in the past.

It is suspected that one motive behind this shift has been the desire to decouple general nuclear warfare from theater warfare, primarily as a result of the Soviet achievement of strategic nuclear parity with the United States.

> The changing realities of the world situation are forcing the supporters of the "from-a-position-of-strength" policy to maneuver. They cannot avoid dealing with the main reality - the change in the correlation of forces in the world. (68)

> Even when compared with the very recent past the present international situation has important distinguishing features.

> First, the correlation of world forces has changed fundamentally in favor of socialism and to the detriment of capitalism. (69)

Throughout much of the 1960s, limited nuclear war was clearly to the Soviets' disadvantage as a result of obvious United States nuclear superiority. The United States nuclear threshold or firebreak appears to have been well recognized and accepted simply because the strategic balance of forces virtually dictated such a strategy. As long as United States strength gave it a clear superiority in limited theater nuclear war capability, such a war was undesirable for the Soviet Union.

Perhaps the most definitive Soviet statement on the advantages of superiority is in the 1969 edition of Methodological Problems of Military Theory and Practice, published by the Lenin Political-Military Academy. Outlined below is the relationship between strategic superiority and freedom of action within the theater.

> Military history teaches that only those tactical successes are durable which express the tendency of the overall superiority of one side over another. Analogous is the matter with the relationship of forces of troops which are conducting military actions of an operational nature or of a strategic scale.

> In this dialectical interconnection of various levels in the relationship of forces two important, moments focus attention on themselves. The first is that superiority in the relationship of forces of the higher level creates favorable conditions for the successful military actions of lower levels, and the possibility of supplying the superiority of forces in the military actions of a lower level

contributes to the change in the relationship of the forces of the higher level. (70)

The following focuses upon the importance of superiority at any level - strategic or theater.

> The determining role of the relationship of forces in the course of military actions is revealed in a general form in the ability of each of the battling sides to preserve its forces and to destroy the enemy's forces.   Superiority in numbers and equipment creates favorable real possibilities for active and decisive action on the enemy for the purpose of suppressing him and disrupting his combat formations, and the disorganization of all his activity. On the other hand a deficiency of forces substantially limits the combat actions of troops and deprives the commander of the possibility of imposing his will over the enemy.

> Superiority over the enemy creates conditions for a variety of combat actions, makes it possible to manifest flexibility in the creation of combat formations and operational organization of the troops, and the ways and forms of their effective utilizations; it enlarges the range for a combination of fire (nuclear strike) and maneuver,and also increases the effectiveness of the utilization of space, time and other factors included one way or another in military actions. (71)

As stated in Voyennaya mysl' in 1969:

> Superiority accelerates the process of the physical and moral defeat of the enemy and makes it possible to operate more daringly and decisively and to impose one's will on the enemy and to attack him more successfully. It promotes the development of flexibility in the selection of scales, forms and methods for coordinating the delivery of nuclear fires and air attacks with the maneuver of troops and increases the effectiveness of using space, time and other factors which influence the course of military operations. Conceivably, an obvious shortage of forces substantially limits capabilities for organizing the repulsing of the enemy. (72)

Simultaneously, there has been the gradual development in the Soviet literature of a theme that is faintly reminiscent of the United States literature in the 1950s wherein the Soviets refer to their nuclear forces as a nuclear sword and shield.

> The defensive might of the countries of the socialist community, the reliable shield of which is the nuclear potential of the Soviet Union, proved to be, and continues to prove to be, a deterrent to the aggressive circles of imperialism. (73)

> A cardinal change in the correlation between war and politics at the present time is that fact that the growth in the might of socialism

and other peace-loving forces, as well as the fact that the U.S.S.R. wields a mighty "nuclear sword," make it possible to check the forces of aggression: world war has ceased to be an inevitability. (74)

Despite the enormous disparity in meaning of statements issued by the Soviet Union and the United States, both countries' literature currently stresses the dangers of general nuclear war and, as a national objective, the need to prevent it. Should war develop in Europe, it is clearly in the interests of both parties to keep it from escalating into general nuclear war. While Europeans understandably resent any suggestion that the superpowers might try to limit a nuclear war to Europe, they also realize that Europe itself probably stands to suffer even more damage in a general nuclear war. Moreover, the Soviets vigorously challenge any approach that they believe would increase the "coupling" between theater and general nuclear war or that would lower the threshold for general nuclear war, which appears to be their interpretation of the Schlesinger selective targeting strategy.

Yet, there remains a strong if not dominant position in the Soviet Union that appears to connect theater nuclear war and intercontinental nuclear war. While one can attempt to separate these conflicting positions (on both sides) as declaratory and operational policies, this can be dangerous insofar as the two appear inextricably connected. Perhaps the lowest common denominator is that it is to the European, American and Soviet advantage first, to limit an actual war to whatever extent possible; second, to recognize that the risk of escalation to world nuclear war will be ever present — independent of declaratory statements to the contrary — and will grow with the conflict and its goals; third, to realize that Soviet military objectives in Europe may be very similar in both the global nuclear and major theater war contexts; and fourth, that it is the scenario which ultimately will determine the risk of escalation and whether the situation is coupled or decoupled. Without knowing the scenario, any assessment of the risks is strictly academic.

SUPERIORITY AND WAR INITIATION

Most analysts portray the Soviets as extremely conservative and therefore unlikely to start a major war or become directly involved in an armed confrontation with NATO or the United States. Although their military capability in Eastern Europe and the western military districts of the Soviet Union has been growing steadily, an attack on Western Europe is considered unlikely.

Perhaps a most critical question for the future is: To what extent has the past behavior of Soviet policy makers been conditioned by the Soviet Union's position of economic, political and military inferiority, and will they play a more active role should they really begin to perceive themselves as superior? All of our assumptions derived from historical evidence may need to be qualified to reflect this possible new condition of superiority.

In the past, the Soviets have not been adverse to taking risks; they demonstrated this in Berlin, Cuba, and to a lesser extent, the Middle East and Southeast Asia. Yet, in all cases, it would appear that the risks they were willing to take had definite limits. Furthermore, they have employed force in mass in Eastern Europe on several occasions - Hungary and Czechoslovakia being the best examples - in which the local correlation of forces was overwhelmingly in their favor.

Great concern has been focused on the correlation of forces and on turning it to the Soviets' favor. The drive for superiority - political, economic, scientific-technical, and military - has been a major Soviet preoccupation, not the least because it provides them with necessary flexibility of maneuver. At the same time, they are striving to curtail improvements to Western forces, which is one of the major objectives of their "peace strategy." They are by definition opposed to any development in the West that may undermine their position. One of the best such examples is usable theater nuclear forces that counter the traditional Soviet strength in ground forces.

The Soviets may recognize that encouraging the West to curtail unilaterally its own military programs is one of the best, if not the only means for the Soviets to attain superiority. They appear to have recognized what the West can accomplish if there is a "cause" - a Berlin, a bomber gap, a missile gap. They stand to reap enormous long-term benefits if they are careful in playing out their hand while encouraging arms control restraints. They need only examine the graph of United States strength deployed in Europe over time to note that the downward trend is only reversed following Soviet-instigated crises involving their use of armed force. The impact of Sputnik along with Khrushchev's rhetoric on delivering nuclear warheads anywhere on earth shocked the United States out of its self-imposed constraint, and opened the doors for long-range missile development, which had been previously blocked by the manned-bomber proponents within the United States Air Force. Apparent Soviet recognition of such events may have been one motive behind their concern over a possible United States awareness - beginning in 1975 - of a civil defense gap following its 15-year neglect of the subject. (75)   These lessons serve as well to increase the significance of surprise and the need to develop secret weapons and plans.

At present, major United States decision makers openly acknowledge the existence of strategic parity or equivalency; some are even beginning to recognize Soviet theater superiority - nuclear and conventional - as an accomplished fact. Of greater importance, however, is the Soviet perception of that correlation. Soviet assessments of the correlation of forces are not, as argued previously, deterrence oriented in the Western sense; rather, they are oriented toward war fighting. Included in such assessments are those factors that are most critical to war fighting - command/control, reconnaissance capability, countermeasures, rear area support, and the employment strategy itself. In contrast to Western perceptions, the Soviet drive is not limited simply to "mass" or to quantitative superiority, which perhaps has been achieved in some areas. Rather, it emphasizes qualitative as well as quantitative superiority - superiority that is available for selective, flexible or controlled use at all levels of conflict, nuclear and conventional, worldwide and local. Such "fingertip use" (76) is therefore not merely massive application of force, but includes perhaps more importantly, its political use or threat of use.

Such qualitative superiority has perhaps not yet been achieved, but when the Soviets believe it to be available, what behavior patterns, if any, will change? How will Berlin or Cuba be replayed in the future? This will be a crucial unknown to observe and evaluate over the next 10 to 20 years.

THE SCENARIO

Perhaps the single most important variable affecting the prospects for conventional war, limited or selective nuclear war and escalation, is the scenario. It is dangerous to attempt to foretell or even rationally hypothesize situations without a detailed understanding of the events that lead up to the conflict and the complete political, economic and military context of the scenario. Any assessment of what is likely or unlikely to happen is, of necessity, highly scenario dependent.

Former Secretary of Defense Schlesinger put it this way:

> ...doctrines control the minds of men only in periods of non-emergency. They do not necessarily control the minds of men during periods of emergency. In the moment of truth, when the possibility of major devastation occurs, one is likely to discover sudden changes in doctrine. (77)

Or, as expressed by the Soviets in 1971:

> During war, military doctrine withdraws somewhat into the background because in armed conflict they are guided primarily by military-political and military-strategic considerations and by the conclusions and generalizations which follow from the conditions of a specific situation. Consequently, war and armed conflict are guided not by doctrine, but by strategy. (78)

This theme can be traced back to Sokolovskiy's Military Strategy:

> The features of the interrelations between politics and strategy in time of war arise from the fact that in a war period the center of gravity of the political struggle is transferred from non-military to military form. Politics, it is said, "exchanges the pen for the

sword," and new relations and laws become operative. "Once the
military movements on land and on sea have been started, they are
no longer subject to the desires and plans of diplomacy, but rather to
their own laws, which cannot be violated without endangering the
entire expedition."

Pointing out the certain independence enjoyed by strategy, F. Engels
did not intend to stress its independence from politics. He only
warned that if policy violates or ignores the laws of military
strategy, this can lead to the defeat of the army and to the
destruction of the state. During a war, strategic concepts often
have a reverse effect on policy. Cases even arise when the military
factor acquires decisive significance. V. I. Lenin pointed out
during the Civil War in the U.S.S.R. that the outcome of the
revolution depended entirely on "who won" the Civil War.

Therefore, in time of war, politics must often conform its actions
with this fact: to what degree do these actions favor the
achievement of strategic results, which in the final analysis lead to
the accomplishment of political aims in war. Of course the
diplomatic and economic struggle does not stop in wartime, but
these forms of political struggle are entirely dependent on the
decisive form, that of armed conflict, and at times are also waged
by its means. (79)

In considering the importance of the yet unknown scenario on the
prospects for limited nuclear or conventional war, several points
warrant attention. First, the Soviets will probably seek to operate
within the limits of their political objectives.

A nuclear missile war consequently cannot go beyond the bounds of
politics, lose contact with it, lose its class-political content and
social character. At the same time it will unquestionably be in
many ways different in comparison with past wars, particularly as
regards its concrete political, class content and character, in means
and methods of warfare, as well as in its social, psychological, moral
and other consequences. (80)

Second, the major uncertainty of the scenario will lie in the political
decision to go to war. Given the scenario, the nature of the war will be
much less uncertain and most strongly influenced by military-strategic
considerations. These, in turn, will have had considerable influence on
the political decision to go to war, and therefore, should not be
underestimated. Unlike the United States, where the two orders have
traditionally been kept separate in theory and in practice, politics and
the military are closely integrated in the Soviet Union. As stated in
The People, the Army, the Commander:". . .the Communist Party and
Soviet government focus considerable attention on securing a unity of
political and military leadership."(81)
    This applies to the political decision as well which is made with a
thorough understanding of the military laws of war.

Leadership in war can be successful only if crucial decisions are in conformity with the demands of the laws of war; if the political party, government, and military command actively and vigorously alter to their country's advantage those conditions on the basis of which the laws of war are in effect; if political and military leaders are aware of the realistic potential for victory and intelligently transform this potential into actuality.

In order to ensure victory in war it is necessary to know not only its objective laws and to act in conformity with their demands, but also to observe those principles and fundamental rules of leadership in a war which derive from these laws. Political and military leaders who ignore these principles cannot count on victory by their armed forces. (82)

Third - and derived from those laws - the basic determinant, criterion, and objective for success both in peace and in war is a superiority in the correlation of forces, and particularly, the nuclear forces. (83) This is the law of the dependence of the course and outcome of the war on the correlation of military power. The Soviet objective is not equivalence or even superiority, but rather, a "preponderance of forces."

The law of relationship between the course and outcome of war and the correlation of military might of the belligerant nations enables a given country, depending on the forces and resources at its disposal, to select the most expedient methods and forms for military operations. The most important and decisive factor is the question of which side will be able to achieve both a quantitative and qualitative preponderance of forces over those of the adversary. (84)

The assessment of the correlation of forces is an essential input to the "political" process because it is one of the crucial factors that will influence the method and form of armed struggle in a future scenario.

Thus a principle of and essential condition for correct political leadership is scientific substantiation of plans and their conformity with the realistic capabilities of the belligerent nation. Ignoring this vital requirement leads to failure and defeat.

The experience of history and analysis of the present situation teach us that sober calculation of the correlation of forces between us and our adversary constitutes an important principle of leadership in a war. Correct calculation of the correlation of forces of the warring parties enables the political and military leadership to determine what is possible and what is impossible in the course of war, to foresee the adversary's probable actions and to select the most effective methods and forms of armed struggle under various conditions. (85)

The fourth likely component of the scenario consists of preemption, mass, in-depth strikes and surprise, particularly in the use of nuclear weapons - all central concepts in the Soviet strategy of survival and victory.

The last consideration is that nuclear weapons and the direction for their employment will be under the control of the top "political" authorities.

Despite such probable considerations, the actual scenario remains obscure. Yet, if there is a single dominating factor, it is believed to be the bilateral assessments by each party of the other's goals. Such evaluations may be extremely complex because of the different meanings attached to words such as doctrine, war, and so forth, unequal familiarity with concepts, radically different information base, highly varied nature of external influencing factors and pressure groups, and disparate analytical approaches to the problem. In short, both parties may simply arrive at an assessment "on faith" that a particular course of action is the most sensible path, coupled with the hope that the opposition agrees.

The definition of goals may serve to delineate the theater of operations, i.e., the geography of the conflict. If and when the geography is established, the pressure will be to strike first at all major acquired and even suspected targets. Anyone who has seriously grappled with the practical problems of limited nuclear war sooner or later seems to acknowledge the enormous problems, costs and risks associated with any known strategy which does not seek decisive effects in the first strike before all the uncertainties and unknowns pour forth. The decisive, mass, simultaneous, first nuclear strike either at the beginning or in the course of the war at the most favorable time is the simplest and cheapest approach known. There does not yet appear to be any accepted second approach in sight in Soviet doctrinal literature, or even in Western strategic writing, for that matter.

8 Conclusions and Issues for NATO

In terms of NATO's security interest in Europe, how should one view the major continuing Soviet expansion in military capabilities? This is the basic question today. While probably no one in the Western world can state with any degree of certainty what the Soviet intentions actually are, there are a few observations which appear to be particularly important as they relate to considerations of NATO strategy and force planning on the one hand, and to various arms control negotiations on the other.

The first point is that the Warsaw Pact forces are combined arms forces. The concept of combined arms emphasizes the use of all forces and especially the combination of nuclear firepower and maneuver - strike plus exploitation. This tends to be neglected in Western discussions because of the propensity to ascribe to Soviet capabilities the manner in which Western military thought is often structured - strategic nuclear, tactical nuclear and conventional. The placement of the Warsaw Pact forces in these categories ignores their crucial combined arms nature and the political context of the war in which they are to be employed.

While it is fashionable to speak of a conventional shift in Soviet strategy and a buildup in Soviet conventional capabilities, precious little evidence that would support unequivocally this contention has been identified in any of the material examined in the course of this study.. At best, there can be found an acknowledgement of a <u>possible conventional phase,</u> which is expected to undergo transition into nuclear war. Such a phase is therefore designed with this transition in mind, with instructions to keep to a minimum any effort expended on missions that do not directly contribute to the second and decisive nuclear phase. Further, if they would maintain proper perspective, Western analysts ought to recognize that the emerging dialogue on the possibility of a conventional phase still represents only a small portion of the Soviet military literature. An examination of the new equipment introduced since 1967 reveals little, if any, that is neither required nor designed for nuclear and chemical war. Moreover, in addition to the major developments in the so-called "conventional equipment," there have been equally, if not more impressive improvements in theater nuclear systems of all yields, ranges and delivery means and associated nuclear survivable command and control.

If there is a major change in the Soviet/Warsaw Pact capabilities, it is believed to be a long-term trend toward an effective, usable, preemptive offensive nuclear war-fighting capability. While in the late 1950s and early 1960s the Soviet forces may have been principally defense, deterrent or retaliation oriented, and indeed may have lacked the capability to undertake a major offensive operation due to logistics and other infrastructure limitations, that is no longer the case. From the mid-1960s to the present, the overall improvements have contributed to a basic upgrade in their capability to conduct an effective offensive campaign. It is expected that these improvements will continue and that over the next few years NATO will see further Warsaw Pact nuclear improvements at the tactical level matching those at the operational-strategic level. Moreover, such improvements will be integrated with requisite combined arms command and control and target acquisition capabilities and made effective down to the critical regimental level.

The aspects of the developing threat that appear to be especially underrated or often ignored in assessments of NATO vulnerabilities include: first, chemical warfare; second, counter-C_3I capabilities; third, the tactical nuclear balance; and fourth, Soviet C^3I. In the first area, impressive Soviet gains, coupled with noticeable NATO declines, have created not only major vulnerabilities, but also incentives for Soviet employment. The importance of this asymmetry bears heavily not only on nuclear warfare, but perhaps more directly on the conventional phase. Implicit in its assessments of the counter C^3I problem is a Western propensity to think only in terms of its electronic superiority, rather than in terms of the total integrated Soviet threat to NATO C^3I. That threat includes not merely electronic warfare capabilities, but also the use of chemical, conventional, nuclear and both airborne and ground-based assault forces, together with passive measures, including decoy, cover and deception techniques. The third area also requires a revision in Western thinking which for two decades has held to the notion of United States superiority. Conventional estimates that place the Soviet tactical nuclear stockpile in the range of 3,000 nuclear weapons may, indeed, be another serious underestimate of Soviet capability, as it fails to take fully into account the large expansion in Soviet theater nuclear capabilities referred to in the Soviet literature, the relative senescence of NATO capabilities, and the associated command and control that is essential to any effective employment. The fourth concerns the flexibility of Soviet attack planning and command and control. If the Soviet C^3I system eventually meets or even approaches its design criteria, it will provide the Soviets with a real-time battle management capability that can respond to rapid changes in the situation and direct the type of fast-pace porous war situation that modern technology — high-mobility forces and effective munitions, such as nuclear, precision guided and other — makes possible. This is another example in which the West leads in technology while the Soviets lead in having the capabilities in the field ready for war.

In examining the deployments of Soviet forces, it must be stressed that their critical capabilities are not limited to the NATO guidelines area or to Eastern Europe, but also exist throughout the Western military districts of the Soviet Union itself. Such capabilities of particular importance centered in the Soviet Union would include medium-range aviation, IRBMs, airborne assault forces, most of the second-echelon strategic forces, and especially, C^3I capabilities. Any assessment of the Warsaw Pact threat to NATO in the European area must include consideration of all those aspects of the threat that are deployed outside Eastern Europe.

In comparing Western discussion of NATO strategy with discussions of strategy in the Soviet literature, several important asymmetries emerge that may also warrant serious consideration. In Western discussions of NATO strategy, the NATO triad — strategic forces, tactical nuclear forces, and conventional forces — is stressed. The manner in which it is emphasized, however, raises some interesting questions. On the one hand, the United States continually emphasizes the need to focus on the conventional defense aspect. With equal fervor, the Europeans, particularly the West Germans, stress the need to focus on the strategic nuclear element. At the same time most NATO nations, while supporting the need for the tactical nuclear option, in effect strive to avoid it, deemphasize it and focus on other options. In contrast, to the extent that there is an emphasis in the Soviet strategy, it is on the nuclear offense.

A second and increasingly apparent distinction is that between NATO deterrent and Soviet war fighting strategies. The NATO strategy of deterrence was formulated during a period of overwhelming United States nuclear strength. This strength has now eroded to the point of rough equivalence, at best. The implications of this erosion need to be seriously addressed, particularly the distinctions between war fighting and deterrence, and the future role of external forces.

A third potential asymmetry that has appeared in the course of this study concerns the conventional phase, the advantages of that phase as perceived by the Soviet Union, and the question of when and how the war may go nuclear. A NATO strategy that emphasizes the need to meet conventional aggression with a conventional defense, that agonizes over the decision to go nuclear, that attempts to postpone that decision for as long as possible and that intends to employ nuclear weapons as a "last resort" means of warding off an imminent defeat, greatly facilitates the Soviet problem of transitioning and automatically passes to the Soviets the advantages that stand to be gained from a decisive first nuclear strike. It is difficult to see how such a NATO strategy could succeed when faced with a Soviet action strategy as described in their literature, practiced in their exercises, and for which their capabilities are designed and adequate.

Finally, in assessing NATO strategy in Europe, it should be recognized that coupling and decoupling is not likely to be a two-way process. While it is possible to conceive of a war in the theater that does not involve external strategic forces, the reverse does not seem to be true. A world war will undoubtedly encompass Europe and the Soviet strategies relative to Europe employed in such a war may not be too dissimilar from those discussed in the preceding pages. European defense requirements for world war are as important as those for theater war and as such are worthy of much closer attention than they have heretofore received.

In the past, the West has produced some great writers in the realm of military strategic theory. But with the growth of nuclear stockpiles and the assumptions of rational restraint that underlie the doctrine of deterrence, strategic theory has atrophied in the West, while it has continued to flourish within the Soviet Union. Such an asymmetry can prove fatally dangerous to the military preparedness and, in the long run, even to the political viability of NATO. It will not be enough for the governments of the Atlantic Allies to hope for the best - namely that rational decisionmaking will always prevail, as prescribed according to the canons of Western cost-benefit calculus. Rationality has a way of collapsing just when it is most taken for granted.

Notes

PREFACE

(1) W.T. Lee, The Estimation of Soviet Defense Expenditures, 1955-1975 (New York: Praeger, 1977); and Soviet Defense Expenditures in the 10th FYP," Osteuropa Wirtschaft, no. 4, 1977.

(2) For a discussion of the emerging capabilities, see John M. Collins, American and Soviet Military Trends since the Cuban Missile Crisis (Washington, D.C.: Center for Strategic and International Studies, Georgetown University, 1978).

(3) V.D. Sokolovskiy, Soviet Military Strategy, 3rd ed., ed. and trans. Harriet Fast Scott (New York: Crane, Russak, 1975), [hereafter referred to as Scott trans.]; and V.D. Sokolovskii, Soviet Military Strategy, trans. Herbert Dinerstein, Leon Goure, and Thomas Wolfe (Englewood Cliffs, N.J.: Prentice-Hall, 1963) (hereafter referred to as RAND trans.).

(4) Maj. Gen. V. Voznenko, Col. I. Korotkov, and Col. M. Skovorodkin, "Military Strategy in the Works of Soviet Authors," Voyennaya mysl', no. 4, 1967, FPD 1135/67, November 24, 1967, p. 97.

(5) These five books have been translated in the U.S. Air Force's translation series, "Soviet Military Thought" (SMT). The numbers and years listed with each book refer to publication in this series by the Government Printing Office. Maj. Gen. S.N. Kozlov, ed., The Officer's Handbook (A Soviet View), SMT no. 13, 1977; B. Byely et al., Marxism-Leninism War and Army (A Soviet View), SMT no. 2., 1974; N.A. Lomov, ed., Scientific-Technical Progress and the Revolution in Military Affairs (A Soviet View), SMT no. 3, 1974; V.V. Druzhinin and D.S. Kontorov, Decision Making and Automation - Concept, Algorithm, Decision (A Soviet View), SMT no. 6, 1975; Dictionary of Basic Military Terms (A Soviet View), SMT no. 9, 1976.

(6) These three books are also in the USAF "Soviet Military Thought" series. Marshal A.A. Grechko, The Armed Forces of the Soviet State (A Soviet View), SMT no. 12, 1977; A.A. Sidorenko, The Basic Offensive (A Soviet View), SMT no. 1, 1973; V. Ye Savkin, Basic Principles of Operational Art and Tactics (A Soviet View), SMT no. 4, 1974.

(7) "50 Years of Voyennaya mysl'," Military Thought, no. 6, 1968), FPD 0005/69, January 16, 1969, p. 26. Throughout the text the Russian title of this journal will be used to avoid confusing it with the USAF "Soviet Military Thought" series.

(8) Raymond L. Garthoff, "The Soviet Military," Problems of Communism (September-October 1977), p. 104.

(9) See William F. Scott, Soviet Sources of Military Doctrine and Strategy (New York: Crane, Russak, 1975), p. 14, for an excellent description of these and other Soviet sources, especially important books, since 1960.

(10) "50 Years of Voyennaya mysl'," p. 26.

CHAPTER 1

(1) Oleg Penkovskiy, The Penkovskiy Papers (New York: Doubleday, 1965, 1965), pp. 252-253.

(2) Byely, et al., Marxism-Leninism on War and Army (Moscow, 1972), SMT no. 2, 1974, p. 1.

(3) "To Meet the Centennial of the Birth of Vladimir Ill'ich Lenin," Voyennaya mysl', no. 10, 1968, FPD 0084/69, August 29, 1969, p. 8.

(4) Vladimir I. Lenin, Collected Works, vol. 30, p. 152, cited in Byely, et al., p. 9.

(5) Byely,et al., Marxism-Leninism on War and Army, pp. 9-10.

(6) A.S. Milovidov, The Philosophical Heritage of V.I. Lenin and Problems of Contemporary War (A Soviet View) (Moscow: 1972); and Soviet Military Thought, no. 5, trans. U.S. Air Force (Washington, D.C.: GPO, 1974), p. 37.

(7) Byely, et al., Marxism-Leninism on War and Army, p. 70.

(8) "The Ideological Struggle and the Military-Theoretical Front," Voyennaya mysl', no. 5, 1969, FPD 0117/69, December 18, 1969, p. 1.

(9) "To Meet the Centennial," p. 6.

(10) Col. S. Tyushkevich, "Development of the CPSU Marxist-Leninist Doctrine of War and the Army," Voyennaya mysl', no. 8, 1967, FPD 0125/68, August 26, 1968, p. 7.

(11) U.S. Congress, Senate, Committee on International Relations, The Soviet Union: Internal Dynamics of Foreign Policy, Present and Future (Washington, D.C.: GPO, 1978), p. 34.

(12) Col. V. Morozov, "Book on Laws of Armed Conflict," Voyennaya mysl', no. 7, 1965, FPD 962, May 25, 1969, pp. 79-80.

(13) Maj. Gen. N. Vasendin and Col. N. Kuznetsov, "Modern Warfare and Surprise Attack," Voyennaya mysl', no. 6, 1968, FPD 0005/69, January 16, 1969, pp. 46-47.

(14) Project on Soviet Perceptions of the Role and Utility of Military Power in War and Peace, draft report (Washington, D.C.: Advanced International Studies Institute, September 7, 1978), p. 19.

(15) Morozov, "Books on Laws," p. 80.

(16) G. Miftiyev and Col. V. Vasin, "On the Question of the Role of Economics in Nuclear Warfare," Voyennaya mysl', no. 11, 1965, FPD 953, March 8, 1966, p. 28.

(17) Maj. Gen. N. Sushko and Lt. Col. V. Kozlov, "The Development of Marxist-Leninist Teaching on War and the Army," Voyennaya mysl', no. 4, 1968, FPD 0052/69, May 27, 1969, p. 95.

(18) Byely, et al., Marxism-Leninism on War and Army, p. 257.

(19) Sokolovskiy, Soviet Military Strategy (Scott trans.), p. 38.

(20) Maj. Gen. S.N. Kozlov, ed., Spravochnik Ofitsera [The Officer's Handbook] (Moscow: Voyenizdat, 1971), trans. U.S. Air Force, Foreign Technology Division, AD 733-207, October 26, 1971, pp. 25, 109.

(21) See Harriet F. Scott, "The Making of Soviet Military Doctrine" (Paper prepared for CFIA-PSIA-RRC Seminar at Harvard University, March 13, 1978).

(22) Army Gen. S. Ivanov, "Soviet Military Doctrine and Strategy," Voyennaya mysl', no. 5, 1969, FPD 0017/69, December 18, 1969, p. 45.

(23) Kozlov, Officer's Handbook (USAF trans.), p. 116; and Joseph D. Douglass, Jr., The Soviet Theater Nuclear Offensive (Washington, D.C.: GPO, 1976), p. 10.

(24) Sidorenko, The Offensive, p. 3.

(25) Ivanov, "Soviet Military Doctrine and Strategy," p. 46.

(26) Sokolovskiy, Soviet Military Strategy (Scott trans.), p. 242.

(27) Ivanov, "Soviet Military Doctrine and Strategy," p. 46.

(28) Ibid., p. 47.

(29) Ibid., p. 48.

(30) Sokolovskiy, Soviet Military Strategy (RAND trans.), p. 299.

(31) Maj. Gen. S.N. Kozlov, Spravochnik Ofitsera [The Officer's Handbook] (Moscow: Ministerstra Oborony, 1971), trans. Harriet F. Scott, pp. 73-74.

(32) Sokolovskiy, Soviet Military Strategy (RAND trans.), p. 298.

(33) Marshal Su M. Zakharov, "Soviet Military Science over Fifty Years," Voyennaya mysl', no. 2, 1968, FPD 0042/69, April 25, 1969, p. 49.

(34) A.S. Zheltov, T.R. Kondratkov, and Ye. A. Khomenko, Metodologicheskiye Problemy Voyennoy Teorii i Praktiki [Methodological Problems of Military Theory and Practice] (Moscow: Voyenizdat, 1969), trans. B. Tauber et al., FTD-MT-24-87-71 (NTIS: 1971), AD 738 734, p. 321.

(35) Vasendin and Kuznetsov, "Modern Warfare and Surprise Attack," p. 45; see also, Maj. Gen. V. Zemskov, "Characteristic Features of Modern Wars and Possible Methods of Conducting Them," Voyennaya mysl', no. 7, 1969, FPD 0022/70, April 6, 1970, p. 19.

(36) Kozlov, Officer's Handbook (USAF trans.), p. 116.

(37) Ibid., pp. 82-83.

(38) Zheltov et al., Methodological Problems, pp. 327-328.

(39) Sokolovskiy, Soviet Military Strategy (Scott trans.), p. 38.

(40) Kozlov, Officer's Handbook (USAF trans.), p. 115.

(41) Sokolovskiy, Soviet Military Strategy (Scott trans.), p. 7.

(42) Ivanov, "Soviet Military Doctrine and Strategy," p. 45.

(43) Marshal Su V. Sokolovskiy and Maj. Gen. M. Cherednichenko, "Military Strategy and Its Problems," Voyennaya mysl', no. 10, 1968, FPD 0084/69, August 29, 1969, p. 35.

(44) Sokolovskiy, Soviet Military Strategy (Scott trans.), pp. 8-9.

(45) Kozlov, Officer's Handbook (USAF trans.), p. 101.

(46) V.G. Reznichenko, Taktika [Tactics] (Moscow: Voyenizdat, 1966), trans. FTD-MT-67-35 (NTIS: 1967), AD 659-928, p. 3.

(47) Zheltov et al., Methodological Problems, p. 313.

(48) Sokolovskiy, Soviet Military Strategy (Scott trans.), p. 40.

(49) Kozlov, Officer's Handbook (USAF trans.), p. 101.

(50) Ibid., p. 116.

(51) Reznichenko, Tactics, p. 3.

(52) Ibid.

(53) Kozlov, Officer's Handbook (USAF trans.), p. 103.

(54) Reznichenko, Tactics, p. 3.

(55) Kozlov, Officer's Handbook (USAF trans.), p. 103.

CHAPTER 2

(1) Maj. Gen. Ye. Nikitin and Col. S. Baranov, "The Revolution in Military Affairs and Measures of the CPSU for Raising the Combat Might of the Armed Forces," Voyennaya mysl', no. 6, 1968, FPD 0005/69, January 16, 1969, p. 4.

(2) Maj. Gen. S. Kozlov, "The Development of Soviet Military Science After World War II," Voyennaya mysl', no. 2, 1964, FDD 934, July 20, 1965, p. 29.

(3) Marshal Su R. Malinovskiy, "Historical Exploits of the Soviet People and their Armed Forces in the Great Patriotic War," Voyennaya mysl', no. 5, 1965, FDD 949, November 5, 1965, p. 24.

(4) Kozlov, "Development of Soviet Military Science," p. 39.

(5) Harriet F. Scott, The Making of Soviet Doctrine, pp. 7-8.

(6) Penkovskiy, Penkovskiy Papers, p. 251.

(7) Kozlov, "Development of Soviet Military Science," p. 29.

(8) N.A. Sbitov, "The Revolution in Military Affairs and Its Results," Krasnaya Zvezda [Red Star] (February 15, 1963), quoted in William R. Kintner and Harriet F. Scott, The Nuclear Revolution in Soviet Military Affairs (Norman: University of Oklahoma Press, 1968), p. 27.

(9) This is a particularly interesting book. It is a collection of the most important articles that had appeared in Red Star in the early sixties in a column that was headed with the same title. As pointed out by William F. Scott, Soviet Sources of Military Doctrine and Strategy (New York: Crane, Russak, 1975), p. 10, while prepared under Khrushchev, the book was revised and printed under Brezhnev, with only minor changes, an indication of the continuity in military thought that spanned the two administrations.

(10) K.S. Bochkarev, I.P. Prusanov, and A.A. Babkov, The Modern Revolution in Military Affairs and its Meaning - The Program of the CPSU on the Defense of the Soviet Fatherland (Moscow: Voyenizdat, 1965), p. 143, quoted in Kintner and Scott, The Nuclear Revolution, p. 115.

(11) Kozlov, "Development of Soviet Military Science," p. 28.

(12) The problem of introducing change in the absence of war is discussed in Brig. Gen. R.C. Richardson III, USAF (Ret.), "Can NATO Fashion a New Strategy?" Orbis (Summer 1973), pp. 415-438.

(13) S.I. Krupnov, "According to the Laws of Dialectics," Krasnaya Zvezda (January 7, 1966), quoted in Kintner and Scott, The Nuclear Revolution, p. 242.

(14) Sokolovskiy, Soviet Military Strategy (Scott trans.), p. 282.

(15) Reznichenko, Tactics, p. 6.

(16) Sidorenko, The Offensive, p. 41.

(17) Savkin, Basic Principles of Operational Art and Tactics, p. 202.

(18) Sidorenko, The Offensive, p. 58.

(19) Ibid.

(20) Ibid., p. 41.

(21) S.V. Malyanchikov, "The Character and Features of Nuclear Rocket War," Kommunist Vooruzhennykh Sil (November 1965), quoted in Kintner and Scott, The Nuclear Revolution, p. 178.

(22) A.A. Grechko, Na Strazhe Mira i Stroitel'stva Kommunizma [On Guard for Peace and the Building of Communism] (Moscow: Voyenizdat, 1971); trans. JPRS 54602 (NTIS: 1971), p. 33.

(23) Reznichenko, Tactics, p. 229.

(24) Sokolovskiy, Soviet Military Strategy (Scott trans.), p. 291.

(25) I. Zavyalov, "New Weapons and the Art of War," Krasnaya Zvezda, October 30, 1970; trans. in FBIS, Daily Report: Soviet Union, November 4, 1970, pp. F2, F4.

(26) Ibid., p. F4.

(27) Ibid.

(28) Ibid., p. F5.

(29) Sokolovskiy, Soviet Military Strategy (Scott trans.), p. 205.

(30) Savkin, Basic Principles of Operational Art and Tactics, pp. 190-191.

(31) Ibid., pp. 165-166.

(32) Sidorenko, The Offensive, p. 111.

(33) Savkin, Basic Principles of Operational Art and Tactics, p. 107.

(34) Byely et al., Marxism-Leninism on War and Army, p. 255.

(35) Sokolovskiy, Soviet Military Strategy (RAND trans.), p. 301.

(36) Sokolovskiy, ibid (Scott trans.), p. 198.

(37) Marshal Su M. Zakharov, "The Increasing Role of Scientific Troop Leadership," Voyennaya mysl', no. 2, 1967, PFD 0018/68, January 9, 1968, p. 16.

(38) Druzhinin et al., <u>Decision Making and Automation: Concept, Algorithm, Decision</u>, p. 3.

(39) V. Bondarenko, "Scientific-Technical Progress and Troop Control," <u>Kommunist Vooruzhennykh Sil</u>, trans. in <u>USSR Military Affairs</u>, no. 929, JPRS 59370, June 27, 1973, pp. 1-2.

(40) Druzhinin et al., <u>Decision Making and Automation: Concept, Algorithm, Decision</u>, pp. 58-59.

(41) N.A. Lomov, <u>Scientific-Technical Progress</u>, p. 182.

(42) D.D. Gorbatenko, <u>The Time Factor in a Modern War</u> (Moscow: 1972); trans. U.S. Air Force, Soviet Press Selected Translations, nos. 73-75, June 27, 1973, p. 11.

(43) Col. V. Trofimov and Capt. 2nd Rank G. Kadomstev, "Methodology of Scientific Foresight," <u>Voyennaya mysl'</u>, no. 2, 1967, FPD 0018/68, January 9, 1968, p. 32.

(44) Ibid., p. 29.

(45) Druzhinin et al., <u>Decision Making and Automation: Concept, Algorithm, Decision</u>, p. 5.

(46) N.A. Lomov, <u>Scientific-Technical Progress</u>, p. 165.

(47) Sokolovskiy, <u>Soviet Military Strategy</u> (Scott trans.), p. 242.

(48) Army Gen. A. Yepishev, "The CPSU and the Soviet Armed Forces," <u>Voyennaya mysl'</u>, no. 1, 1968, FPD 0093/68, May 22, 1968, p. 10.

(49) Nikitin and Baranov, "The Revolution in Military Affairs," p. 7.

(50) V. Bondarenko, "Soviet Science and Strengthening of the Defense of the Country," <u>Kommunist Vooruzhennykh Sil</u> (September 1974), pp. 22-30, trans. U.S. Air Force, Soviet Press Selected Translations, February 1, 1975, p. 4.

(51) Maj. Gen. V. Prokhorov and Lt. Gen. G. Semenov, "Scientific-Technical Progress and Some Questions of Strategy," <u>Voyennaya mysl'</u>, no. 2, 1969, FPD 0060/69, June 18, 1969, p. 27.

(52) Ibid., p. 32.

CHAPTER 3

(1) Savkin, <u>Basic Principles of Operational Art and Tactics</u>, p. 52.

(2) Sokolovskiy and Cherednichenko, "Military Strategy and Its Problems," p. 41.

(3) 1st Rank Capt. Kulakov, "Problems of Military-Technical Superiority," Voyennaya mysl', no. 1, 1964, FDD 939, August 4, 1965, p. 12.

(4) Savkin, Basic Principles of Operational Art and Tactics, p. 52.

(5) Col. V. Morozov and Col. S. Tyushkevich, "On the System of Laws of Military Science and Principles of Militlary Art," Voyennaya mysl', no. 3, 1967, FPD 122/67, December 26, 1967, p. 14.

(6) Ibid., p. 17.

(7) Ibid.

(8) Ibid.

(9) Ibid.

(10) Savkin, Basic Principles of Operational Art and Tactics, pp. 89-90.

(11) Morozov and Tyushkevich, "On the System of Laws," pp. 18, 19.

(12) Ibid., p. 19.

(13) Morozov, "Book on Laws," p. 82.

(14) Col. M. Popov, "The Laws of Armed Conflict are the Objective Basis of the Leadership of Combat Operations," Voyennaya mysl', no. 10, 1964, FDD 914, May 20, 1965, p. 24.

(15) Savkin, Basic Principles of Operational Art and Tactics, p. 99.

(16) Ibid., pp. 105-106.

(17) Ibid., p. 109.

(18) Ibid., p. 110.

(19) Ibid., p. 111.

(20) Popov, "The Laws of Armed Conflict," p. 25.

(21) Trofimov and Kadomstev, "Methodology of Scientific Foresight," p. 31.

(22) "The Ideological Struggle and the Military-Theoretical Front," p. 6.

(23) Savkin, Basic Principles of Operational Art and Tactics, p. 1.

(24) Ibid., p. v.

(25) Ibid., p. 167.

(26) Ibid., p. 169.

(27) Ibid., pp. 184-185.

(28) Army Gen. V. Kurasov, "On the Question of Troop Leadership," Voyennaya mysl', no. 9, 1963, FDD 963, July 14, 1966, p. 52.

(29) Savkin, Basic Principles of Operational Art and Tactics, p. 201.

(30) Ibid., p. 202.

(31) Sidorenko, The Offensive, p. 58.

(32) Savkin, Basic Principles of Operational Art and Tactics, p. 226.

(33) Ibid., p. 227.

(34) Ibid., p. 234.

(35) Dictionary of Basic Military Terms, p. 35.

(36) Savkin, Basic Principles of Operational Art and Tactics, p. 230.

(37) Sidorenko, The Offensive, p. 42.

(38) N.A. Lomov, Scientific-Technical Progress, p. 152.

(39) Savkin, Basic Principles of Operational Art and Tactics, p. 239.

(40) N.A. Lomov, Scientific-Technical Progress, p. 151.

(41) D.F. Loza, G.I., Garbuz, and I.F. Sazonoy, Motostrelkovyy Batal'on v Sovremennom Boyu (Motorized Rifle Battalion in Modern Combat) (Moscow: Voyenizdat, 1965), trans. FSTC-HT-23-175-73, AD 748-873, August 10, 1972, p. 26.

(42) Sidorenko, The Offensive, p. 200.

(43) Savkin, Basic Principles of Art and Tactics, p. 240.

(44) Ibid., pp. 240-241.

(45) Col. V. Mochalov, "Types of War According to the Pentagon," Voyennaya mysl', no. 9, 1964, FDD 896, March 2, 1965, p. 92.

(46) Savkin, Basic Principles of Operational Art and Tactics, p. 241.

(47) Ibid., p. 255.

(48) Ibid., p. 249.

(49) Ibid., p. 241.

(50) Ibid., p. 248.

(51) Ibid., p. 253.

(52) A.A. Grechko, The Armed Forces of the Soviet State (A Soviet View) (Moscow: 1975: 1975), "Soviet Military Thought" series no. 12, trans. U.S. Air Force (Washington, D.C.: GPO, 1977), p. 275.

(53) Savkin, Basic Principles of Operational Art and Tactics, p. 241.

(54) Ibid., p. 283.

(55) Ibid., p. 253.

(56) Ibid., p. 255.

(57) Ibid., p. 258.

(58) Ibid., p. 260.

(59) Ibid., p.266.

(60) Ibid., p. 273.

(61) Ibid., p. 275.

(62) I.G. Pavlovskiy, "In the Battles for the Motherland," Izvestiya (March 13, 1975), trans. U.S. Air Force, Soviet Press Selected Translations, no. 75-5, May 1975, p. 25.

(63) Sokolovskiy, Soviet Military Strategy (Scott trans.), p. 291.

(64) Savkin, Basic Principles of Operational Art and Tactics, p. 275.

(65) Sidorenko, The Offensive, pp. 114-115.

(66) Savkin, Basic Principles of Operational Art and Tactics, p. 279.

CHAPTER 4

(1) Planning U.S. General Purpose Forces: The Theater Nuclear Forces, Congressional Budget Office, January 1977, p. 22.

(2) Maj. Gen. George J. Keegan, Jr., "New Assessment Put on Soviet Threat," Aviation Week and Space Technology (March 28, 1977), p. 46.

(3) Planning U.S. General Purpose Forces, p. 22; and John Erickson, Soviet-Warsaw Pact Force Levels, United States Strategic Institute, Report 76-2, p. 30.

(4) Jeffrey Record, Sizing Up the Soviet Army (Washington, D.C.: The Brookings Institution, 1974), p. 40.

(5) Ibid.

(6) Maj. Gen. V. Kruchinin, "Contemporary Strategic Theory on the Goals and Missions of Armed Conflict," Voyennaya mysl', no. 10, 1963, FDD 965, July 20, 1966, p. 17.

(7) Congressional Record, vol. 123, no. 135, part III, p. S14102.

(8) Koslov, Officer's Handbook (SMT series), pp. 116-117; see also John Erickson, "Some Developments in Soviet Tactical Aviation [Frontovaya Avistsiya]," RUSI, September 1975.

(9) Maj. Gen. A. Kravchenko, "Trends in the Development of Military Aviation," Voyennaya mysl', no. 6, 1966, FPIR 0503/67, May 26, 1967, p. 39.

(10) Kozlov, Officer's Handbook (USAF trans.), pp. 117-119.

(11) Ibid., pp. 110-114.

(12) Ibid., p. 114.

(13) Lt. Col. Ye. Galitskiy, "The Coordination of Civil Defense with

Units of the Armed Forces," Voyennaya mysl', no. 4, 1968, FPD 0052/69, May 27, 1969, p. 48; and Col. Gen. Avn. O. Tolstikov, "Civil Defense in Nuclear-Rocket War," Voyennaya mysl', no. 2, 1964, FDD 939, August 4, 1965, p. 36.

(14) Tolstikov, "Civil Defense in Nuclear-Rocket War," p. 36.

(15) U.S. Congress, Senate, Nuclear Weapons and Foreign Policy, Hearings before Subcommittees of the Committee on Foreign Relations, March 7, 14, and April 4, 1974 (Washington, D.C.: GPO, 1974), p. 62.

(16) Sokolovskiy, Soviet Military Strategy (Scott trans.), p. 310.

(17) Maj. Gen. Kh. Dzhelaukhov, "The Augmentation of Strategic Efforts in Modern Armed Conflict," Voyennaya mysl', no. 1, 1964, FDD 939, August 4, 1965, p. 21.

(18) Sokolovskiy, Soviet Military Strategy (Scott trans.), pp. 313-314.

(19) Ibid., p. 245.

(20) Savkin, Basic Principles of Operational Art and Tactics, p. 89.

(21) Kruchinin, "Contemporary Strategic Theory," p. 18.

(22) Maj. Gen. K. Sevast'yanov, Maj. Gen. N. Vasendin, and Capt. 1st Rank N. V'Yunenko, Comments on the Article "Augmenting Strategic Efforts in Modern Armed Conflict," Voyennaya mysl' no. 9, 1964, FDD 896, March 2, 1965, p. 35.

(23) Maj. Gen. M. Dahalaukhov, "Combating Strategic Reserves in a Theater of Military Operations," Voyennaya mysl', no. 11, 1964, FDD 924, June 30, 1965, p. 7; see also Sokolovskiy, Soviet Military Strategy (Scott trans.), p. 311.

(24) Ivanov, "Soviet Military Doctrine," p. 50.

(25) Sokolovskiy, Soviet Military Strategy (Scott trans.), p. 323.

(26) Ibid., p. 311.

(27) Engr. Col. B. Mikhaylov, "Improvements of Systems for Protection of Troops from Weapons of Mass Destruction," Voyennaya mysl', no. 7, 1967, FPD 0120/68, July 1967, p. 63.

(28) Maj. Gen. Tank Troops A. Zhilin, "Some Questions of Meeting Engagements of Large Tank Groupings," Voyennaya mysl', no. 2, 1964, FDD 934, July 20, 1965, p. 6; and Maj. Gen. A. Skovoroda, "Logistical Support for Troop Regroupings," Voyennaya mysl', no. 1, 1966, p. 46.

(29) Loza et al., "Motorized Rifle Battalion," p. 33.

(30) Sokolovskiy, Soviet Military Strategy (Scott trans.), p. 317.

(31) Col. M. Shirokov, "Military Geography at the Present Stage," Voyennaya mysl' no. 11, 1966, FPD 0730/67, July 27, 1967, pp. 60-61.

(32) Dzhelaukhov, "Augmentation of Strategic Efforts," p. 15.

(33) Kruchinin, "Contemporary Strategic Theory," p. 20.

(34) Sokolovskiy, Soviet Military Strategy (Scott trans.), p. 312; see also Dzhelaukhov, "Augmentation of Strategic Efforts," p. 25.

(35) Kruchinin, "Contemporary Strategic Theory," p. 21.

(36) Sevast'yanov et al., "Augmenting Strategic Efforts," p. 36.

(37) Sidorenko, The Offensive, p. 89.

(38) Ibid., p. 111.

(39) Reznichenko, Tactics, p. 186.

(40) Sokolovskiy, Soviet Military Strategy (Scott trans.), pp. 292, 291.

(41) N.A. Lomov, Scientific-Technical Progress, p. 147.

(42) Savkin, Basic Principles of Operational Art and Tactics, p. 282.

(43) Zheltov et al., Methodological Problems, p. 512.

(44) Savkin, Basic Principles of Operational Art and Tactics, p. 255.

(45) Reznichenko, Tactics, p. 160.

(46) Maj. Gen. N. Komkov and Col. P. Shemanskiy, "Certain Historic Trends in the Development of Troop Control," Voyennaya mysl', no. 10, 1964, FDD 914, May 20, 1965, p. 13.

(47) Maj. Gen. Kh. Dzhelaukhov, "The Infliction of Deep Strikes," Voyennaya mysl', no. 2, 1966, FPD 0763/67, August 9, 1967, pp. 43-44.

(48) In a war which the Soviets might hope to confine to the European Theater, it is almost certain that among the highest priority targets will be those nuclear weapons systems which have a capability that extends - however hypothetically - to Soviet territory.

(49) Dzhelaukhov, "Infliction of Deep Strikes," p. 44.

(50) Col. M. Skovorodkin, "Some Questions on Coordination of Branches of Armed Forces in Major Operations," Voyennaya mysl', no. 2, 1967, FPD 0018/68, January 9, 1968, p. 40.

(51) Dzhelaukhov, "Infliction of Deep Strikes," p. 42.

(52) Maj. Gen. Engr.-Tech. Serv I. Anureyev, "Determining the Correlation of Forces in Terms of Nuclear Weapons," Voyennaya mysl', no. 6, 1967, July 11, 1968, FPD 0012/68, p. 35.

(53) Col. M. Shirokov, "The Question of Influences on the Military and Economic Potential of Warring States," Voyennaya mysl', no. 4, 1968, FPD 0052/69, April 1968, p. 36.

(54) Rear Adm. V. Andreyev, "The Subdivision and Classification of Theaters of Military Operations," Voyennaya mysl', no. 11, 1964, FDD 924, June 30, 1965, p. 15.

(55) Ibid., p. 19.

(56) Ibid., pp. 16-17.

(57) Shirokov, "Question of Influences," p. 33.

(58) Ibid., p. 39.

(59) Ibid.

(60) Col. I. Vorob'yev, "Maneuver in Operations and in Combat," Voyennaya mysl', no. 9, 1963, FDD 963, July 14, 1966, p. 25; and "Types and Forms of Combat Operations," Voyennaya mysl', no. 8, 1965, FPD 958, April 22, 1966, p. 32.

(61) Penkovskiy, Penkovskiy Papers, p. 252; Sokolovskiy, Soviet Military Strategy (Scott trans.), p. 195; and Marshal S.S. Biryuzov, "The Lessons of the Beginning Period of the Great Patriotic War," Voyennaya mysl', no. 8, 1964, FDD 904, April 23, 1965, p. 27.

(62) Col. L. Korzun, "Certain Questions on High Speeds and Continuity of Attack," Voyennaya mysl', no. 5, 1966, FPD 0665/67, May 26, 1967, pp. 51-52.

(63) Sokolovskiy, Soviet Military Strategy (Scott trans.), p. 202.

(64) Col. M. Fedulov, Col. M. Shmelev, Col. A. Sinyayev, and Col. I. Lyutov, "Problems of Modern Combined-Arms Combat," Voyennaya mysl', no. 10, 1964, FDD 914, May 20, 1965, p. 37.

(65) Ibid., p. 28.

(66) Sidorenko, The Offensive, p. 90.

(67) Ibid., pp. 42-43.

(68) Ibid., p. 148.

(69) Bochkarev et al., Modern Revolution in Military Affairs, p. 131.

(70) I.A. Grudinin, "The Time Factor in Modern War," Kommunist Vooruzhennykh Sil, February 1966; quoted in Kintner and Scott, The Nuclear Revolution, p. 253.

(71) Bochkarev et al., Modern Revolution in Military Affairs, p. 144.

(72) Savkin, Basic Principles of Operational Art and Tactics, p. 172.

(73) Sokolovskiy, Soviet Military Strategy (Scott trans.), pp. 291-292.

(74) "The Task, Important for All" (editorial), Voyennyi Vestnik [Military Herald], June 6, 1967; unpublished trans. by Harriet F. Scott, August 6, 1967.

(75) Sidorenko, The Offensive, p. 61.

(76) Milovidov, Philosophical Heritage of V.I. Lenin, p. 199.

(77) L. Goure, F.D., Kohler, and M.L. Harvey, The Role of Nuclear Forces in Current Soviet Strategy (Coral Gables, Fla.: University of

Miami, Center for Advanced International Studies, Monographs in International Affairs, 1974), p. 10.

(78) Col. B. Samorukov, "Combat Operations Involving Conventional Means of Destruction," Voyennaya mysl', no. 8, 1967, FPD 0125/68, August 26, 1968, p. 38.

(79) Sidorenko, The Offensive, pp. 79-80.

(80) A.A. Grechko, Vooruzhennyye Sily Sovetskogo Gosudarstva [Armed Forces of the Soviet State] (Moscow: Voyenizdat, 1974), p. 175.

(81) Maj. Gen. B. Golovchiner, Encirclement and Annihilation of Groupings of Defending Troops," Voyennaya mysl', no. 8, 1964, FDD 904, April 23, 1965, p. 48.

(82) Ibid.

(83) Lt. Gen. B. Arushanyan, (Res.), "Combat Operations by Tank Units Against Operational Defense Reserves," Voyennaya mysl', no. 1 1966, FPD 966, August 23, 1966, p. 30.

(84) Samorukov, "Combat Operations," p. 35.

(85) Col. M.A. Jan Szyszkowski, "Penetration of the Enemy Defense: A Form of Offensive Operation," Zolnierz Wolnosci (February 6, 1978), p. 3 [in Polish].

(86) Sidorenko, The Offensive, p. 113.

(87) Ibid., p. 88.

(88) Reznichenko, Tactics, p. 175.

(89) U.S. Congress, Senate, The Consideration of Military Applications of Nuclear Technology, Hearings before the Senate Subcommittee on Military Applications of the Joint Committee on Atomic Energy, 93rd Cong., 1st sess., May 22 and June 29, 1973, p. 62.

(90) Savkin, Basic Principles of Operational Art and Tactics, p. 225.

(91) Sidorenko, The Offensive, p. 66.

(92) Sokolovskiy, Soviet Military Strategy (Scott trans.), p. 293.

(93) Sidorenko, The Offensive, p. 62.

(94) Fedulov et al., "Problems of Modern Combined-Arms Combat," p. 34; and Golovchiner, "Encirclement and Annihilation," p. 45.

(95) Lt. Gen. G. Semenov, "The Content of the Concept of an Operation (Reply to Readers)," Voyennaya mysl', no. 1, 1968, FPD 0093/68, May 22, 1968, p. 92.

(96) Sidorenko, The Offensive, p. 114.

(97) Ibid., pp. 66-67.

(98) Savkin, Basic Principles of Operational Art and Tactics, p. 226.

(99) Loza et al., "Motorized Rifle Battalion," p. 26.

(100) Grechko, The Armed Forces, p. 227.

(101) Army Gen. P. Kurochkin, "Operations of Tank Armies in Operational Depth," Voyennaya mysl', no. 11, 1964, FDD 924, June 30, 1965, pp. 50-73.

(102) Ibid., pp. 61-62.

(103) Col. I. Vorob'yev, "Forward Detachments in Offensive Operations and Battles," Voyennaya mysl', no. 4, 1965, FDD 957, April 6, 1966, pp. 12-22.

(104) Ibid., p. 14.

(105) Ibid., p. 15.

(106) Ibid., p. 19.

(107) Ibid., p. 16; and Col. V. Kuznetsov and Col. B. Andreyev, "Coordination between Aviation and Tanks," Voyennaya mysl', no. 8, 1966, FPD 0761/67, August7, 1967, p. 51.

(108) Maj. Gen. S. Begunov, "The Maneuver of Forces and Materiel in an Offensive," Voyennaya mysl', no. 5, 1968, FPD 0013/69, February 4, 1969, p. 44.

(109) Col. A. Shlyapkin, "Air Support of Ground Troops," Voyennaya mysl', no. 8, 1968, FPD 0019/70, March 30, 1970, p. 40.

(110) Vorob'yev, "Forward Detachments," p. 16.

(111) Biryuzov, "Lessons of the Beginning Period," p. 27.

(112) Sokolovskiy, Soviet Military Strategy (Scott trans.), p. 291.

(113) Reznichenko, Tactics, p. 43.

(114) Sidorenko, The Offensive, p. 60.

(115) Begunov, "Maneuver of Forces," p. 44.

(116) For an excellent detailed discussion of Soviet "desant" (assault) operations, see C.N. Donnelly, "The Soviet Concept of The Desant," RUSI/RMAS Research Center Bulletin, September 1971.

(117) Sokolovskiy, Soviet Military Strategy (Scott trans.), p. 292.

(118) N.A. Lomov, Scientific-Technical Progress, pp. 146-147.

(119) Savkin, Basic Principles of Operational Art and Tactics, pp. 184, 194.

(120) S. Goryachkin, "Communications during a Tactical Airborne Assault Landing," Voyennyi Vestnik, no. 12, 1974, JPRS K-5363, p. 203.

(121) I.M. Nikishin and B.A. Vvedenskiy, Long Distance Movement of Small Units (Moscow: 1967); trans. U.S. Army, OACS (I), no. J-8454, December 7, 1970, p. 17.

(122) Goryachkin, "Communications," p. 203.

(123) V. Margelov, "Airborne Troops," Voyennyi Vestnik, no. 7, 1967, unpublished trans. by H.F. Scott, August 10, 1967.

(124) Sokolovskiy, Soviet Military Strategy (Scott trans.), pp. 293-294.

(125) Col. I. Andrukhov and Col. V. Bulatnikov, "The Growing Role of Air-Borne Troops in Modern Military Operations," Voyennaya mysl', no. 7, 1966, FPIR 0475/67, p. 26.

(126) Sidorenko, The Offensive, p. 50.

(127) Reznichenko, Tactics, p. 180.

(128) Sidorenko, The Offensive, pp. 149-150.

(129) Sokolovskiy, Soviet Military Strategy (Scott trans.), p. 293.

(130) Savkin, Basic Principles of Operational Art and Tactics, p. 193.

(131) Zheltov et al., Methodological Problems, p. 312.

(132) Savkin, Basic Principles of Operational Art and Tactics, p. 260.

(133) Col. K. Lapshin, "Engineering Support of the Combat Operations of Rocket Troops in an Offensive," Voyennaya mysl', no. 9, 1965, FPD 960, May 10, 1966, p. 1.

(134) Zhilin, "Some Questions," p. 1.

(135) Arushanyan, "Combat Operations," p. 31; and Maj. Gen. N. Reut, "The Meeting Engagement in Nuclear War," Voyennaya mysl', no. 9, 1966, FPD 0558/67, June 12, 1967, p. 34.

(136) Kuznetsov and Andreyev, "Coordination between Aviation and Tanks," p. 51.

(137) Marshal of Aviation, S. Krasovskiy, "Trends in the Use of Aircraft in a Nuclear War," Voyennaya mysl', no. 3, 1967, FPD 122/67, December 26, 1967, p. 26.

(138) Col. F. Shesterin, "The Experience of the Battle for Air Superiority in World War II and Its Significance under Modern Conditions," Voyennaya mysl', no. 2, 1969, FPD 0060/69, June 18, 1969, p. 73.

(139) Ibid., p. 75.

(140) Krasovsky, Aviation and Cosmonautics of the USSR, p. 4.

(141) Sokolovskiy, Soviet Military Strategy (Scott trans.), p. 253.

(142) N. Zhuplatov, "In the Air - Reconnaissance Pilots," Aviatsiya i Kosmonavtika [Aviation and Cosmonautics], April 1975, trans. in USSR Military Affairs, no. 1150, JPRS 64927, June 5, 1975, p. 1.

(143) Ibid., p. 2.

(144) Krasovskiy, "Trends in the Use of Aircraft," p. 27.

(145) Ibid.

(146) Skovorodkin, "Some Questions," p. 41; and Shesterin, "Experience of the Battle for Air Superiority," p. 74.

(147) Shesterin, "Experience of the Battle for Air Superiority," p. 72.

(148) Col. K. Lapshin, "Surmounting Obstacles and Zones of Destruction and Radioactive Contamination of the Offense," Voyennaya mysl', no. 10, 1963, FDD 964, July 18, 1966, p. 18.

(149) Col. A. Martynov, "Comprehensive Protection of Troops from Weapons of Mass Destruction," Voyennaya mysl', no. 6, 1968, FPD 0005/69, January 16, 1969, p. 70.

(150) Kuznetsov and Andreyev, "Coordination between Aviation and Tanks," p. 53.

(151) Krasovskiy, "Trends in Use of Aircraft," p. 28.

(152) Kruchinin, "Contemporary Strategic Theory," p. 19.

(153) Sokolovskiy, Soviet Military Strategy (Scott trans.), p. 254.

(154) Krasovsky, Aviation and Cosmonautics of the USSR, p. 4.

(155) Sokolovskiy, Soviet Military Strategy (Scott trans.,) p. 254.

(156) Sidorenko, The Offensive, p. 47.

(157) Krasovsky, Aviation and Cosmonautics of the USSR, p. 3.

(158) Zheltov et al., Methodological Problems, pp. 351-352.

(159) Reznichenko, Tactics, p. 193.

(160) Kuznetsov and Andreyev, "Coordination between Aviation and Tanks," pp. 50-53.

(161) Col. I. Andrushkevich, "Combat against Tanks in Modern Operations," Voyennaya mysl', no. 4, 1969, FPD 0004/70, January 22, 1970, p. 40.

(162) Maj. Gen. of Aviation S. Sokolov, "Air Support of Ground Troops," Voyennaya mysl', no. 7, 1965, FPD 962, May 25, 1966, pp. 39-40.

(163) Vorob'yev, "Forward Detachments," p. 21.

(164) Kuznetsov and Andreyev, "Coordination between Aviation and Tanks," p. 52.

(165) Krasovskiy, "Trends in Use of Aircraft," p. 30; and Vorob'yev, "Forward Detachments," p. 21.

(166) Kuznetsov and Andreyev, "Coordination between Aviation and Tanks," p. 54; and Sokolov, "Air Support of Ground Troops," p. 44.

(167) Chief Marshal of Aviation K. Vershinin, "The Influence of Scientific Technical Progress on the Development of the Air Force and Its Strategy in the Postwar Period," Voyennaya mysl', no. 5, 1966, FPD 0665/67, May 26, 1967, p. 36.

(168) Sokolov, "Air Support of Ground Troops," p. 44.

(169) John Erickson, Soviet Military Power (Whitehall, London: The Royal United Services Institute, 1971), p. 68.

(170) Col. A. Postovalov, "Modeling the Combat Operations of the Ground Forces," Voyennaya mysl', no. 3, 1969, FPD 0101/69, October 30, 1969, pp. 28-29.

(171) Fedulov et al., "Problems of Modern Combined-Arms Combat," p. 29.

(172) Maj. Gen. S. Shtrik, "The Encirclement and Destruction of the Enemy During Combat Operations Not Involving the Use of Nuclear Weapons," Voyennaya mysl', no. 1, 1968, FPD 0093/68, May 22, 1968, p. 57.

(173) Ibid.

(174) Samorukov, "Combat Operations."

(175) Shtrik, "Encirclement and Destruction."

(176) "The Secret Arsenal of the USA," Voyennaya mysl', no. 6, 1969, FPD 0008/70, January 30, 1970.

(177) Samorukov, "Combat Operations," p. 32.

(178) Col. Yu. Bryukhanov, "The Massed Employment of Aircraft," Voyennaya mysl', no. 6, 1969, FPD 0008/70, January 30, 1970, p. 45.

CHAPTER 5

(1) P.N. Tkachenko, et al., Mathematical Models of Combat Operations (Moscow: 1969); trans., FSTC-HT-23-270-73, NTIS, AD764109.

(2) U.S. Congress, Senate, Nuclear Weapons and Foreign Policy, Hearings.

(3) "Command and Staff Exercises - One of the Most Important Types of Training for Troops and Staffs" (editorial), Voyennaya mysl', no. 7, 1969, FPD 0022/70, April 6, 1970, p. 5.

(4) Ibid.

(5) Engr. Col. A. Tatarchenko, "The Critical Time and Operativeness of Troop Control," Voyennaya mysl', no. 7, 1965, p. 30.

(6) Grechko, The Armed Forces, p. 208.

(7) Savkin, Basic Principles of Operational Art and Tactics, pp. 147-148.

(8) N.A. Lomov, Scientific-Technical Progress, p. 167; and Savkin, Basic Principles of Operational Art and Tactics, p. 174.

(9) Lt. Col. G. Lukava, "Contradictions in the Leadership of Troops and Methods of Resolving Them," Voyennaya mysl', no. 6, 1966, FPIR 0503/67, May 26, 1967, p. 29.

(10) N.A. Lomov, Scientific-Technical Progress, p. 166.

(11) Ibid., p. 167.

(12) Ibid.

(13) Col. D. Samorukov and Col. L. Semeyko, "The Increase of Efforts in Nuclear Warfare Operations," Voyennaya mysl', no. 10, 1968, FPD 0084/69, August 29, 1969, p. 52.

(14) Skovorodkin, "Some Questions," p. 42.

(15) Lt. Gen. V. Mernov and Lt. Col. A. Bogomolov, "Characteristics of the Perception of Truth in Military Operations," Voyennaya mysl', no. 7, 1966, FPIR 0475/67, May 17, 1967, p. 24.

(16) Col. N. Popov, Col. A. Kukushkin, and Col. M. Perevalov, "Employment of Defense by the Ground Forces under Modern Conditions," Voyennaya mysl', no. 7, 1969, FPD 0022/70, April 6, 1970, p. 57.

(17) Komkov and Shemanskiy, "Certain Historic Trends," p. 6.

(18) Ibid.

(19) Mose L. Harvey and Foy D. Kohler, eds., Soviet World Outlook (December 1977), p. 6; and Harriet F. Scott, "The Soviet High Command," Air Force Magazine (March 1977), pp. 52-56.

(20) Komkov and Shemanskiy, "Certain Historic Trends, p. 6.

(21) Ibid.

(22) Savkin, Basic Principles of Operational Art and Tactics, pp. 185-186.

(23) Gen. S.M. Shtemenko, The Soviet General Staff at War (Moscow: Progress Publishers, 1970), p. 118; and M.P. Skirdo, "Leadership, Management of a Modern War Effort," in People, Army, Military Leader (Moscow: Voyenizdat, 1970), chapt. 3, trans. in Military Affairs, no. 1063, JPRS 62749, August 16, 1974, pp. 15-21.

(24) Sokolovskiy, Soviet Military Strategy (Scott trans.).

(25) Col. Trevor N. Dupuy, USA (Ret.), "The Current Implications of German Military Excellence," Strategic Review (Fall 1976), pp. 87-93.

(26) Scott, "The Soviet High Command," p. 54.

(27) Reznichenko, Tactics, pp. 3-7.

(28) Skovorodkin, "Some Questions," p. 36.

(29) For the importance of this coordination to airborne operations see

Andrukhov and Bulatnikov, "Growing Role of Air-Borne Troops," p. 26.

(30) Skovorodkin, "Some Questions," p. 36.

(31) Milovidov, The Philosophical Heritage, p. 228.

(32) Sokolovskiy, Soviet Military Strategy (Scott trans.), p. 303.

(33) Reznichenko, Tactics, p. 63.

(34) Savkin, Basic Principles of Operational Art and Tactics, pp. 185-186.

(35) Col. S. Tyushkevich, "The Methodology for the Correlation of Forces in War," Voyennaya mysl', no. 6, 1969, FPD 0008/70, January 30, 1970, p. 35.

(36) Kruchinin, "Contemporary Strategic Theory," p. 22.

(37) Skovorodkin, "Some Questions," p. 39.

(38) Col. Gen. M. Lomov,"Several Problems of Control in Modern Warfare," Voyennaya mysl', no. 1, 1966, FDD 0762/67, August 8, 1967, p. 16.

(39) Komkov and Shemanskiy, "Certain Historic Trends," p. 11.

(40) Lukava, "Contradictions," p. 32.

(41) The regiment, incidentally, in Grechko's The Armed Forces of the Soviet State, is considered to be the most important integrated (combined arms) fighting unit. The battalion is the critical subunit that leads the assault and opens the battle.

(42) Savkin, Basic Principles of Operational Art and Tactics, pp. 252-253.

(43) I. Pavlovskiy, "Independence - a Commander's Most Important Attribute," Voyenni Vestnik, no. 2, 1974, pp. 8-15; trans. OACS (I) K-4677, June 4, 1974, pp. 10-12, 18.

(44) See also Maj. Gen. A. Surchenko, "Instilling Resolute Qualities in Soviet Commanders," Voyennaya mysl', no. 8, 1964, FDD 904, April 23, 1965, p. 36.

(45) Sidorenko, The Offensive, p. 88.

(46) Col. V. Bilaonov and Col. I. Kabachevskiy, "Air Defense of Ground Troops in Offensive Operations," Voyennaya mysl' no. 10, 1966, FPIR 0504/67, May 29, 1967, p. 37.

(47) Sidorenko, The Offensive, pp. 142, 144.

(48) A.K. Shovkolovich, F.I. Konasov, and S.I, Tkach, Boyevyye Deystiviya Motostrelkovogo Batal'ona v Gorode [Combat Action of a Motorized Rifle Battalion in a City] (Moscow: Voyenizdat, 1971), trans. OACS (I) K-1400, January 12, 1972, p. 110.

(49) Skovorodkin, "Some Questions," p. 38.

(50) Krasovskiy, "Trends in the Use of Aircraft," p. 27.

(51) Sidorenko, The Offensive, p. 202.

(52) Ibid., p. 200.

(53) A.M. Adgamov, et al., Voprosy Nauchnogo Rukovodstva v Sovetskikh Vooruzhennykh Silakh [Problems of Scientific Leadership in the Soviet Armed Forces] (Moscow: Voyenizdat, 1973); trans. OACS (I) K-4674, IR 6901003974, July 29, 1974, pp. 195-196.

(54) Col.Gen. M. Kozlov, "An Important Factor in the Might of the Armed Forces," FBIS, USSR National Affairs, Military Developments, part III, May 5, 1976, v. 5.

(55) Bondarenko, "Scientific-Technical Progress," p. 6-7.

(56) Ibid.,p. 5.

(57) "The Construction and Use of Nomograms For Operational-Tactical Computations," Voyennaya mysl', no. 11, 1965, FPD 953, March 8, 1966, p. 1.

(58) Maj. Gen., Signal Troops, G. Zakharov, "Modern Views on Organization of Communications in Offensive Operations," Voyennaya mysl', no. 10, 1966, FPIR 0504/67, May 29, 1967, pp. 54-55.

(59) Mikhaylov, "Improvement of Systems," p. 59.

(60) Col. V. Savel'yev and Col. P. Shemanskiy, "Assuring the Stability of Troop Control," Voyennaya mysl', no. 8, 1968; FPD 0019/70, January 16, 1969, p. 26.

(61) Zakharov, "Modern Views on Organization," pp. 54-55.

(62) N.A. Lomov, Scientific-Technical Progress, p. 186.

(63) Savel'yev and Shemanskiy, "Assuring the Stability," p. 23.

(64) Komkov and Shemanskiy, "Certain Historic Trends," p. 8.

(65) "Types and Forms of Combat Operations," p. 31.

(66) Zakharov, "The Increasing Role of Scientific Troop Leadership," p. 17.

(67) Shirokov, "Military Geography," p. 63.

(68) Col. N. Semenov, "Gaining Supremacy in the Air," Voyennaya mysl', no. 4, 1968, FPD 0052/69, May 27, 1969, p. 43.

(69) Ibid., p. 44.

(70) Krasovskiy, "Trends in the Use of Aircraft," p. 31.

(71) Semenov, "Gaining Supremacy," p. 44.

(72) Zakharov, "Modern Views on Organization," p. 51.

(73) Samorukov, "Combat Operations," p. 39.

(74) Col. I. Lyutov, "Some Problems of Defense without the Use of

Nuclear Weapons," Voyennaya mysl', no. 7, 1966, FPIR 0475/67, May 17, 1967, p. 41.

(75) Sokolov, "Air Support," p. 42.

(76) Vasendin and Kuznetsov, "Modern Warfare and Surprise Attack," p. 44.

(77) Engr. Col. S. Vol'nov, "Space and Electronic Warfare," Voyennaya mysl', no. 9, 1966, FPD 0558/67, June 12, 1967, p. 82.

(78) Col. I. Grudinin, "Essence and Phenomenon in Military Affairs," Voyennaya mysl', no. 1, 1966, FPD 966, August 23, 1966, p. 27.

(79) Ibid., p. 24.

(80) Maj. Gen., Engineer Troops, V. Makarevskiy, "Forcing Water Barriers From the March," Voyennaya mysl', no. 3, 1968, FPD 0160/68, November 21, 1968, p. 53.

(81) Vasendin and Kuznetsov, "Modern Warfare and Surprise Attack," p. 44.

(82) Ibid., p. 45.

CHAPTER 6

(1) G. Biryukov and G. Melnikov, Antitank Warfare, trans. D. Myshne, ed. R. Daglish (Moscow: Progress Publishers, 1972) pp. 69, 105.

(2) Ibid., p. 5.

(3) Milovidov, The Philosophical Heritage of Lenin, pp. 106-107.

(4) Sokolovskiy, Soviet Military Strategy (Scott trans.), p. 188.

(5) Sidorenko, The Offensive, p. 132.

(6) Col. B. Aleksandrov and Col. A. Yur'yev, "Air and Space Reconnaissance in Armed Conflict," Voyennaya mysl', No. 10, 1965, FPD 961, May 11, 1966, p. 1.

(7) Sidorenko, The Offensive, p. 135.

(8) Ibid.

(9) Ibid.

(10) Ibid.

(11) Ibid., p. 114.

(12) Ibid., p. 134.

(13) Savkin, Basic Principles of Operational Art and Tactics p. 169.

(14) Sidorenko, The Offensive, p. 72.

(15) N.N. Astakhov, et al., The Soldier and War (Moscow: Voyenizdat, 1971), trans. OACS (I) K-5111, December 19, 1944, p. 7.

(16) Sidorenko, The Offensive, pp. 71-72.

(17) Savkin, Basic Principles of Operational Art and Tactics, p. 229.

(18) Reznichenko, Tactics, pp. 42, 74, 137.

(19) Sidorenko, The Offensive, p. 80.

(20) Col. L. Belansov and Col. L. Sapozhnikov, "Troop Combat Operations Under Conditions of Radioactive Contamination of Terrain," Voyennaya mysl', no. 7, 1963, FDD 956, March 30, 1966, p. 49.

(21) Ibid., p. 59.

(22) Lapshin, "Surmounting Obstacles," p. 15.

(23) See, for example, Col. K. Lapshin and Lt. Col. Ye. Galitskiy, "Calculating a March When Rubble and Obstacles Block March Routes," Voyennaya mysl', no. 10, 1964, FDD 914, May 20, 1965, p. 42.

(24) Emphasis in original of Kuznetsov and Andreyev, "Coordination between Aviation and Tanks," p. 49.

(25) Maj. Gen. M. Dahalaukhov, "Combating Strategic Reserves in a Theater of Military Operations," Voyennaya mysl', no. 11, 1964, FDD 924, June 30, 1965, pp. 5-6.

(26) Druzhinin et al., Decision Making and Automation: Concept, Algorithm, Decision, p. 3.

(27) Ibid., p. 7.

(28) Col. Gen. M. Kozlov, "An Important Factor in the Might of the Armed Forces," Krasnaya Zvezda (April 21, 1976), trans. in FBIS USSR National Affairs, May 5, 1976, III, p. V4.

(29) Grechko, The Armed Forces, p. 217; and Maj. G.M. Cherednichenko, "Scientific-Technical Progress and Some Problems of Military Science," Kommunist Vooruzhennykh Sil (July 1976), trans. in USSR Military Affairs, JPRS L/6520, October 13, 1976, p. 7.

(30) N. Khrushchev, Khrushchev Remembers: The Last Testament, ed. and trans. Strobe Talbott (Boston: Little, Brown, 1974), p. 52.

CHAPTER 7

(1) Byely et al., Marxism-Leninism on War and Army, p. 17.

(2) Skirdo, "Leadership, Management," p. 26.

(3) Quoted in "The Third Edition of 'Marxism-Leninism on War and Army'," Voyennaya mysl', no. 7, 1963, FDD 956, March 30, 1966, p. 81.

(4) Zemskov, "Characteristic Features of Modern Wars," p. 22.

(5) Kruchinin, "Contemporary Strategic Theory," p. 14.

(6) Shirokov, "Military Geography," p. 59.

(7) General Alexander M. Haig, quoted in F. Clifton Berry, Jr., "Tactical C3 - Bringing Order out of Chaos," Armed Forces Journal (April 1978).

(8) Byely et al., Marxism-Leninism on War and Army, p. 19.

(9) V. Kulikov, "The Soviet Armed Forces and Military Science," Kommunist (February 1973), unpublished trans. by Harriet F. Scott, p. 13.

(10) Ibid., p. 10.

(11) Ibid., p. 11.

(12) Sidorenko, The Offensive, p. 134.

(13) Zheltov et al., Methodological Problems, p. 101.

(14) Savkin, Basic Principles of Operational Art and Tactics, p. 253.

(15) N.A. Lomov, Scientific-Technical Progress, p. 147.

(16) Milovidov, Philosophical Heritage of Lenin, p. 261.

(17) Savkin, Basic Principles of Operational Art and Tactics, p. 254.

(18) Shirokov, "The Question of Influences," pp. 36, 39.

(19) Shovkolovich et al., Combat Action, p. 12.

(20) Druzhinin et al., Decision Making and Automation: Concept, Algorithm, Decision, p. 41.

(21) Shirokov, "The Question of Influences," p. 39.

(22) See C.N. Donnelly, "Fighting in Built-up Areas: A Soviet View - Part II," RUSI; and "Soviet Techniques for Combat in Built-up Areas," International Defense Review (February 1977).

(23) Tyushkevich, Necessity and Accident in War, p. 99.

(24) Grechko, Armed Forces, p. 173; and Sidorenko, The Offensive, p. 222.

(25) Maj. Gen. G. Kublanov, "Airborne Landings and the Struggle Against Them," Voyennaya mysl', no. 8, 1965, FPD 958, April 22, 1966, p. 62.

(26) Zheltov et al., Methodological Problems, p. 405.

(27) V.M. Bondarenko, "The Modern Revolution in Military Affairs and

the Combat Readiness of the Armed Forces," Kommunist Vooruz-hennykh Sil, no. 24, ed. and trans. Harriet F. Scott, January 20, 1969, p. 8.

(28) Capt. Yu Nepodayev, "On 'Nuclear Threshold' in NATO Strategy," Voyennaya mysl', no. 6, 1966, FPIR 0503/67, May 22, 1967.

(29) Dzhelaukhov, "The Augmentation of Strategic Efforts," p. 25.

(30) Samorukov, "Combat Operations," p. 29.

(31) Zemskov, "Characteristic Features," p. 22.

(32) William F. Scott, "Are we Underrating the Soviet Military Manpower?" Air Force Magazine (April 1974), p. 28.

(33) Gurov, "Economics and War," p. 8.

(34) "A Prominent Event of Our Time" (editorial), Voyennaya mysl', no. 5, 1966, FPD 0665/67, May 26, 1967, p. 6.

(35) U.S. Secretary of Defense Posture Statement for FY79, p. 74.

(36) Ibid., pp. 75-76.

(37) Ibid., p. 76.

(38) Ibid., pp. 76-77.

(39) Army General A. Radziyevskiy, "The Development of Combined Arms Tactics," Voyenno-Istoricheskiy Zhurval, no. 2, 1978, JPRS 70923, April 7, 1978, p. 55.

(40) Ibid., pp. 55-56.

(41) U.S. Secretary of Defense Posture Statement for FY79, p. 34.

(42) Vasendin and Kuznetsov, "Modern Warfare and Surprise Attack," p. 45.

(43) Ibid.

(44) Col. Gen. F. Gayvoronskiy, "The Development of Soviet Opera-tional Art," Voyenno-Istoricheskiy Zhurval, no. 2, 1978, p. 46.

(45) Zemskov, "Characteristic Features," pp. 22-23; see also, Sidorenko, The Offensive.

(46) Col. Gen. M. Povaliy, "Development of Soviet Military Strategy," Voyennaya mysl', no. 2, 1967, FPD 0018/68, January 9, 1968, p. 71.

(47) Tyushkevich, "The Methodology for the Correlation of Forces in War," pp. 35-36.

(48) Zemskov, "Characteristic Features," p. 22.

(49) Anureyev, "Determining the Correlation of Forces," p. 35; and William T. Lee and Harriet F. Scott, "Evolution of USSR Military Doctrine on the Issue of Non-Nuclear War, 1960-1970," Stanford Research Institute, Technical Note SSC, TN-8260-10, July 10, 1970, p. 84.

228 SOVIET MILITARY STRATEGY IN EUROPE

(50) Anuryev, "Determining the Correlation of Forces," p. 45.

(51) Ibid., p. 42.

(52) Samorukov, "Combat Operations," p. 31.

(53) Marshal of the Soviet Union N. Krylov, "The Nuclear-Missile Shield of the Soviet State," Voyennaya mysl', no. 11, 1967, FPD 0157/68, November 18, 1968, p. 18; and Zemskov, "Characteristic Features of Modern Wars," p. 19.

(54) Postovalov, "Modeling the Combat Operations," p. 22.

(55) U.S. Secretary of Defense Posture Statement for FY78, p. 22.

(56) Samorukov, "Combat Operations," p. 31.

(57) Ibid., p. 30.

(58) Vasendin and Kuznetsov, "Modern Warfare and Surprise Attack," p. 45.

(59) Based on Amoretta M. Hoeber and Joseph D. Douglass, Jr., "Chemical Warfare: Issues and Decisions for the United States," prepared for the New York Arms Control Seminar, April 18, 1978.

(60) Edward A. Miller and Lt. Gen. Howard H. Cooksey, "Speaking on...Evaluation of Soviets' Overall Threat: Analysis of Potential Factors," Army Research and Development News Magazine (March-April 1977), p. 22.

(61) Miosis is contraction of the pupil of the eye, resulting in dimmed vision.

(62) Henry A. Kissinger, The Necessity for Choice: Prospects of American Foreign Policy (New York: Harper and Row, 1960), p. 56.

(63) Sokolovskiy, Soviet Military Strategy (Scott trans.), pp. 283-284.

(64) Milovidov, Philosophical Heritage of Lenin, p. 36.

(65) See, for example, Sokolovskiy, Soviet Military Strategy (Scott trans.), chapt. 2.

(66) Lt. Col. Ye. Rybkin, "A Critique of the Book On Peace and War," Voyennaya mysl', no. 7, 1966, FPIR 0475/67, May 17, 1967, p. 83.

(67) Sokolovskiy, Soviet Military Strategy (Scott trans.), p. 188.

(68) L. Semeyko, "New Forms, but the Same Content," Krasnaya Zvezda, April 8, 1975; trans. U.S. Air Force, Soviet Press Selected Translations, no. 75-6, June 1975, p. 25.

(69) Ye. Ye. Mal'tsev, "Leninist Concepts of the Defense of Socialism," Krasnaya Zvezda (February 14, 1974), trans. U.S. Air Force, Soviet Press Selected Translations, no. 74-9, October 1, 1974, p. 3.

(70) Zheltov et al., Methodological Problems, p. 336.

(71) Ibid., p. 339.

(72) Tyushkevich, "The Methodology for the Correlation of Forces in War," p. 32.

(73) Ye. A. Boltin et al., Sovetskaya Vneshnyaya Politika i Yevropey-skaya Bezopasnost' [Soviet Foreign Policy and European Security] (Moscow: Izdatel'stvo Mezhdunarodnyye Otnosheniya, 1972); trans. in JPRS-57815, December 20, 1972, p. 5.

(74) Milovidow, Philosophical Heritage of Lenin, p. 37.

(75) Henry Trofimenko, "The 'Theology' of Strategy," Orbis (Fall 1977), pp. 497-515.

(76) Kozlov, "The Development of Soviet Military Science," p. 23.

(77) U.S. Congress, Senate, U.S. Nuclear Weapons in Europe and U.S.-U.S.S.R. Strategic Doctrines and Policies, Hearings, pp. 160, 183.

(78) Kozlov, Officer's Handbook, p. 116.

(79) Sokolovskiy, Soviet Military Strategy (Scott trans.), pp. 19-20.

(80) Milovidow, Philosophical Heritage of Lenin, p. 47.

(81) Col. M.P. Skordo, "The People, the Army, the Commander" (Moscow: 1970); "Soviet Military Thought" series, no. 14, trans. U.S. Air Force (Washington, D.C.: GPO, 1978), p. 83.

(82) Ibid., p. 80.

(83) Ibid., pp. 86-91.

(84) Ibid., pp. 79-80.

(85) Ibid., p. 89.

Index

About the Author

JOSEPH D. DOUGLASS, JR. (Ph.D. - Cornell University) is Director of the Policy and Strategy Analysis Division of System Planning Corporation in Arlington, Virginia. He has been engaged in European defense studies - nuclear, conventional, chemical, command/control - over the past decade. Prior to his current position, he was Deputy Director of the Tactical Technology Office of the Defense Advanced Research Projects Agency, where he was instrumental in focusing attention on the problems of collateral damage in a European conflict and the development and impact of precision guided munitions. He also has been associated with the Institute for Defense Analyses, the Research Triangle Institute, and Sandia Corporation. Dr. Douglass is the author of The Soviet Theater Nuclear Offensive, published in 1976 under the auspices of the U.S. Air Force as the first volume in the Studies in Communist Affairs Series, and co-author of Soviet Strategy for Nuclear War, published in 1979 by the Hoover Institution Press. He has lectured on various aspects of Soviet strategy and U.S./NATO nuclear policy at universities, military academies, and numerous research institutes.